Journalistic Stance in Chinese and Australian Hard News

Changpeng Huan

Journalistic Stance in Chinese and Australian Hard News

上海交通大學出版社
SHANGHAI JIAO TONG UNIVERSITY PRESS

Springer

Changpeng Huan
School of Foreign Languages
Shanghai Jiao Tong University
Shanghai
China

ISBN 978-981-13-0790-4 ISBN 978-981-13-0791-1 (eBook)
https://doi.org/10.1007/978-981-13-0791-1

Jointly published with Shanghai Jiao Tong University Press, Shanghai, China

The printed edition is not for sale in China Mainland. Customers from China Mainland please order the print book from Shanghai Jiao Tong University Press.

Library of Congress Control Number: 2018942923

Printed on acid-free paper

This Springer imprint is published by the registered company Springer Nature Singapore Pte Ltd.
The registered company address is: 152 Beach Road, #21-01/04 Gateway East, Singapore 189721, Singapore

In memory of Chris Candlin,
a superb supervisor and a visionary linguist.

Foreword

It is a great pleasure to write the foreword to this new volume on Chinese and Australian hard news. In this book, Changpeng Huan innovatively combines a multitude of perspectives to compare journalistic stance taking practices in "risk-focused" news stories in Chinese and Australian newspapers:

First, the author brings together discourse and corpus analysis of news stories with ethnographic fieldwork, interviewing a range of Chinese industry professionals, from journalists to sub-editors to senior editors as well as a government official. The insights from this field site alone will be fascinating to many.

Second, he brings together an analysis of Appraisal with corpus linguistics, enabling him to present quantitative tendencies in Attitude and Engagement realizations across the Chinese and Australian datasets. In so doing, this book makes a contribution to the important field of corpus-based Appraisal analysis. But there is also no shortage of qualitative examination of examples from the corpus throughout the book, ensuring that the analysis goes beyond numbers.

Third, the author combines analysis of Attitude with analysis of grammatical structures, including part-of-speech variation and grammar patterns. This enables more detailed insights into *how* Attitude is expressed rather than focussing only on the evaluative meanings that are realized.

Fourth, Changpeng Huan draws on the important concept of news values from journalism research, studying news values in media policy documents, editorial meetings, interviews, and news items. It is no small feat to gain access to and analyze such varied texts and sites of engagement.

Finally, throughout the book the author compares Chinese and Australian news contexts, enabling him to investigate both cultural similarities and variability. This is particularly important given the significance of the Chinese–Australian relationship in the Asia-Pacific region.

By building on and developing the work that has gone before, Changpeng Huan shows himself to be working at the interface of many complementary perspectives on news discourse and developing new insights into Australian and Chinese contexts. He is adding new stepping stones on the road toward bringing together discourse analysis, corpus linguistics, and ethnographic analysis, showing how each can enrich the other. This book establishes Changpeng Huan as a new voice in news analysis, and will be of relevance to all readers interested in cross-cultural analysis, Appraisal, and news discourse.

Sydney
April 2018

Associate Professor Monika Bednarek

Acknowledgements

This book is only made possible with academic and spiritual support from many people who have in one way or another inspired me to carry on my research and life.

Among them, first I would like to express my sincere gratitude to the late Emeritus Prof. Christopher N. Candlin at Macquarie University, Sydney. His meticulous scholarship, great passion for research, formidable erudition, and unfailing support have been priceless legacies to me. I could not have made so much sense of the study of language in social life without his programmatic vision. I am proud of having been able to work closely with him and to be influenced by him, as evidenced in this book. It is through talking to him, reading him, and working with him that I have desired to become a scholar just like him in future. This book is dedicated to Chris.

I must also give special thanks to Prof. Monika Bednarek, Prof. Susan Hunston, Dr. John Knox, Prof. Daniel Perrin, and Dr. Canzhong Wu for their careful edits and constructive comments on earlier versions of this book. I am greatly indebted to my colleagues in Sydney and elsewhere around the world who have provided support through discussion, constructive feedback, scholarly inspiration, or encouragement, in particular Prof. Marcel Burger, Dr. Helen Caple, Dr. Alexanne Don, Prof. Sue Hood, Prof. Geert Jacobs, Dr. Annabelle Lukin, Prof. Jim Martin, Prof. Kristen Precht, Dr. Tom van Hout, Dr. Peter White, and many other scholars whose work has inspired my own.

The writing up of this book has witnessed the commencement of a romantic life with Menghan Deng. Her love, patience, innocence, and passion for life have been my main source of happiness and accorded my life new meanings.

The publication of this book is sponsored by the Humanities and Social Sciences Research Grant (Culture Research Project) (grant number: 16JCWH13) at Shanghai Jiao Tong University and the Shanghai Pujiang Program (grant number: 17PJC058).

Contents

List of Figures

List of Tables

Chapter 1
Introduction

This research examines journalistic stance taking practices in Chinese and Australian hard news reporting in relation to discourses of Risk. Previous studies on stance in news discourse have largely focused on its discursive aspect through analyzing semiotic realizations of stance in news texts (e.g. Bednarek, 2006; Pounds, 2010, 2012; Thomson, White, & Kitley, 2008; White, 1998, 2012). This line of scholarly inquiry, albeit with abundant linguistic evidence of stance in news texts, does not suffice to analyze journalistic stance taking practices (e.g. Fairclough, 1995; Perrin, 2013; Van Dijk, 1997; Vertommen, Vandendaele, & Van Praet, 2012). This is because these studies have paid insufficient attention to the social aspect of journalistic stance which brings into view journalistic stance taking as social and professional practices afforded and/or constrained by the associated social-institutional context in which journalists operate. However, studies interrogating journalistic stance as social interaction (e.g. Scollon, 1998) often ignore the discursive aspect of stance in the processes and the products of news writing.

In order to better explain the manifold aspects of the concept of journalistic stance, it is useful to probe more fully into the semiotic cycle (Scollon & Scollon, 2003, 2004) or the entextualizing process (Park & Bucholtz, 2009) of a nexus of discourses in the enactment of journalistic stance (for a similar position, see Perrin, 2012; Vertommen et al., 2012). This challenge constitutes the central task of my research in the interrogation of journalistic stance. This research brings together ethnographic research involving interviews with journalism practitioners, participant observation of their professional practices and examination of the associated social-institutional and professional contexts in which journalists operate, along with close textual analysis drawing on newly created corpora of Chinese and Australian news texts. This integrated mixed-methods study, I hope, could afford a richer and deeper analysis and understanding of journalists' stance taking practices than can be provided by textual analysis alone.

The purpose of this chapter is to explain some key terms—hard news, discourses of Risk and journalistic stance—and to provide an overview of *why* and *how* journalistic stance is to be problematized in this research.

C. Huan, *Journalistic Stance in Chinese and Australian Hard News*,
https://doi.org/10.1007/978-981-13-0791-1_1

1.1 Research Objectives

Evaluative language is a significant resource to construct authorial personae (Martin & White, 2005). As such, analyzing discursive realizations of journalistic stance in news texts opens a window into understanding of how journalists' professional perception of news values, personal beliefs, and social-institutional values and ideologies are resemioticized (Iedema, 2003) into news stories. Hence, my research objective is twofold:

(1) To describe linguistic realizations of journalistic stance in the corpora of Chinese and Australian hard news reporting in relation to discourses of Risk;
(2) To explore how discursive stance markers are made possible in relation to other social factors, especially the (re)articulation of news values and the exercise of symbolic power in daily professional practices of journalism practitioners.

1.2 Delineating Discourses of Risk

This section will neither provide a historical account of risk nor list approaches to risk studies, since these studies abound in the literature (e.g. Bernstein, 1996; Boyne, 2001; Firkins, 2011; Lupton, 1993). In the context of Beck's (1992) formulation of risk society, the late twentieth century has been marked by rising hazards associated with risk and uncertainty in many professional practices (Sarangi & Clarke, 2002, p. 142).

The central issue of risk society concerns "the ability [of human beings] to define what may happen in the future and to choose among alternatives" (Bernstein, 1996, p. 2). Negotiating risk is therefore linked to the ways "that lay actors and technical specialists organise the social world" (Giddens, 1991, p. 3). As Candlin and Candlin (2002, p. 128) put it succinctly, it may be not so much the ontological underpinning of risks that is contestable and controversial but rather the epistemological representation or negotiation of discourses of risk. In light of this, this research detaches itself from studies of relational and rational nature of risk per se. Rather, it conceives risk as a negotiable construct demanding sustained negotiation between different voices with a focus on Chinese and Australian news discourses. Such a view is premised on the subjectivity (Lupton, 1999) and uncertainty of risk (e.g. Sarangi & Clarke, 2002). Negotiating risk through news discourse is inevitably subject to journalistic (inter)subjective stance taking practices in their mediating of various voices. Each stance taking implies a process of knowledge negotiation of risk "between different epistemologies and subcultural forms, amongst different discourses" (Beck, 1992, p. 5). As such, this research highlights the role of journalistic stance in mediating risk communication in the Chinese and Australian press. The specific risk events to be interrogated in this work will be explicated in next Section.

1.3 Delineating Hard News Reporting

Hard news is often applied in linguistic studies without a rigorous definition and defined in relation to one or two of its dimensions that are identified by Reinemann et al. (2011) (e.g. Lehman-Wilzig & Seletzky, 2010; Shoemaker & Cohen, 2005; Tuchman, 1973). Despite its contestable definitional scope, scholars generally agree on the view that hard news and soft news constitute a continuum of news reporting rather than a dichotomy (Baum, 2002; Curran, Salovaara-Moring, Cohen, & Iyengar, 2010; Reinemann, Stanyer, Scherr, & Legnante, 2011). The location of each type of news in this continuum may be measured by the dimensions involved in news reports. Reinemann et al. (2011) identify five such multi-dimensions for differentiating hard news from soft news: topics/events, news production, news focus, news style, and news reception. Topics refer to the subject matters of news events, such as politics, economy, or sports. News production means the timeliness of news events, such as whether there is an urgency for the news be published. News focus alludes to the frame of news events, such as societal-relevance (hard news) or individual relevance (soft news) of the news reports. News style of hard news is indicated by factual and text-oriented presentation of news events. News reception refers to the audience-related features. Focusing on three measurable characteristics of news texts per se: topics, focus and style, Reinemann et al. (2011) defined hard news and soft news as follows:

> The more a news item is politically relevant, the more it reports in a thematic way, focuses on the societal consequences of events, is impersonal and unemotional in its style, the more it can be regarded as hard news. The more a news items [sic] is not politically relevant, the more it reports in an episodic way, focuses on individual consequences of events, is personal and emotional in style, the more it can be regarded as soft news (Reinemann et al., 2011, p. 233).

On this premise, the risk events to be included in each corpus must be reported in print media hard news reporting with a focus on the societal consequences of the events and in a detached instead of sensational or interpretive fashion. To be specific, I am particularly concerned with risk events of food safety, earthquake and bush fires that were covered in Chinese and Australian press. Individuals or institutions who are involved in the production of these risk events are considered risk makers.

1.4 What Is Journalistic Stance: A Working Definition

It is widely acknowledged that evaluative language (e.g. stance markers) is pervasive in communication and that it is fluid and flexible in social life (e.g. Bednarek, 2006; Conrad & Biber, 2000; Hunston, 2011; Martin & White, 2005). There is however no consensus on the definition of stance, and its associated categorization. The main approaches to the study of stance will be presented and discussed in Chap. 2.

In attempting a working definition of journalistic stance, I intend to highlight both social and semiotic aspects of stance. It has a social aspect because journalistic stance is always undertaken within a particular social-institutional context. For this reason, an isolated interpretation of journalistic stance without taking into account its associated contexts would be biased.

However, any stance taking practices eventually need to be enacted in certain semiotic forms, linguistic or multimodal. This constitutes the semiotic aspect of journalistic stance, as language in news texts is the primary semiotic medium for journalists to anchor their stances. For this reason, this research will examine discursive patterns of stance taking in newly constructed corpora of hard news reporting (see Chaps. 5–8 for corpus findings).

This research holds that each aspect of journalistic stance deserves careful examination in its own right without a priori subordinating one to the other. What is equally important is that the investigation of each aspect demands careful consideration of the other aspects, and vice versa. For instance, the analysis of linguistic stance markers should extend well beyond the identification of the markers per se but requires recontextualizing journalistic stance in its associated social-institutional and (inter)personal contexts in order to achieve a fuller understanding of the mechanism through which stance is produced, sustained and changed over the course of social changes (Blommaert, 2005; Perrin, 2012; Richardson, 2007; Vertommen et al., 2012). However, it very much misses the central tenet of journalistic stance to simply consider its social aspect as social-institutional and (inter) personal contexts which provide better understanding of the discursive aspect. Instead, this research firmly believes that journalistic stance is enacted in a nexus of practices including, but not limited to, news values that are (re)produced daily in institutional and professional practices in each context (see Chap. 9) and the exercising of symbolic power (see Chap. 10).

On this view, this research proposes a working definition to problematize the concept of journalistic stance. It refers to discursive and social practices undertaken by journalism practitioners to express their affect towards, judgement upon, and appreciation of news events, news actors or any propositions in question. The other aspect of journalistic stance incorporates how journalism practitioners evaluate and engage with different news sources. The enactment of such stance taking practices is governed by social, institutional and (inter)personal factors of values and belief.

Evaluative language and social-institutional and (inter)personal orders are considered in the research as mediational means (Scollon, 1998, 2001; Scollon & Scollon, 2003, 2004) by which journalistic stance is enacted. Mediational means refer to the semiotic means through which mediated actions (e.g. journalistic stance taking practices) are conducted. As Scollon (2001, p. 14) pointed out, meditational means are "neither external or internal psychological constructs alone but rather are a dialectical relationship between objective materiality and psychonological or intramental process". This point will be discussed in greater detail in Chap. 3.

1.5 Why Study Journalistic Stance: Motivational Relevancies and Practical Relevance

The reasons why this research probes into the concept of journalistic stance in news discourse are manifold. From a linguistic perspective, the mechanism of linguistic articulation of journalistic stance has largely been unclear. Despite some research efforts in this regard (Bednarek, 2008, 2009; Hunston, 2011; Precht, 2000, 2003, 2008), we have as yet limited knowledge about the relationship between semantic patterns of stance (e.g. attitudinal features), and the associated social-institutional and (inter)personal orders. This is particularly true in Chinese news discourse.

A related point is that news discourse does inform readership of news events of relevance and significance. But news discourse is also ideological (e.g. Fairclough, 2014; Habermas, 1967), in the sense that it is a site of struggle in which a nexus of discourses and ideologies competing and struggling for dominance (Jones & Norris, 2005). Discursive patterns of journalistic stance in news texts are thus carriers of the patterns of affordances and constraints of the dominant power relations and ideologies. On this view, discursive stance taking practices mediate journalistic stances in news texts, and at the same time perpetuates the status quo. In so doing, journalism practitioners enact certain identities by means of conformity with or resistance to the rule of games in the sense of Wittgenstein (1953/2001). However, the fast changing face of journalism in Australia and China has called for updated research on journalistic professional practices. The choice of the Australian context for comparison is simply a choice of convenience because I was conducting a doctoral project at Macquarie University in Sydney. This issue then leads to the practical relevance (Roberts & Sarangi, 1999) of this research.

The practical relevance of this research is not simply to better understand journalistic practices in each context, but to provide insights into understanding of the potential stance taking practices to effect positive social change (see also Candlin & Sarangi, 2004; Fairclough, 2010; Jones & Norris, 2005; Sarangi & Candlin, 2001; Scollon & Scollon, 2004; Van Dijk, 2006). This is particular the case in recognition of the highly concentrated media ownership in Australia and updated mechanism of press control in China (see Chap. 10). However, this is not to naively suggest that the research findings could directly promote positive social changes. The central canon is that it describes, interprets and explains the ways stance taking practices are linked in social life to constitute a nexus of practice in which dominant values, ideologies and power relations reside.

It is worth emphasizing that news discourse is not the prime unit of analysis of this research. Rather, it forms a site of engagement (Scollon, 1998) through which journalistic stance taking practices are enacted and interconnected to other social practices. Hence, the focal point of analytical attention is journalistic stance in this research.

Additionally, this research intends to confine its analytical focus on hard news reporting in relation to discourses of Risk. Thus, it is unable to show possible variation of stance across news genres, such as editorials, features, infotainment news (e.g. Bednarek, 2006), across news media (e.g. TV news vs. print media) (e.g. Perrin, 2012). However, the restriction on the Chinese and Australian hard news reporting dedicated to Risk in newspapers has given me a detailed insight into the mechanism of journalistic stance taking practices that I would not get in the same way with a broader focus.

1.6 How to Study Journalistic Stance: A Multiperspectival Approach

The challenge posed by the manifold aspects of journalistic stance is how to adopt an appropriate research approach that can capture them all. To do so, this research will adopt a multiperspectival (MP) approach (e.g. Candlin, 1997, 2006; Candlin & Crichton, 2011, 2013; Crichton, 2010), which will be presented and discussed in detail in Chap. 3. As a linguistic project, this research takes discursive realizations of journalistic stance in news texts as the analytical point of entry to appreciate the mechanism of stance taking practices in each context of news production.

In this research, I have constructed a comparable corpus of Chinese and Australian hard news reporting in relation to discourses of Risk (see Chap. 4 for the process of corpus construction) to examine discursive articulation of stance in news texts in line with the APPRAISAL framework (Martin & White, 2005).

To examine the semiotic aggregates (Scollon & Scollon, 2003) of journalistic stance taking practices in a nexus of practice, this research focuses on the (re) articulation of news values (Chap. 9) and the exercises of symbolic power (Chap. 10). In this sense, I will investigate how news values and symbolic power are resemioticized (Iedema, 2003) as mediational means (Scollon, 1998) by which journalism practitioners undertake certain stances.

In recognition of the dynamic and elusive nature of journalistic stance, this research accepts that 100% precision of identifying stance markers in corpus is not possible, and that the reading (Martin & White, 2005) of journalistic stance in news discourses, together with subsequent analysis, necessarily involves researchers' subjectivity and a priori positions. To minimize the effect of researcher subjectivity, this research has documented in detail the methodologies followed in the study of journalistic stance.

References

Baum, M. A. (2002). Sex, lies, and war: How soft news brings foreign policy to the inattentive public. *American Political Science Review, 96*(01), 91–109.

Beck, U. (1992). From industrial society to the risk society: Questions of survival, social structure and ecological enlightenment. *Theory, Culture & Society, 9*(1), 97–123.

Bednarek, M. (2006). *Evaluation in media discourse: Analysis of a newspaper corpus*. London/New York: Continuum.
Bednarek, M. (2008). *Emotion talk across corpora*. Basingstoke/New York: Palgrave Macmillan.
Bednarek, M. (2009). Language patterns and ATTITUDE. *Functions of Language, 16*(2), 165–192.
Bernstein, P. L. (1996). *Against the gods: The remarkable story of risk*. New York: Wiley.
Blommaert, J. (2005). *Discourse: A critical introduction*. Cambridge: Cambridge University Press.
Boyne, R. (2001). Cosmopolis and risk: A conversation with Ulrich Beck. *Theory, Culture & Society, 18*(4), 47–63.
Candlin, C. N. (1997). General editor's preface. In *The construction of professional discourse* (pp. ix–xiv). London: Longman.
Candlin, C. N. (2006). Accounting for interdiscursivity: Challenges to professional expertise. In M. Gotti & D. S. Giannoni (Eds.), *New trends in specialized discourse analysis* (pp. 21–45). Bern: Peter Lang.
Candlin, C. N., & Candlin, S. (2002). Discourse, expertise, and the management of risk in health care settings. *Research on Language and Social Interaction, 35*(2), 115–137.
Candlin, C. N., & Crichton, J. (2011). Introduction. In C. N. Candlin & J. Crichton (Eds.), *Discourses of deficit* (pp. 1–22). Basingstoke: Palgrave Macmillan.
Candlin, C. N., & Crichton, J. (2013). From ontology to methodology: Exploring the discursive landscape of trust. In C. N. Candlin & J. Crichton (Eds.), *Discourses of trust* (pp. 1–20). Basingstoke: Palgrave Macmillan.
Candlin, C. N., & Sarangi, S. (2004). Making applied linguistics matter [Editorial]. *Journal of Applied Linguistics, 1*(1), 1–8.
Conrad, S., & Biber, D. (2000). Adverbial marking of stance in speech and writing. In S. Hunston & G. Thompson (Eds.), *Evaluation in text: Authorial stance and the construction of discourse* (pp. 56–73). Oxford: Oxford University Press.
Crichton, J. (2010). *The discourse of commercialization: A multi-perspectived analysis*. Basingstoke/New York: Palgrave Macmillan.
Curran, J., Salovaara-Moring, I., Cohen, S., & Iyengar, S. (2010). Crime, foreigners and hard news: A cross-national comparison of reporting and public perception. *Journalism, 11*(1), 3–19.
Fairclough, N. (1995). *Media discourse*. New York: Arnold.
Fairclough, N. (2010). *Critical discourse analysis: The critical study of language*. Harlow: Pearson Education Limited.
Fairclough, N. (2014). *Language and power* (3rd ed.). London: Longman.
Firkins, A. S. (2011). *Discourse and the framing of risk* (Doctoral thesis), Macquarie University, Sydney.
Giddens, A. (1991). *Modernity and self-identity: Self and society in the late modern age*. Cambridge: Polity Press.
Habermas, J. (1967). *Erkenntnis und Interesse [Knowledge and interest]*. Frankfurt am Main: Suhrkamp.
Hunston, S. (2011). *Corpus approaches to evaluation: Phraseology and evaluative language*. New York: Routledge.
Iedema, R. (2003). Multimodality, resemiotization: Extending the analysis of discourse as multi-semiotic practice. *Visual Communication, 2*(1), 29–57.
Jones, R. H., & Norris, S. (Eds.). (2005). *Discourse in action: Introducing mediated discourse analysis*. New York: Routledge.
Lehman-Wilzig, S. N., & Seletzky, M. (2010). Hard news, soft news, 'general'news: The necessity and utility of an intermediate classification. *Journalism, 11*(1), 37–56.
Lupton, D. (1993). Risk as moral danger: The social and political functions of risk discourse in public health. *International Journal of Health Services, 23*(3), 425–435.
Lupton, D. (1999). *Risk: Key ideas*. London: Routledge.
Martin, J. R., & White, P. R. R. (2005). *The language of evaluation*. Basingstoke: Palgrave Macmillan.

Park, J. S.-Y., & Bucholtz, M. (2009). Public transcripts: Entextualization and linguistic representation in institutional contexts. *Text & Talk, 29*(5), 485–502.
Perrin, D. (2012). Stancing: Strategies of entextualizing stance in newswriting. *Discourse, Context & Media, 1*(2–3), 135–147.
Perrin, D. (2013). *The linguistics of newswriting*. Amsterdam: John Benjamins Publishing.
Pounds, G. (2010). Attitude and subjectivity in Italian and British hard-news reporting: The construction of a culture-specific 'reporter' voice. *Discourse Studies, 12*(1), 106–137.
Pounds, G. (2012). Multimodal expression of authorial affect in a British television news programme. *Discourse, Context & Media, 1*(2–3), 68–81.
Precht, K. (2000). *Patterns of stance in English* (Unpublished Ph.D. thesis), Northern Arizona University, Arizona.
Precht, K. (2003). Stance moods in spoken English: Evidentiality and affect in British and American conversation. *TEXT, 23*(2), 239–258.
Precht, K. (2008). Sex similarities and differences in stance in informal American conversation1. *Journal of Sociolinguistics, 12*(1), 89–111.
Reinemann, C., Stanyer, J., Scherr, S., & Legnante, G. (2011). Hard and soft news: A review of concepts, operationalizations and key findings. *Journalism, 13*(2), 221–239.
Richardson, J. E. (2007). *Analysing newspapers: An approach from critical discourse analysis*. Basingstoke: Palgrave Macmillan.
Roberts, C., & Sarangi, S. (1999). Hybridity in gatekeeping discourse: Issues of practical relevance for the researcher. In S. Sarangi & C. Roberts (Eds.), *Talk, work and institutional order: Discourse in medical, mediation and management settings* (pp. 473–503). Berlin: Mouton de Gruyter.
Sarangi, S., & Candlin, C. N. (2001). Motivational relevancies: Some methodological reflections on social theoretical and sociolinguistic practice. In *Sociolinguistics and social theory* (350–388).
Sarangi, S., & Clarke, A. (2002). Constructing an account by contrast in counselling for childhood genetic testing. *Social Science and Medicine, 54*(2), 295–308.
Scollon, R. (1998). *Mediated discourse as social interaction: A study of news discourse*. New York: Routledge.
Scollon, R. (2001). *Mediated discourse: The nexus of practice*. London: Routledge.
Scollon, R., & Scollon, S. W. (2003). *Discourses in place: Language in the material world*. London: Routledge.
Scollon, R., & Scollon, S. W. (2004). *Nexus analysis: Discourse and the emerging internet*. London: Routledge.
Shoemaker, P. J., & Cohen, A. A. (2005). *News around the world: Content, practitioners, and the public*. New York: Routledge.
Thomson, E., White, P. R. R., & Kitley, P. (2008). "Objectivity" and "hard news" reporting across cultures: Comparing the news report in English, French. *Japanese and Indonesian Journalism. Journalism Studies, 9*(2), 212–228.
Tuchman, G. (1973). Making news by doing work: Routinizing the unexpected. *American Journal of Sociology*, 110–131.
Van Dijk, T. A. (1997). *Discourse as social interaction*. London: Sage.
Van Dijk, T. A. (2006). Ideology and discourse analysis. *Journal of Political Ideologies, 11*(2), 115–140.
Vertommen, B., Vandendaele, A., & Van Praet, E. (2012). Towards a multidimensional approach to journalistic stance. Analyzing foreign media coverage of Belgium. *Discourse, Context & Media, 1*(2), 123–134.
White, P. R. R. (1998). *Telling media tales: The news story as rhetoric* (Unpublished Ph.D. Thesis), University of Sydney, Sydney.
White, P. R. R. (2012). Exploring the axiological workings of 'reporter voice'news stories—attribution and attitudinal positioning. *Discourse, Context & Media, 1*(2), 57–67.
Wittgenstein, L. (1953/2001). *Philosophical Investigations*. Hoboken: Blackwell.

Chapter 2
Linguistic Modelling of Journalistic Stance

2.1 Introduction

The primary aim of this chapter is to construct a linguistic model for analyzing journalistic stance in news texts, largely based on the APPRAISAL[1] framework proposed by Martin and White (2005).

In the next section (Sect. 2.2), I will present the APPRAISAL framework with a focus on its ATTITUDE and ENGAGEMENT systems (Sect. 2.2.1). The analytical affordances of this framework for addressing my research concerns will be discussed in relation to the other two most competing frameworks—'evaluation' (e.g. Hunston, 2011) in Sect. 2.2.2 and 'stance' (e.g. Biber, Johansson, Leech, Conrad, & Finegan, 1999; Precht, 2000) in Sect. 2.2.3. A modified linguistic model of journalistic stance will be presented and justified in Sect. 2.3 after discussing the affordances and constraints of each framework.

2.2 APPRAISAL, Evaluation and Stance

Concepts and approaches to the investigation of evaluative language are abundant in the literature, such as affect (e.g. Caffi & Janney, 1994), subjectivity (e.g. Finegan, 1995; Lyons, 1982), modality (e.g. Nuyts, 2001; F. R. Palmer, 2001; Papafragou, 2000), evidentiality (Aikhenvald, 2004; Chafe & Nichols, 1986; Plungian, 2001) and hedging (e.g. Hyland, 1998), to name only the most obvious. Review of these concepts has been conducted elsewhere (e.g. Bednarek, 2006), and I will not duplicate such scholarly efforts.

---

[1]Following the convention in presenting the APPRAISAL framework, from this point onward I will use small caps to refer to the APPRAISAL framework itself, and the systems of ATTITUDE, ENGAGEMENT and GRADUATION.

C. Huan, *Journalistic Stance in Chinese and Australian Hard News*,
https://doi.org/10.1007/978-981-13-0791-1_2

Hunston (2011) has briefly discussed four approaches to evaluative language—stance (Biber et al., 1999; Conrad & Biber, 2000), APPRAISAL (Martin, 2000; Martin & White, 2005), metadiscourse (Hyland, 2005a), and the Status, Value and Relevance approach (Hunston, 2000, 2011). Her account has prioritized "researchers whose work takes individual texts (written or spoken) as the raw material, and uses methodologies appropriate to those data" (Hunston, 2011, p. 10). In addition, her primary interest is in evaluative language in academic discourses rather than that in news discourse. As Hunston puts it succinctly, in academic discourse the process of knowledge-formation is prior, whereas in news discourse the priority is given to the argument function and the position of readers is crucial in the argument (Hunston, 2011, p. 49). For this reason, a discussion of metadiscourse frameworks is excluded since metadiscourse is unsatisfactory in addressing stance in news discourse due to its inclusion of linguistic resources such as text organizers (e.g. in addition, finally) and the ways writers interact with readers in academic discourse (e.g. I, you, we).

In recognition of these points, this section will focus on the three most relevant concepts to the key concern of journalistic stance—APPRAISAL (Martin & White, 2005), evaluation (Hunston, 2011; Hunston & Thompson, 2000) and stance (Biber, 2006; Biber et al., 1999; Du Bois, 2007; Jaffe, 2009). Dissimilar from Hunston's (2011) prioritizing of those studies on evaluative language in academic discourses, this section (Sect. 2.2) will pay special attention to the affordances and constraints of each approach under investigation in the study of journalistic stance (e.g. evaluative language) in news texts. In view of the fact that the APPRAISAL framework is more successful in accounting for news discourse than other approaches (Hunston, 2011, p. 49), this section will establish the point of reference for comparison to the APPRAISAL framework, which I now turn to.

2.2.1 *APPRAISAL*

APPRAISAL framework concerns the dynamic process of personae construction and ongoing negotiation of interpersonal meaning among interlocutors. It is deeply rooted in systemic functional linguistics (SFL) (Halliday & Matthiessen, 2014) in which language is considered as social semiotics organized around several strata or levels (Halliday, 1978). However, I have to claim from the outset that this research is not situated in SFL, but rather adapts the conceptualization of evaluative meaning from SFL, without subscribing to its other tenets. Central to SFL is its tripartite distinction of three major functions of language—construing a world of experience (i.e. ideational), enacting relationships between interlocutors (i.e. interpersonal), and organizing individual instances of language into cohesive discourse (i.e. textual). The corresponding meanings (i.e. ideational, interpersonal and textual meanings) constitute the discourse-semantic stratum of language, which realizes its higher level of context (field, tenor and mode), and which is in turn realized by its lower level of lexico-grammar (transitivity, mood and modality, and cohesion and coherence). Appraisal is one of three major discourse semantic resources construing interpersonal meaning alongside 'negotiation' and 'involvement' (Martin & Rose, 2003; Martin & White, 2005). As Martin and Rose (2003, p. 219) point out "negotiation is concerned with interaction as an exchange between speakers: how speakers adopt and assign roles to each other in dialogue and how moves are organized in relation to one another". 'Involvement' looks at non-gradable resources, e.g. anti-language (Halliday, 1976), address terms, jargons and various markers of social dialect, inter alia, (Eggins & Slade, 1997; Martin & White, 2005, pp. 33–34) to align or alienate with addressees, and therefore construct in-group and out-group. Appraisal has been designed to account for "the semantic resources used to negotiate emotions, judgement, and valuations, alongside resources for amplifying and engaging with these evaluations" (Martin, 2000, p. 145).

The appraisal framework itself is categorized into three systems: attitude, engagement, and graduation (see Fig. 2.1). "**Attitude** is concerned with our feelings, including emotional reactions, judgement of behaviour and evaluation of things. **Engagement** deals with sourcing attitudes and the play of voices around opinions in discourse. **Graduation** attends to grading phenomena whereby feelings are amplified and categories blurred" (Martin & White, 2005, p. 35).

The graduation system is divided into **force** and **focus**. **Force** is concerned with quantifying things and intensifying quality (e.g. extraordinarily intelligent) and process (e.g. greatly inspired), whereas **Focus** adjusts the boundaries of categories (e.g. they play jazz, sort of). Attitude may be intensified or weakened through gradable language, however, these gradable sources alone are not always evaluative. Further justification for excluding graduation will be provided in Sect. 2.3 below. This research will exclusively focus on attitude and engagement.

The attitude system incorporates three sub-systems: 'affect', 'judgement' and 'appreciation' (see Fig. 2.2). 'Affect' differs in kind from 'judgement' and

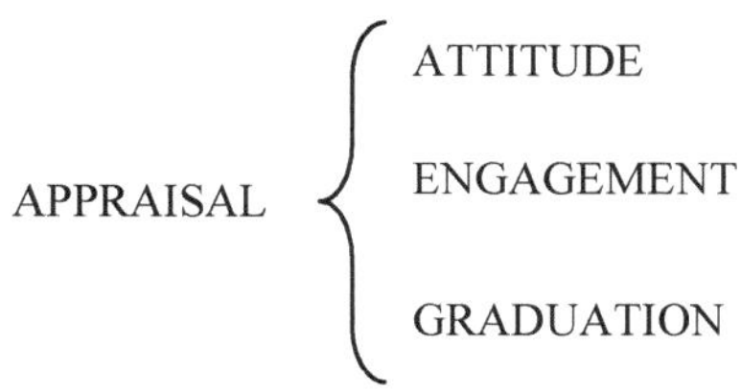

Fig. 2.1 Outlining the appraisal framework (after Martin & White, 2005)

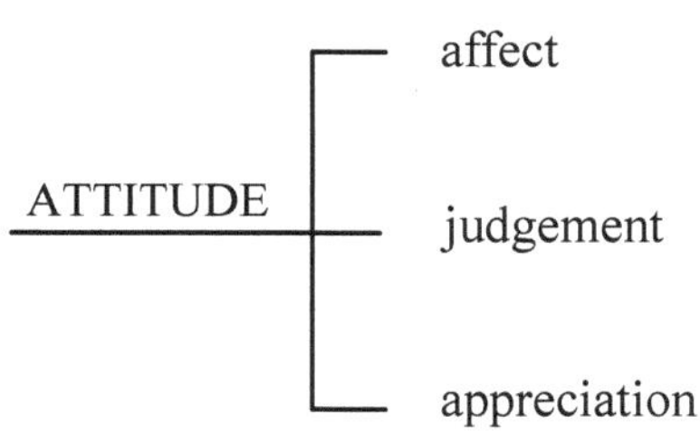

Fig. 2.2 An outline of the attitude system

'appreciation' (Hunston, 2011, p. 21) as 'affect' is appraiser-oriented (i.e. who is appraising) subjective reaction to something, while 'judgement' and 'appreciation' are appraised-adjusted (i.e. what is appraised) evaluation of the social value of something (Martin & White, 2005). 'Judgement' and 'appreciation' express institutionalized feelings (Martin, 2000, p. 147). 'Judgement' is human behaviour oriented ethic assessment by reference to a set of conventionalized social norms. 'Appreciation' orients to evaluating objects and entities by reference to their aesthetic values (Martin & White, 2005).

At the heart of ATTITUDE is 'affect', which is concerned with semantic resources for registering emotions. Affect is a four-fold subsystem consisting of 'un/happiness', 'dis/satisfaction', 'in/security' and 'dis/inclination'. '**Un/happiness**' concerns emotional affairs of the heart (e.g. sadness, hate, happiness and love). '**Dis/satisfaction**' is related to eco-social well-being (e.g. anxiety, fear, confidence and trust). '**In/security**' involves the pursuit of goals (e.g. ennui, displeasure, curiosity, and respect) (Martin & White, 2005). These three features are realis emotions, in contrast to an irrealis attitude of '**dis/inclination**' (e.g. fear, desire). The difference between realis and irrealis emotions is that with the former the trigger (or stimulus) is realis whereas with the latter the trigger is irrealis (i.e. hasn't happened yet, isn't 'actualised').

'Judgement' concerns resources for ethically evaluating human behaviour. It is divided into '**social esteem**' and '**social sanctionb**'. Each subsystem is further divided. As (Martin, 2000, p. 156) puts it succinctly: "social esteem involves admiration and criticism, typically without legal implications; if you have difficulties in this area you may need a therapist. Social sanction on the other hand involves praise, and condemnation, often with legal implications; if you have problems in this area you may need a lawyer" (also see Martin & White, 2005). The 'judgement' categories are presented in Table 2.1, with some examples of the corresponding realizations in lexicogrammar.

'Appreciation' is organized around three features: 'reaction', 'composition', and 'valuation'. '**Reaction**' is glossed as the impact of objects or entities on an individual, and their emotional response accordingly; '**composition**' is referred to as the constitutive structure and consistence or harmoniousness of the whole; while '**valuation**' means the aesthetical, socio-cultural and economical weight of certain objects or state of affairs.

In this research, 'reaction' will be moved out from 'appreciation' as a feature in parallel with 'affect', 'judgement' and 'appreciation', the reasons for which will be provided in Sect. 2.3 below.

However, it should be noted that although the distinction between 'judgement' and 'appreciation' is clear, the borderline is blurred between 'affect' and 'judgement'/ 'appreciation' (Martin & White, 2005). Such an issue poses some problems to determine which feature is prioritized (Bednarek, 2008, 2009a; White, 2012) and caused redundancy of the ATTITUDE system (e.g. Hunston & Thompson, 2000, p. 142). The mapping of ATTITUDE meanings as envisaged by Martin and White are derived from English texts only. For this reason, the ATTITUDE system remains as

Table 2.1 Judgement categories (after Martin, 2000, p. 156)

Social Esteem (venial)	Positive (admire)	Negative (criticise)
normality (fate) 'is the person's behaviour unusual, special, customary?'	lucky, charmed... standard, everyday, average... fashionable, avant-garde...	unlucky, unfortunate... eccentric, odd, maverick... dated, unfashionable...
capacity 'is the person competent, capable?'	skilled, clever, insightful... athletic, strong, powerful... sane, together...	stupid, slow, simple-minded... clumsy, weak, uncoordinated... insane, neurotic...
tenacity (resolve) 'is the person dependable, well disposed?'	plucky, brave, heroic... reliable, dependable... indefatigable, resolute...	cowardly, rash, despondent... unreliable, undependable... distracted, lazy, unfocussed...
Social sanction (mortal)	**Positive (praise)**	**Negative (condemn)**
veracity (truth) 'is the person honest?'	honest, truthful, credible...; authentic, genuine...; frank, direct ...;	deceitful, dishonest...; bogus, fake...; deceptive, obfuscatory...
propriety (ethics) 'is the person ethical, beyond reproach?'	good, moral, virtuous...; law abiding, fair, just...; caring, sensitive, considerate...	bad, immoral, lascivious...; corrupt, unjust, unfair...; cruel, mean, brutal...

> Hypotheses about the organisation of the relevant meanings – offered as a challenge to those concerned with developing appropriate reasoning, as a reference point for those with alternative classifications and as a tool for those who need something to manage the analysis of evaluation in discourse. (Martin & White, 2005, p. 46; White, 2002, p. 4)

'Appreciation' will be discussed in passing in Chaps. 5–7 in that this research is mainly concerned with journalistic stance taking practices through the presentation and representation of 'affect' towards and 'judgment' upon news actors rather than news events. Readers can refer to Huan (2015) for more detailed discussion of 'appreciation'.

The system of ENGAGEMENT has shifted the focus of appraisal research from static investigation of personal attitudinal meaning to a position highlighting the dynamic processes of meaning negotiation between interlocutors (e.g. how writers attend to other voices). It concerns the ways speakers/writers project themselves onto the ongoing text and the ways they take a certain stance vis-à-vis various voices both within and beyond discourses at issue. The entire system of ENGAGEMENT is presented in Fig. 2.3.

Writers have the choice of either contracting (i.e. 'contract') or expanding (i.e. 'expand') the dialogic spaces in discourse through allowing other voices to be heard for purposes of warranting, confirming, fending off or challenging. For instance,

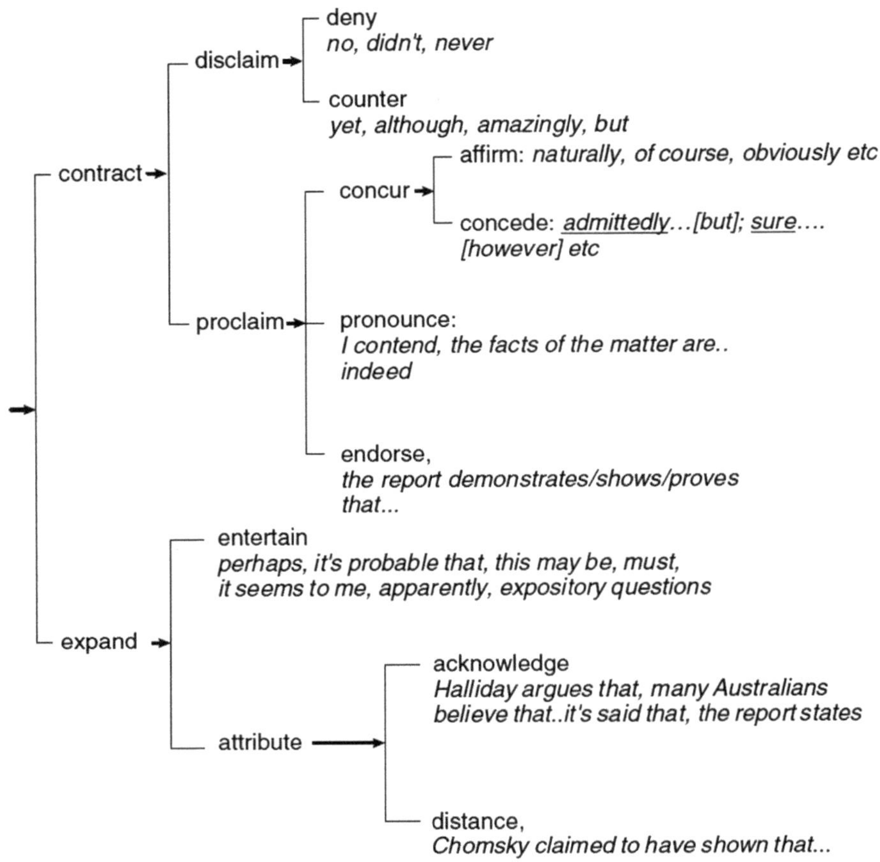

Fig. 2.3 The ENGAGEMENT system (Martin & White, 2005, p. 134)

writers may choose to contract the dialogic space by virtue of directly rejecting or replacing other dialogic alternatives (i.e. 'disclaim'), or by means of offering a preferable voice over others (i.e. 'proclaim'). 'Disclaim' is divided into 'deny' and 'counter', while 'proclaim' consists of 'concur', 'pronounce', and 'endorse'. 'Concur' involves semantic values which explicitly project the writer as affirming the voice or positioning of the putative readers. 'Pronounce' concerns explicit authorial intrusion into the dialogue so as to de/value one positioning over another. It differs from 'endorse' which "refers to those formulations by which propositions sourced to external sources are construed by the authorial voice as correct, valid, undeniable or otherwise maximally warrantable" (Martin & White, 2005, p. 126).

Under 'expand', dialogic voices are construed as more negotiable, contingent, contestable or challengeable, and degree of writer subjectivity moves down to approach objectivity. This covers two types of expansive values—'entertain' and 'attribution'. According to (Martin & White, 2005, pp. 104–105), 'entertain' mainly concerns those meanings "by which speaker/writer makes assessment of likelihood via modality". Attributing one utterance to other sources, writers have the choice of either declining to make a choice/indication of preferred voice, but simply acknowledging the voice as one of a range of possible voices (i.e. 'acknowledge'), or even explicitly detaching/alienating from the position being advanced (i.e. 'distance').

Since this research is more concerned with how journalists explicitly quoting or attributing to different sources in communicating risk, I will deliberately exclude the analysis of 'disclaim', 'concur' and 'entertain'. Further justification to do so will be provided in Sect. 2.3 below, and in Chap. 8.

The ENGAGEMENT system allows journalists or authors of texts to intrude into their ongoing texts by inserting authorial attitudes or stances, or to quote other sources to do so. Although non-authorial stance markers seem to merely describe the speaker's attitude (Bednarek, 2006, p. 32), it is generally believed that journalists excel in putting their words in the mouth of the sources quoted (e.g. Bell, 1991; Sleurs, Jacobs, & Van Waes, 2003). In this sense, non-authorial stance markers constitute a parameter of evaluation as important as the authorial equivalent for understanding journalistic stance (Hunston, 2003).

The APPRAISAL framework highlights the fact that the expression of ATTITUDE means more than a personal subjective matter of opinion or emotion, but a social and interpersonal matter of alignment or alienation in communication, in the sense that "advancing an opinion is to elicit a response of solidarity from the addressee" (Hunston & Thompson, 2000, p. 143). Construing interpersonal relationship is prosodic, and APPRAISAL meanings are scattered throughout a text or a clause. Since APPRAISAL features are semantic, rather than lexico-grammatical, features, there is no one-to-one correspondence of attitudinal lexis with APPRAISAL features. As such, it is important to take into account the co-text in which evaluative language at issue is embedded, rather than presenting isolated analysis of single items (Martin & Rose, 2003, p. 36).

There is inevitably considerable subjectivity involved in coding a given expression to its corresponding appraisal feature, and there might be some dispute over the coding. In fact, as Martin and White (2005) make it clear, what the APPRAISAL framework offers is a reading of a text that is open to debate rather than an analysis that is a definitive account. That is to say, appraisal analyses of text "are always socially positioned readings and we need to declare our 'interest' as best as we can" (Martin & White, 2005, p. 25). In this sense, this research does not claim that my reading is completely value-free.

2.2.2 *Evaluation*

The approaches to evaluative language under the overriding concept of evaluation in the literature can be broadly divided into two groups. One group is parameter-based approaches by virtue of presenting a taxonomy of evaluative features. The other, and perhaps the most widely cited work under evaluation, is the one associated with Hunston (Hunston, 2008, 2011; Hunston & Thompson, 2000) in her framework of Status, Value and Relevance (SVR).

Parameter-based approaches to evaluation are closely connected with Greenbaum (1969), Francis (1995), Lemke (1998), and Bednarek (2006, 2009b) in their corpus-informed studies of English texts. However, the features included in each approach differ considerably from each other. Although Francis (1995) and Lemke (1998, p. 6) claim their respective lists as comprehensive and exhaustive, these parameter-based approaches have not been widely adopted in the literature. For this reason, this section will concentrate on discussing Hunston's (2011) SVR framework of evaluation.

Evaluation is delimited as "the broad cover term for the expression of the speaker or writer's attitude or stance towards, viewpoint on, or feelings about the entities or propositions that he or she is talking about" (Thompson & Hunston, 2000, p. 5). This definition is preferred because of "its syntactic and morphological flexibility: not only does it express a user-orientation [...], but it also allows us to talk about the values ascribed to the entities and propositions which are evaluated" (Thompson & Hunston, 2000, p. 5). The SVR approach to the analysis of evaluation proposed by Hunston implies a three-move evaluative act: "identifying and classifying the status of an object to be evaluated; ascribing a value to that object; and identifying the significance of the information" (Hunston, 2011, p. 21).

The central tenet inherent in this approach is that all statements in texts are evaluated in terms of how they are aligned with the world (i.e. on interactive plane) and how the world is labelled (i.e. on the autonomous plane). Status, value and relevance are functions rather than mere dimensions of evaluation in texts (Hunston, 2000, 2008, 2011). Simply put, every proposition carries with it a particular 'status', and the 'status' determines the extent to which its associated 'value' can be ascribed. The ascribed 'value' is "context-dependent, often implicit, and cumulative" (Hunston, 2011, p. 22). "Significance, on the other hand, is indicated only at relatively infrequent intervals in the text and is identified through items of encapsulation among other features" (Hunston, 2011, p. 22).

Hunston extrapolates from her corpus-based studies of evaluation a limited taxonomy of attitudinal meanings which incorporates four basic parameters: good-bad/positive-negative, certainty, expectedness/obviousness, and relevance/importance (Thompson & Hunston, 2000, pp. 22–23). Drawing on Sinclair's (1981) autonomous and interactive planes of discourse, Hunston (2000) identifies some general types of 'status' in these two planes. On the interactive plane, writers inform readers of the structure of the text, while on the autonomous plane, writers show readers the content of the text (Hunston, 2000, p. 183). In this sense, 'status' on the autonomous plane ascribes thing-ness, for example the labelling of a person as *terrorist* or *freedom fighter*, and its value is therefore typically linked to the good-bad parameter. In comparison, 'status' on the interactive plane mainly concerns epistemic values, whereas 'status' on the autonomous plane primarily focuses on attitudinal values. 'Status' on the interactive plane can be determined by checking types and sources of statement.

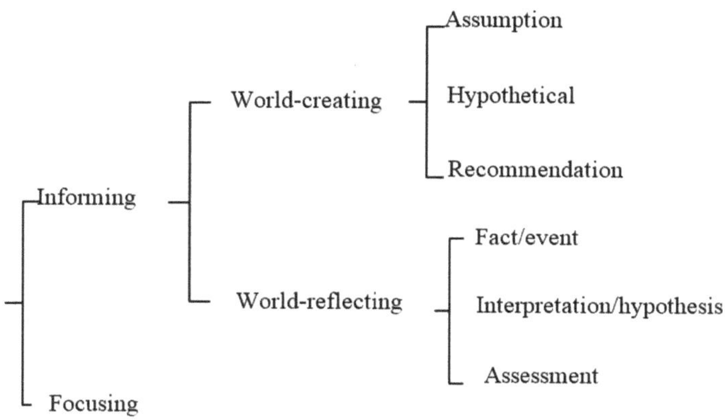

Fig. 2.4 Statement types (Hunston, 2000, p. 187)

The statement types (as shown in Fig. 2.4) present several useful distinctions. The basic one is that made between propositions which focus on the text itself (e.g. *Figure X provides a summary of...*) and those which align with the world. The type of focusing statement is equivalent to metadiscourse in its narrow sense (e.g. Ädel, 2006) which focuses on the ongoing text only. In this sense, statements are not aligned in any way with the world outside the discourse in question and therefore the evaluation of status does not apply to them (Hunston, 2011, p. 32). Unfortunately, this 'focusing' feature has as yet received scant scholarly attention, and the explanatory affordances of this feature remain unclear.

Drawing on Searle's (1985, p. 18) concept of "direction of fit", Hunston distinguishes under 'informing' statements 'world-creating' propositions from 'world-reflecting'. There are a number of important distinctions between these two types of propositions. 'World-reflecting' statements, as its name suggests, fit and reflect the world. Thus, a dialogic space is left open for debating the issue whether such an alignment of statements with the worlds remains true or reliable. 'World-creating' statements create an irrealis language world and make the world outside the texts fit these statements. Writers have the choice of creating a hypothetical world, as it were for the time being, which can be simply assumed, hypothesized or recommended. Accordingly, 'world-creating' statements discourage further tests on the alignment of a statement with the actual world. "For example, '*the virus could claim up to 7.4 million lives*' is a statement that fits the world, whereas '*Let's assume a worst-case scenario in which avian flu has taken hold*' creates a (hypothetical) world that fits the assumption" (Hunston, 2011, p. 32).

Hunston (2000, p. 187; 2011, p. 33) suggests three categories of 'world-reflecting propositions': 'fact/event', 'interpretation/hypothesis', and 'assessment' [see examples (1–3) below]:

(1) I belong to a spiritual movement called the Wild Goose Company, some of whose members live at Energy World, a community in rural France. [**Fact/event**]
(2) Energy World was recently invaded by police without warning at seven one morning. [**Interpretation**]
(3) It does not seem outrageously liberal to allow a group of people to gather together…[**Assessment**] (Hunston, 2000, pp. 187–188)

A writer may employ evaluative resources to align with what the world actually is (i.e. 'fact/event'), with what the world possibly is or is said to be (i.e. 'interpretation/hypothesis') and with a subjective world (i.e. 'assessment'). While 'fact/event' implies a writer's high investment to the proposition and thus discourages further evaluation of its truth-value, assessment indicates that such statements are open to verification and accordingly invite further evaluation of their truth values. 'Interpretation/hypothesis' is placed between 'fact/event' and 'assessment' in that interpretation/hypothesis statements are perceived by writers as possibly being true, and thus readers are invited to evaluate the truth values.

Let us now turn to the sources of statement in which Hunston (2000, p. 190) distinguishes between 'averral' (i.e. attributed to self) and 'others' (i.e. attributed to other sources). When it is attributed to others, writers have the choice to either delegate/divert the responsibility to the sources (e.g. *X said…*), or to reclaim the responsibility for the statement (e.g. *X proved…*). Alternatively, writers can project themselves onto the propositions with explicit presence of author (e.g. *I have to say…*) or implicit presence (e.g. *The present paper suggests…*). However, averred statements only differ in form rather than in substance since it is the authors who eventually are held responsible for the statements being advanced, although the author's self as the source of a statement may be disguised in various forms.

Hunston's SVR approach provides a detailed account of interaction between texts and the world. As mentioned above, she emphasizes that the value given to an object is determined by the status of the object in the world of discourse or in the material world. Hunston (2011, p. 21) makes it clear that her work mainly focuses on "an area where evaluation is usually highly implicit" and that, like most metadiscourse frameworks, her classification of 'status' and 'value' primarily focuses on written academic genres which "in essence give information about the real world" (Hunston, 2008, p. 67). However, this approach may preclude conducting corpus-based exploration of evaluative language on the ground that "the analysis of a text would turn out to be a great deal more than the text per se" (Hunston, 2000, p. 198).

'Status' on the autonomous plane ascribes thing-ness and 'value' ascribes quality, but such a distinction is not always clearly discernible (Hunston, 2000, p. 198). The complex interplay between statuses and values, in addition to the elusive evaluative resources present in real texts, ultimately makes attempts to create more delicate categories of status on the interactive plane not wholly successful (Hunston, 2011, p. 33). In general, she feels that "a taxonomy of status is probably at least premature and possibly ultimately not a useful exercise" (Hunston,

2011, p. 33). However, this, in my view, is in part caused by her belief that "all propositions in texts are evaluated in terms of how they are aligned with the world" (Hunston, 2011, p. 27). In comparison of 'status' with ENGAGEMENT, she admits that "Engagement provides a more rewarding reading of the newspaper text while Status offers a more revealing interpretation of the academic text" (Hunston, 2011, p. 49).

In comparison with the value meanings provided in the APPRAISAL framework or the parameter-based approaches of evaluation, the four parameters of value meanings provided by Hunston seem rather limited. The SVR approach "is probably less useful in the long run than other ways of taxonomising assessments, such as the Appraisal system" (Hunston, 2008, p. 67). Perhaps, this explains why "the work on Value has largely been overtaken by Martin and White's model" (Hunston, 2011, p. 22).

Nonetheless, the considerable values residing in the SVR approach still merits appreciation. Hunston's emphasis on the role of 'status' in determining the 'values' to be ascribed is illuminating, "particularly in cases where the appraisal is highly implicit" (Hunston, 2011, p. 22). This close relationship between status and value has not yet been seriously considered in appraisal studies, but see Bednarek (2008, 2009a) for an exploration of this issue in English. As I will show in the corpus findings (see Chaps. 6–8), the social status of news sources is intimately linked to the APPRAISAL values assigned to evaluate them, and this is particularly the case in the Chinese corpus.

Hunston's SVR approach categorizes Status, Value and Relevance with a focus on "the types and functions of evaluation" (Hunston, 2011, p. 21). In view of this point, the SVR approach could afford more in-depth insights into conceptualizing evaluation in different discourses, which then can be operationalized by various manageable methodological frameworks. As such, its descriptive power increases considerably. For instance, the 'value' system may be operationalized by utilizing the ATTITUDE system in APPRAISAL, or perhaps by evaluative features as advanced in parameter-based studies of evaluation. The 'status' system may be inspired by the categorization of social actors or social actions of the kind conducted by Van Leeuwen (1995, 1996) and Levinson (1979).

2.2.3 Stance

Studies of evaluative language under the rubric of stance can be categorized along two major lines of inquiry, one being stance as a semantic category and the other being stance as a social act. The former line of inquiry of stance is notably linked to Biber's work (e.g. Biber, 2006; Biber et al., 1999; Conrad & Biber, 2000). Hyland's stance and engagement framework (Hyland, 2005b), and Berman's (2004) framework of discourse stance in this line of scholarly inquiry are worth noting as well. However, Hyland's stance and engagement framework, on one hand, only differs from his metadiscourse framework in form but not in substance, while on the other, "whereas the more obvious aspects of evaluative language are limited to the 'attitude markers', almost all the features listed in his model have been discussed under the heading of 'evaluation' by one writer or another" (Hunston, 2011, p. 24). As for Berman's framework, despite its advantage in pinning down whether one has arrived at a "hallmark" of flexibly and appropriately play with different attitudes (Berman, 2004), it fails to proffer a robust, even a clear and explicit definition of its key concern—discourse stance—but simply equates discourse stance with discourse function (Berman, 2004; Berman, Ragnarsdóttir, & Strömqvist, 2002), which seems unsatisfactory as a sound framework. For these reasons, I will mainly focus on Biber's stance framework as an illustration of stance as semantic categories.

Conrad and Biber (2000, p. 57) define stance as "a cover term for the expression of personal feelings and assessments" and adopt a clear tripartite category of stance —epistemic, attitudinal and style stance. **Epistemic stance** indicates speaker's degree of confidence in the reliability of a proposition, and his or her comments on sources of information. **Attitudinal stance** signals speaker's attitudes, feelings, value judgements, or expectations about the utterances, therefore involves two terms—evaluation and emotions. **Style stance** conveys the way or manner of speaking (Biber et al., 1999; Conrad & Biber, 2000). The studies of stance by Biber and his colleagues are often associated with a quantitative corpus-based approach to a large amount of data. Precht (2000, 2003) has even developed a relatively reliable computational tool named 'StanceSearch' to assist in the automatic identification of stance markers. Unfortunately, 'StanceSearch' needs to run on a Pentium PC (old) with an old programing language, and even its designer does not have a working computer to run it on at the time of writing (personal communication, 14 Feb. 2014). Additionally, this tool can only identify and code few frequently occurring stance markers. However, there are two caveats inherent in the framework itself. On one hand, as Hunston (2011, p. 22) points out, it focuses on identifying linguistic markers of stance, rather than investigating a more abstract concept per se. On the other, it ignores some types of stance markers of which the most obvious is that of non-authorial stance, and this ignorance has resulted in their ignoring 60% of stance markers in affect nouns (Dry, 1992, cited in Bednarek, 2008).

Despite these caveats, this approach is able to provide insights into understanding the linguistic expressions of stance and the associated power relations. For instance, Precht (2003, p. 240), citing Fairclough (1992, p. 159), maintained that

> Expressing high affinity may have little to do with one's commitment to a proposition, but a lot to do with a desire to show solidarity. Conversely…low affinity with a proposition may express lack of power, rather than lack of conviction or knowledge.

The other line of inquiry of stance delimits stance as a social act that can be realized through various semiotic systems. The research focus of stance has accordingly been shifted away from purely linguistic description or a matter of personal emotions to an area that highlights the social aspect of stance taking practices. In this sense, stance is "the smallest unit of social action" (Du Bois, 2007, p. 173). Stance is defined by Du Bois (2007, pp. 163, 169) as:

> A public act by a social actor, achieved dialogically through overt communicative means, of simultaneously evaluating objects, positioning subjects (self and others), and aligning with other subjects, with respect to any salient dimension of the sociocultural field.

Stance, as viewed by Du Bois (2007), involves three key aspects of social life: Who is responsible for the current act of stance-taking? What is the object of stance? What is the value being assigned to the object? On this view, while we are assigning values to or evaluating an object, we are simultaneously positioning ourselves and seeking (dis)alignment. Although Du Bois' ideas on stance triangle are not necessarily new or different from what previous researchers on evaluation/appraisal have suggested, research in this line has tended to foreground the social aspect of stance taking. They argue that by mobilizing social-cultural values and conducting discursive stance taking, an individual stance taker is situated within the broad sociocultural values, and linked to other members of community of practice, and object or state of affairs at issue. Hence, stance is "a socially recognized disposition" (Ochs, 1990, p. 2), and "a process of assigning situational, i.e., indexical, meanings to particular forms" (Ochs, 1996, p. 410).

The stance so defined from a sociolinguistic perspective is intimately linked to my concern of journalistic stance taking practices in the Chinese and Australian hard news reporting. This is because, as Ochs (1996, p. 408) shows, language, as a symbolic tool (Vygotsky, 1978), encodes stance to shape, reshape, form, and transform social practices, and the social order. In this sense, stance taking indexes social identities: participant roles, positions, relationships, and reputation (Ochs, 1996, p. 424). In such "processes of indexicalization" (Jaffe, 2009, p. 13), stance taking is a "nexus where the linguistic and social are implicated in a number of ways" (Jaffe, 2009, p. 5) and it also bridges the connection between individual acts and social meanings. Overall, the sociolinguistic perspective on stance broadens the spectrum of resources to enact stance, ranging from speaker's footing (i.e. principal, author, animator) (Goffman, 1981) to multiple contextualisation cues (Gumperz, 1982). The key insight offered by this line of inquiry on stance is the understanding of journalistic stance as discursively constructed rather than fixed (Jaffe, 2009, p. 11). On this view, stance taking is far from neutral but always ideological by virtue of pursuing 'symbolic capital' (Bourdieu, 1977, 1984, 1986, 1991).

Clearly, Biber's framework of stance has tended to be applied in corpus linguistic investigations and only incorporates a limited number of linguistic realization of stance, whereas the sociolinguistic conceptualization of stance is much broader than that adopted in this book. However, the discursive and social aspects of stance should not to be taken as contradictory to each other. Rather, they supplement each other. Linguistic stance markers in news texts are discursive actions undertaken by journalists in their daily practice of the linguistics of newswriting (Perrin, 2013) and as such they (re)produce the personal attitude or ideological stance upheld by journalists. On this view, one basic tenet of my research is to argue that linguistic stance markers are not determined by language itself, but deeply rooted in journalistic social practices within the social-institutional arrangement of society. This research will take the discursive aspect of stance as the analytical point of departure in revealing the dialogically constructed nature of stance (J. Coupland & Coupland, 2009; Du Bois, 2007; Jaffe, 2009).

2.3 Modeling Journalistic Stance

In order to integrate the affordances of the frameworks outlined above into an applicable and manageable model for the purpose of investigating journalistic stance in this research, it is necessary to have a more fully understanding of what consensuses have been achieved among these approaches. Hunston (2011, pp. 12–19) has listed six points of agreement between various approaches to evaluation, three of which have been emphasized here with a view to highlighting the affordances and constraints of the APPRAISAL framework and eventually presenting a tentative discursive model of journalistic stance.

The primary point of consensus is that evaluation or stance taking is simultaneously attitudinal and epistemic. Hunston's SVR approach (Hunston, 2000, 2011) identifies evaluation operating on two parallel planes: interactive and autonomous. The interactive plane operates on the world of discourse where the primary concern is the writer's epistemic knowledge of the involved propositions. In contrast, the autonomous plane operates on the terrain of the world of physical experiences outside the world of discourse in which the prime focus is on personal attitudinal feeling towards the things at issue. Martin and White (2005) distinguish between personal feelings (i.e. ATTITUDE) and dialogic positioning with respect to propositions (i.e. ENGAGEMENT). Biber et al.'s (1999) stance framework acknowledges the difference between semantic categories that report personal attitude or feelings (i.e. attitude) and those present speaker comments on the status of information in a proposition (i.e. epistemic stance). The same distinction is made in approaches to stance from a sociolinguistic perspective. For instance, Ochs (1990, p. 2) groups stance into "epistemic (a socially recognized way of knowing a proposition) and affective stance (a socially recognized feeling, attitude, mood or degree of emotional intensity)". In recognition of these two primary stance meanings, this research has excluded the GRADUATION system in the APPRAISAL framework from analysis. That is to say, I will focus on journalists' expression of attitudinal and epistemic stances.

The second point of agreement relates to different orientations of the speaker's evaluation. Stance taking can orient to the behavior of human beings, including that of the addressee, or alternatively it may target any entities. In the APPRAISAL framework, this distinction marks the borderline striding between JUDGEMENT and APPRECIATION both of which involve speaker's cognitive and perceptive evaluation of things, entities, and human behaviours. The speaker, in addition to these, may also choose to express their own emotional states, or alternatively describe the feelings of others in order to ward off from being subjective. In the expression of authorial or non-authorial affect, Hunston (2003, p. 353) distinguishes between 'reflective' and 'constitutive' affect:

> I shall also propose that the distinction between reflective and constitutive expression of affect is recognised. One of the complexities of this semantic area is that emotional responses may be indicated as a quality of the responder, as in "Everyone in the school is *distressed* to hear of this tragedy" or as a quality of the thing evaluated, as in "...after the *distressing* events of 1887..." The first of these is reflective evaluation (it attributes evaluation to everyone in the school) while the second is constitutive (it avers an evaluation of the events). (cited in Bednarek, 2009a, p. 166)

The basic tenet of Hunston's distinction here primarily concerns the status of proposition on the interactive plane, that is, whether the affect at stake is attributed to other sources, or averred by the speaker/writer. It also corroborates the distinction between 'affect' and 'reaction' in the APPRAISAL framework where 'affect' resembles reflective evaluation and 'reaction' resembles constitutive evaluation. In addition, Bednarek's (2009a) corpus-based study of 'affect' and language patterns in English texts has provided linguistic evidence to support such a distinction. She makes it clear that:

> The findings suggest that it might be worthwhile to consider covert affect [equivalent to reaction] on its own terms rather than including it in either appreciation or affect, even though it is to be seen as more closely associated with opinion [equivalent to judgement and appreciation] than with emotion (in terms of pattern behaviour). (Bednarek, 2009a, pp. 171–172)

In recognition of this point, I have tentatively separated excluded 'reaction' from the original 'appreciation' system in the APPRAISAL framework. Thus, the ATTITUDE framework to be adopted for data coding and analysis in this book include four features: 'affect', 'judgement', 'appreciation', and 'reaction' (see Fig. 2.5, page XX).

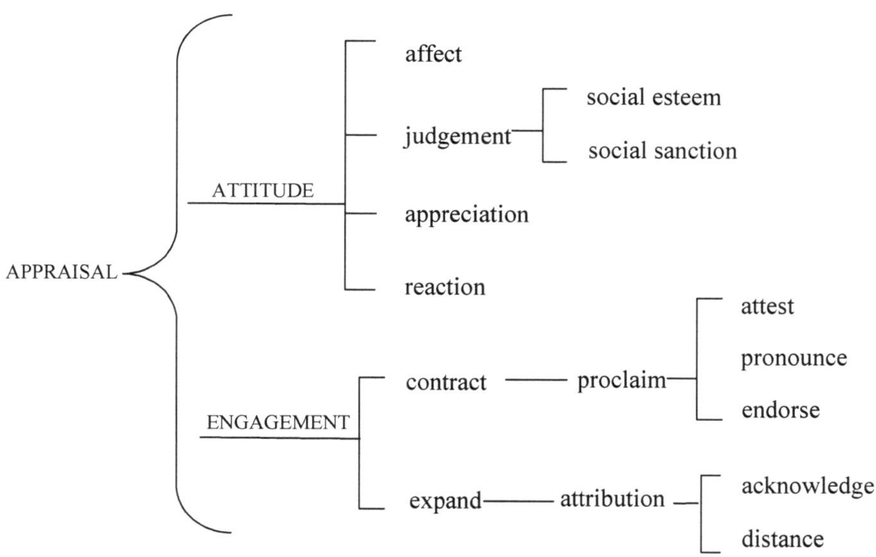

Fig. 2.5 A tentative model for coding stance (modified from Martin & White, 2005)

The third point of consensus is that stance or evaluation essentially involves a source, a target and the evaluation itself. In Hunston's model, the nature of the target (i.e. status) being evaluated determines the choice of evaluative meaning (i.e. value) ascribed to it. In the APPRAISAL framework, Martin and White (2005) identify the appraiser (i.e. source), the appraising item (i.e. evaluation) and the appraised target. For Du Bois (2007), taking a stance constitutes a stance triangle made up of who the stance taker is (i.e. source), what the object of stance is (i.e. target) and what stance the stance taker is responding to (i.e. evaluation). For 'affect' analysis, Bednarek (2008, p. 70) distinguishes between emoter (i.e. the one to whom an emotional response is assigned), emotion (i.e. the particular emotion involved) and trigger (i.e. what causes the emotional response). Analysis of JUDGEMENT comprises three elements as well, and they are the appraiser (i.e. the one who judges other persons' behaviours or characters), the JUDGEMENT itself (i.e. the particular feature of JUDGEMENT involved), and target of JUDGEMENT (i.e. the ones whose behaviours or characters are evaluated).

As for the polarity of attitudinal meanings, I have followed a tripartite distinction proposed by Bednarek (2008), namely positive, negative and neutral. The neutral value will be added to the dichotomy of attitudinal values (e.g. Martin and White, 2005) on the ground that some emotions are not clearly positive or negative although they are still references to emotion (Bednarek, 2008).

The most obvious feature of news discourse is the mediating of different news voices to account for the events at issue. Attested evidence (otherwise known as direct evidence) such as visual (e.g. I saw…) or olfactory evidence (e.g. I smelled…), among others, has been a major concern in the study of evidentiality (Chafe & Nichols, 1986; Dendale & Tasmowski, 2001; Plungian, 2001). It constitutes a substantial means for journalists to show the vividness of the events and to show the audience their presence on site. In so doing, the report is expected to be favourably perceived as true, first-hand, new, and perhaps objective. This notwithstanding, such an important source of evidentiality has not yet been touched upon in APPRAISAL.

In this research, I have however incorporated it in the discursive model of stance (see Fig. 2.5). In the analysis of ENGAGEMENT feature (see Chap. 8) I will provide an overview of the distribution of ENGAGEMENT features in my corpus, but the focus will be laid on those features involving quotation of different news sources. Figure 2.5 presents a tentative model for coding and analysing journalistic stance in this research.

2.4 Summary

To summarize, the APPRAISAL framework, as yet, provides the only systematic, detailed and elaborate framework of evaluative meaning (Bednarek, 2006, p. 32). The tentative model is eventually a marriage of what is ideal and what is practically achievable. The ideal situation is to include in the analysis of comprehensive evaluative meanings, but the practical situation is to be aware of what is manageable and achievable in a single book. With this limitation acknowledged, I now move on to present the ontological perception of journalistic stance in the next chapter.

References

Ädel, A. (2006). *Metadiscourse in L1 and L2 English* (Vol. 24). Amsterdam: John Benjamins Publishing.

Aikhenvald, A. Y. (2004). *Evidentiality*. Oxford: Oxford University Press.

Bednarek, M. (2006). *Evaluation in media discourse: Analysis of a newspaper corpus*. London/New York: Continuum.

Bednarek, M. (2008). *Emotion talk across corpora*. Basingstoke/New York: Palgrave Macmillan.

Bednarek, M. (2009a). Language patterns and ATTITUDE. *Functions of Language, 16*(2), 165–192.

Bednarek, M. (2009b). Polyphony in appraisal: Typological and topological perspectives. *Linguistics and the Human Sciences, 3*(2), 107–136.

Bell, A. (1991). *The language of news media*. Oxford/Cambridge MA: Blackwell.

Berman, R. A. (2004). Introduction: Developing discourse stance in different text types and languages. *Journal of Pragmatics, 37*(2), 105–124.

Berman, R. A., Ragnarsdóttir, H., & Strömqvist, S. (2002). Discourse stance. *Written Language and Literacy, 5*, 255–290.

Biber, D. (2006). Stance in spoken and written university registers. *Journal of English for Academic Purposes, 5*(2), 97–116.

Biber, D., Johansson, S., Leech, G., Conrad, S., & Finegan, E. (1999). *Longman grammar of spoken and written English*. London: Longman.

Bourdieu, P. (1977). The economics of linguistic exchanges. *Social Science Information, 16*(6), 645–668.

Bourdieu, P. (1984). *Distinction: A social critique of the judgement of taste*. Cambridge, MA: Harvard University Press.

Bourdieu, P. (1986). The forms of capital. In J. Richardson (Ed.), *Handbook of theory and research for the sociology of education* (pp. 241–258). New York: Greenwood.

Bourdieu, P. (1991). *Language and symbolic power*. Cambridge, MA: Harvard University Press.

Caffi, C., & Janney, R. W. (1994). Toward a pragmatics of emotive communication. *Journal of Pragmatics, 22*(3–4), 325–373.

Chafe, W., & Nichols, J. (Eds.). (1986). *Evidentiality: The linguistic coding of epistemology*. Norwood, NJ: Ablex.

Conrad, S., & Biber, D. (2000). Adverbial marking of stance in speech and writing. In S. Hunston & G. Thompson (Eds.), *Evaluation in text: Authorial stance and the construction of discourse* (pp. 56–73). Oxford: Oxford University Press.

Coupland, J., & Coupland, N. (2009). Attributing stance in discourses of body shape and weight loss. In A. Jaffe (Ed.), *The sociolinguistics of stance* (pp. 227–249). New York: Oxford University Press.

Dendale, P., & Tasmowski, L. (2001). Introduction: Evidentiality and related notions. *Journal of Pragmatics, 33*(3), 339–348.

Dry, H. (1992). *Evidentiality and affect in the prose of Hanna Arendt*. Paper presented at the International Association of Literary Semantics, Canterbury, England.

Du Bois, J. W. (2007). The stance triangle. In R. Englebretson (Ed.), *Stancetaking in discourse: Subjectivity, evaluation, interaction* (pp. 130–182). Amsterdam: Benjamins.

Eggins, S., & Slade, D. (1997). *Analysing casual conversation*. London/New York: Cassell.

Fairclough, N. (1992). *Discourse and social change* (Vol. 73). Cambridge: Polity Press.
Finegan, E. (1995). Subjectivity and subjectivisation: An introduction. In D. Stein & S. Wright (Eds.), *Subjectivity and subjectivisation* (pp. 1–15). Cambridge: Cambridge University Press.
Francis, G. (1995). Corpus-driven grammar and its relevance to the learning of English in a cross-cultural situation. In A. Pakir (Ed.), *English in education: Multicultural perspectives*. Singapore: Unipress.
Goffman, E. (1981). *Forms of talk*. Philadelphia: University of Pennsylvania Press.
Greenbaum, S. (1969). *Studies in English adverbial usage*. London: Longman.
Gumperz, J. J. (1982). *Language and social identity*. Cambridge: Cambridge University Press.
Halliday, M. A. K. (1976). Anti-languages. *American Anthropologist, 78*(3), 570–584.
Halliday, M. A. K. (1978). *Language as social semiotic*. Maryland: University Park Press.
Halliday, M. A. K., & Matthiessen, C. M. (2014). *An introduction to functional grammar* (4th ed.). New York: Routledge.
Huan, C. (2015). *Journalistic stance in Chinese and Australian hard news* (Doctoral thesis), Macquarie University, Sydney.
Hunston, S. (2000). Evaluation and the planes of discourse: Status and value in persuasive texts. In S. Hunston & G. Thompson (Eds.), *Evaluation in text* (pp. 176–207). Oxford: Oxford University Press.
Hunston, S. (2003). *Frame, phrase or function: A comparison of frame semantics and local grammars*. Paper presented at the Corpus linguistics. University of Lancaster: University Centre for Computer Corpus Research on Language.
Hunston, S. (2008). The evaluation of status in multi-modal texts. *Functions of Language, 15*(1), 64–83.
Hunston, S. (2011). *Corpus approaches to evaluation: Phraseology and evaluative language*. New York: Routledge.
Hunston, S., & Thompson, G. (Eds.). (2000). *Evaluation in text*. Oxford: Oxford University Press.
Hyland, K. (1998). *Hedging in scientific research articles* (Vol. 54). Amsterdam: John Benjamins Publishing.
Hyland, K. (2005a). *Metadiscourse: Exploring interaction in writing*. London: A&C Black.
Hyland, K. (2005b). Stance and engagement: A model of interaction in academic discourse. *Discourse Studies, 7*(2), 173–192.
Jaffe, A. (2009). *Stance: Sociolinguistic perspectives*. Oxford: Oxford University Press.
Lemke, J. L. (1998). Resources for attitudinal meaning: Evaluative orientations in text semantics. *Functions of Language, 5*(1), 33–56.
Levinson, S. C. (1979). Activity types and language. *Linguistics, 17*(5–6), 365–400.
Lyons, J. (1982). Deixis and subjectivity: Loquor, ergo sum. In R. J. Jarvella & W. Klein (Eds.), *Speech, place, and action: Studies in deixis and other related topics* (pp. 101–125). New York: Wiley.
Martin, J. R. (2000). Beyond exchange: Appraisal systems in English. In S. Hunston & G. Thompson (Eds.), *Evaluation in text: Authorial stance and the construction of discourse* (pp. 142–175). Oxford: Oxford University Press.
Martin, J. R., & Rose, D. (2003). *Working with discourse: Meaning beyond the clause*. London/New York: Bloomsbury Publishing.
Martin, J. R., & White, P. R. R. (2005). *The language of evaluation*. Basingstoke: Palgrave Macmillan.
Nuyts, J. (2001). *Epistemic modality, language, and conceptualization: A cognitive-pragmatic perspective*. Amsterdam: John Benjamins.
Ochs, E. (1990). Cultural universals in the acquisition of language. *Papers and Reports on Child Language Development, 29*, 1–19.
Ochs, E. (1996). Linguistic resources for socializing humanity. In J. Gumperz & S. Levinson (Eds.), *Rethinking linguistic relativity* (pp. 407–438). Cambridge: Cambridge University Press.
Palmer, F. R. (2001). *Mood and modality*. Cambridge: Cambridge University Press.
Papafragou, A. (2000). On speech-act modality. *Journal of Pragmatics, 32*(5), 519–538.
Perrin, D. (2013). *The linguistics of newswriting*. Amsterdam: John Benjamins Publishing.

Plungian, V. A. (2001). The place of evidentiality within the universal grammatical space. *Journal of Pragmatics, 33*(3), 349–357.

Precht, K. (2000). *Patterns of stance in English* (Unpublished Ph.D. thesis), Northern Arizona University, Arizona.

Precht, K. (2003). Stance moods in spoken English: Evidentiality and affect in British and American conversation. *TEXT, 23*(2), 239–258.

Searle, J. R. (1985). *Expression and meaning: Studies in the theory of speech acts*. Cambridge: Cambridge University Press.

Sinclair, J. (1981). Planes of discourse. In S. N. A. Rizvi (Ed.), *The two-fold voice: Essays in honour of Ramesh Mohan* (pp. 70–89). Salzburg: University of Salzburg.

Sleurs, K., Jacobs, G., & Van Waes, L. (2003). Constructing press releases, constructing quotations: A case study. *Journal of Sociolinguistics, 7*(2), 192–212.

Thompson, G., & Hunston, S. (2000). Evaluation: An introduction. In S. Hunston & G. Thompson (Eds.), *Evaluation in text* (pp. 1–27). Oxford: Oxford University Press.

Van Leeuwen, T. (1995). Representing social action. *Discourse & Society, 6*(1), 81–106.

Van Leeuwen, T. (1996). The representation of social actors. In C. R. Caldas-Coulthard & M. Coulthard (Eds.), *Texts and practices: Readings in critical discourse analysis* (Vol. 1, pp. 32–70). London: Routledge.

Vygotsky, L. (1978). Interaction between learning and development. In M. Gauvain & M. Cole (Eds.), *Readings on the development of children* (2nd ed., pp. 79–91). New York: W.H. Freeman and Company.

White, P. R. R. (2002). Appraisal: The language of evaluation and stance. In J. Verschueren, J.-O. Östman, J. Blommaert, & C. Bulcaen (Eds.), *The handbook of pragmatics* (pp. 1–27). Amsterdam/Philadelphia: John Benjamins.

White, P. R. R. (2012). Exploring the axiological workings of 'reporter voice'news stories—Attribution and attitudinal positioning. *Discourse, Context & Media, 1*(2), 57–67.

Chapter 3
A Multiperspectival Approach to Journalistic Stance: From Ontology to Methodology

3.1 Introduction

While the linguistic model is necessary for examining the semiotic aspect of journalistic stance, it has yet provided a rather partial view of journalistic stance taking practices. This is because journalistic stance is considered as a nexus of practice (Scollon & Scollon, 2004, 2007; Van Dijk, 1993) rather than textual realization of stance markers per se, a point that will be canvassed below in this chapter. As a nexus of practice, journalistic stance is the result of the convergence of multiple practices, including, but not limited to, social-institutional practices, situated social actions of journalism practitioners and discursive practices. As such, the investigation of journalistic stance is incomplete without having recourse to a systematic examination of its associated nexus of practices.

The primary aim of this chapter is thus to present an ontological approach that can afford insights into systematic interrogation of journalistic stance. The ontological approach is also known as a multiperspectival (MP) approach (e.g. Candlin, 1997, 2006; Candlin & Crichton, 2011, 2013; Crichton, 2010). It is clear that a wide spectrum of approaches have been proposed and applied to news discourse, and other discourses: content analysis, cultural studies, feminist approaches, diachronic approaches, political-economic approaches, critical discourse analysis (CDA), ethnographic approaches, and mediated discourse analysis, to name only the most obvious. A review of approaches to discourse analysis has been provided by researchers such as Bednarek (2006), Bell (1991), Bhatia, Flowerdew, and Jones (2008), Cotter (2010) and Wodak and Busch (2004).

The primary reason for adopting the multiperspectival approach is that it provides insights into conceiving news discourse as social practices rather than pure written or spoken texts. The analysis of news texts offers more on *what* and *whose* ideologies are encoded in news texts at the expense of ignoring the process of *how* ideologies or values are resemioticized in news discourse. The examination of the news production processes can only be afforded by the insights gained from

C. Huan, *Journalistic Stance in Chinese and Australian Hard News*,
https://doi.org/10.1007/978-981-13-0791-1_3

ethnographic research in news institutions by examining journalists' perception of news values, by investigating news selection processes in editorial meetings and by examining the social-institutional and interactional contexts linked to such social practices. Further justification of adopting the MP approach will be provided in the following.

3.2 Ecological Validity of Stance Analysis

Before presenting the MP approach, this section will discuss the 'ecological validity' (Cicourel, 1992, 2007) of research on journalistic stance with a view to revealing the explanatory affordances of the MP approach to address my research concerns. In so doing, it is worth presenting below a long quote about ecological validity as advanced by Cicourel (2007, p. 736)

> Validity in the non-experimental social sciences refers to the extent to which complex organizational activities represented by aggregated data from public and private sources and demographic and sample surveys can be linked to the collection, integration, and assessment of temporal samples of observable (and when possible recordable) activities in daily life settings. Fragments of discourse materials always are shaped and constrained by the larger organizational settings in which they emerge and simultaneously influenced by cognitive/emotional processes despite the convenience of only focusing on extracted fragments independently of the organizational and cognitive/emotional complexity of daily life settings. Social interaction and discourse materials are sometimes portrayed by applied linguists and/or students of conversation as if they have a life of their own (Schegloff, 1987). This latter view, however, ignores the fact that situated social interaction is always embedded in daily life socio-cultural and cognitive/emotional processes that constrain and shape discourse. The challenge remains how daily life activities simultaneously constrain and shape more complex organizational structures.

On this view, journalistic stance, as a nexus of social practice (Scollon & Scollon, 2007), is set within an interpenetrating context (Cicourel, 1992). Journalistic stance is not something that has its own life, but always indexes a relationship between semiotic instances of stance and their social production processes, involving social order, institutional order, interaction order and personal order (i.e. participants' professional experience). Any exploration, interpretation and explanation of journalistic stance are consequently inevitably connected to an understanding of "something about the ethnographic setting, the perception of and characteristics attributed to others, and broader and local social organisational conditions" (Cicourel, 1992, p. 294).

To explore such an interdiscursive concept as journalistic stance requires researchers to adopt appropriate methodologies and different perception and hypotheses concerning the social order, personal order and the mediating role of language. As Candlin (1997, p. xii) puts it succinctly:

> The issue then immediately arises of how to capture these distinct methodological discourses in a workable program of research, not merely harmonizing the different discourses but actively making use of their distinct epistemologies and modes of practice to enrich and expand a grounded analysis" (Candlin, 1997, p. xii).

Following this argument, Candlin and his colleagues (Candlin, 1997, 2006; Candlin & Crichton, 2011, 2013; Crichton, 2010) propose the multiperspectival approach (see Sect. 3.4 below). This research approach holds that analysing discourse/language in social life needs to incorporate semiotic analysis of discursive performances on site (e.g. the discursive aspect of journalistic stance); ethnographically grounded examination of social, institutional and professional practices and interaction order (e.g. the social-institutional aspect of journalistic stance); accumulated accounts of discursive practices by ratified members of the communities of practice under investigation (e.g. the cognitive or personal aspect of journalistic stance); and explicit revelation of analysts' motivational relevancies and practice relevance in relation to participants.

The MP approach seeks to address the fundamental question raised in the applied linguistics and professional practice regarding the relationship among language, social structure and agency (Carter & Sealey, 2000), otherwise known as the macro-micro problem in discourse analysis, and more generally in social sciences (Crichton, 2010). Coupland, Sarangi and Candlin (2001) identified a dilemma in accounting for the situatedness of discursive practice. That is, on one hand, the strength of discourse analysis lies in its close examination of micro-scale language in use, while on the other, such strength is likely to be weakened without reference to its global social context. In a similar vein, Carter and Sealey (2000, p. 11) maintain that:

> Too great an emphasis on structures denies actors any power and fails to account for human beings making a difference. Too great an emphasis on agency overlooks the very real constraints acting on us in time and space. And reducing each to merely a manifestation of the other – a conceptual running-together of difference domains - necessarily results in a theory which is unable to capture the complex relations between them.

The central challenge this dilemma presents concerns the issue of how to synthesize the affordances and characteristics together without a priori subordinating or excluding those of each perspective (e.g. social structure and agency). According to Carter and New (2004), good explanations of social phenomena "are those which account for patterns of phenomena by showing that causal processes are operating at various levels of the social world" (Carter & New, 2004, p. 1). In this sense, the key step to interpret and explain journalistic stance taking practices is to gain insights into locating the source of control of such practices. The sources of control may be arising out of the constraining power of social structures or emerging from the concerted actions of individuals. This issue will be discussed in Sect. 3.4 below.

3.3 Envisaging Consensus

This section identifies six points of consensus shared between the MP approach and other approaches that also focus on the investigation of language in social life, such as critical discourse analysis (Fairclough, 1992, 2010, 2014; Reisigi & Wodak, 2009; Van Dijk, 1993, 2007; Van Leeuwen & Wodak, 1999; Wodak, 1999; Wodak & Meyer, 2009), mediated discourse analysis (Jones & Norris, 2005; Scollon, 1998, 2001; Scollon & Scollon, 2004), and linguistic ethnography (Blommaert, 2009; Blommaert & Dong, 2006; Rampton, 2007; Rampton et al., 2004).

The first point of agreement is that they view language as a set of social resources for meaning making available to human beings in social life. These resources are selected by language users to perform certain functions in relation to the social contexts they engage in. Language is therefore socially and culturally situated. Such an ontological view of language in social life is shared between critical discourse analysis (CDA), mediated discourse analysis (MDA, also known as nexus analysis) and linguistic ethnography. It is also central to Halliday's SFL (Halliday, 1978).

The second point of agreement concerns the epistemological view of the inextricable interconnectedness of language and society. The study of language in parallel with the above ontological view should be closely related to its social and cultural conditions that give rise to the concerned language uses. Language uses are a form of social action performed by language users in a social condition. In this sense, discursive actions are historical and index wider social dimensions. The social and institutional contexts are not deterministic. Instead, language and social life are mutually shaping. In light of this, understanding discursive actions immediately calls into question a scrutiny of its production processes.

Despite the concrete tools that different approaches adopt to address their respective research concerns, they share the same methodological tenet, the third point of agreement. This methodological tenet has been considered as counter-hegemony or democratic (Blommaert & Dong, 2006; Fairclough, 2009; Hymes, 1980; Van Dijk, 1993). The methodological strategy is to locate critical moments (Sarangi & Candlin, 2007) and mediational means (Scollon & Scollon, 2007) by which discursive actions are carried out. This is because, as Rampton et al. (2004, p. 2) point out, "close analysis of situated language use can provide both fundamental and distinctive insights into the mechanisms and dynamics of social and cultural production in everyday activity" (also see Candlin & Sarangi, 2004; Rampton, 2007). The emic perspective is adopted to solicit experience and account of insiders engaging in the identified activities in field sites (Roberts & Sarangi, 1999). The researchers often take case studies as the point of analytical entry to obtaining access to the complex social issues under scrutiny. This is particularly the case for MDA, linguistic ethnographic studies and Van Dijk's approach of CDA. In so doing, it demands researchers to be engaged in a sustained period of participant observation of some cases, interviewing and eliciting narratives from participants, writing up vignettes and field notes of their fieldwork, and collecting other relevant documents or artefacts, if any. However, cases under investigation are not considered as the focus of research but as the entry point to gaining access to understand how activities are organized by and articulated towards the ways the ongoing production and conducting of social, cultural, institutional, professional, and personal processes are made visible and explicated. The essence of studies in this line extends far beyond a method for collecting particular sets of data and a technique through which the analysis of text can be made relevant to contexts, neither can it be reducible to fieldwork techniques or participant observation. Instead, they adopt a holistic view of "the shared conceptual world that is discursively constructed and maintained by the group" (Smart, 2006, p. 58).

The fourth point of agreement concerns the ways of collecting and interpreting data. Discourse analysis has been considered as a set of interpretive practices, highly flexible and creative (e.g. Blommaert, 2005; Candlin & Crichton, 2013; Fairclough, 2010; Rampton et al., 2004; Sarangi & Candlin, 2001; Scollon & Scollon, 2004; Van Dijk, 2007). As such, it is important to avoid drawing rigid divisions between data and interpretation. This requires researchers to pay as much attention to the ways data is interpreted and integrated as to collect a range of data connecting each dataset to the activities and situations under investigation. Rather than simply describing the situations in which participants are involved, ethnographically informed studies involve "joint problematisation" (Roberts & Sarangi, 1999) of these situations between researchers and the researched, acknowledging that "the subjects of ethnographic research are usually more knowledgeable about their practices than are the researchers (Sarangi & Candlin, 2003, p. 283). The insider's experiences and views regarding the concerned situations are of crucial relevance and significance in understanding the activities they engage in, what meanings they ascribe to, and the interaction orders they follow among members of their communities of practice (Lave, 1998; Lave & Wenger, 1991). The process of such joint-problematisation does not however indicate a prior body of existing knowledge and values only to be discovered by the researcher. It denotes an iterative process through which the researcher and researched jointly articulate the knowledge and values inherent in the concerned activities.

The fifth point of consensus is related to the role of discourse analysts in the process of knowledge gathering and production. It is important to recognize the ineradicable role that the researcher's personal subjectivity and motivational relevancies (Sarangi & Candlin, 2001) might play throughout the entire process of research. Analysts are accordingly invited to keep reflexive on their possible partiality of their interpretation of activities under investigation. However, the subjective experience of the researcher is not regarded as a deficit factor impairing discourse studies. Rather, it is a factor that could possibly allow for discovering new knowledge that might be not foreshadowed or foreseen by either participants or researchers at the outset of the study. As pointed out by (Geertz, 1983, p. 57), it is essential for researchers to "take the subject's own concepts and place them in illuminating connection with broader theoretical concepts to produce an interpretation of the life of the group. Researchers, as Geertz argues, must "swim in the stream of the subjects' experience" (Geertz, 1983, p. 58). A sustained engagement with members of the group over an extended period is therefore preferable to achieve thick participation and thick description (Sarangi, 2008).

At the same time, it is equally important to note that researchers must attempt to maintain a balance of engagement with and detachment from the informants' conceptual reality. To achieve this "analytic distance on what's close-at-hand" (Rampton, 2007, p. 590), researchers should move outside the insider's perspective towards an outsider's perspective so as to avoid unnecessarily privileging the relevant interests of any particular participants group or individual over others. While excessive involvement or alignment with participant's perspective may take researchers to a position tending to hedge claims (Rampton, 2007, p. 591), restricted involvement may put researchers in a danger of simply gaining rather rudimentary knowledge of the activities, and thus unable to achieve the levels of understanding of and confidence in producing and articulating the knowledge of complex activities that constitute social actions. In short, researchers are expected to be involved in a collaborative process of interpreting knowledge with the researched and at the same time to balance engagement with detachment.

The last point of consensus is that CDA, MDA, linguistic ethnography and the MP approach are neither a research method of discourse analysis nor a theory with a set of clearly defined tools (e.g. Blommaert & Dong, 2006; Candlin & Crichton, 2011, 2013; Fairclough, 2010; Jones & Norris, 2005; Rampton, 2007; Rampton et al., 2004; Van Dijk, 1993; Wodak & Busch, 2004). Rather, they are a kind of research program that is primarily oriented and geared to understand language in social life and to effect positive social change. Researchers in this line of inquiry often take an explicit social-political position and stance to understand social practices. CDA is perhaps the most obvious approach in this respect by setting out to problematize the ways social inequality and injustice are enacted, sustained, legitimated and/or ignored through various discourses (Fairclough, 2010; Reisigi & Wodak, 2009; Van Dijk, 1993; Van Leeuwen & Wodak, 1999).

3.4 Charting the Research Map of the Multiperspectival Approach

The challenge in the investigation of journalistic stance taking is to explain how journalistic stance is set within its broader social-institutional contexts, and related to the routine of journalist's social practice. To address this issue, a unified and valid ontological framework and a toolkit of manageable methodologies are demanded. Any such enterprises will inevitably raise and demand addressing two fundamental and interrelated questions. The first question concerns the issue of explaining the features and relationship involved in the nexus of journalistic stance taking practices such as social-institutional practices, interaction order and participant's psychobiology. The second one relates to how to consolidate concrete methods at analysts' disposal to establish relevance of journalistic stance taking in the nexus of practice. This section addresses these issues by contouring a research map of the MP approach to journalistic stance taking practices.

3.4.1 Understanding Social Practice in Relation to the Domain Theory

The MP approach draws extensively on Layder's (1993) multi-strategy approach or domain theory (Layder, 2006) towards social research, an intellectual research approach in the field of sociology attempting to link together agency and structure. Domain theory is in part a response to structuration theory (Giddens, 1984), but "rejects the idea that social reality can be properly understood in terms of theories or perspectives that attempt to reconcile or synthesis agency and structure but only succeed in merging or dissolving their distinct characteristics" (Layder, 2006, p. 272). Accordingly, domain theory shuns away from the dualism of agency and structure, but subscribes to the viewpoint that social reality is essentially situated in four interconnected domains to capture its variegated nature (see Fig. 3.1 below).

The psychobiographical domain maps an individual's unique biographies through time and space in social world where their personal feelings, attitudes, ideas, values and dispositions are coloured by their interactions with other experiences. "Every individual's trajectory is unique because his or her life develops in the context of a unique configuration of relationships with others" (Layder, 2006, p. 274). Despite this uniqueness of psychobiographies, any individual, as pre-eminent social actors, will inevitably be involved in and influenced by the face-to-face social interaction, an intersubjective aspect of social life. The social interaction is accounted for by Layder in the domain of situated activity. This domain operates on a different time scale from that of psychobiography, as the former highlights the episodic nature of social interaction from the moment when it is initiated down until the transaction is completed, whereas the latter frames the lifetimes and personal identities of individuals from birth to the present. The

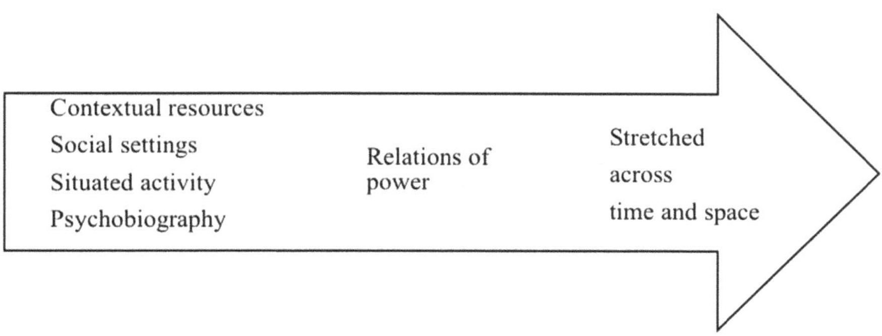

Fig. 3.1 The layering of social domain and power in time and space (after Layder, 2006, p. 273)

domain of psychobiography and that of situated activity foreground respectively the subjective and intersubjective aspect of an individual's social practices. However, all social practices of human beings unfold in the domain of social settings, the immediate environment of situated activity. "Social settings are clearly distinguishable from other domains in that they are local aggregations of reproduced social relations, positions and practices. As such, social settings embody systemic (structural) aspects of social life—the reproduced outcomes of past social activities that influence behaviour in the present" (Layder, 2006, p. 280). Consequently, the focus is shifted away from agency, the subjective and intersubjective aspects of human experience, to structures, the social, cultural and institutional environments where these social interactions arise. Interactions vary in different social settings in tune with different configuration of positions, statuses and other aspects of social relationship. Despite the variegated nature of social settings, there are constraints applied to evaluating the kind of social practices as acceptable/permissible or immoral/illegal at a more global social-cultural level. This brings into view the domain of contextual resources, a set of anterior distributional material and cultural capital (e.g. Bourdieu, 1977b, 1986, 1991) on which social actors draw to sustain social transactions. These cultural resources "furnish the immediate socio-economic context of particular social settings (educational, occupational, domestic/familial, neighbourhood and so on) and their effects are felt and experienced in social activities and the inner mental lives of individuals" (Layder, 2006, p. 281).

Domain theory differs from a structuralism view of perceiving social action as determined and prescribed by social structure. It also speaks against those views that envisage social structure as nothing but the resulting collective outcomes of social interaction. The domain theory presents an alternative to Giddens's structuration theory (e.g. Giddens, 1984) since Giddens views structure and agency as mutually constitutive and as such the possibility of exploring the effects of one on the other is precluded (Carter & Sealey, 2000; Layder, 2006). In contrast, the domain theory identifies and highlights the distinctive features of each domain without losing sight of the links and continuities between them. These domains are considered as inextricably interconnected together in the unfolding process of social practices, whose meaning is "an amalgam of the influences of different domains" (Layder, 2006, p. 278). On this view, structure cannot be taken as identical with or reduced to elements of agency since each domain has their distinctive properties and characteristics. On the other hand, all these elements are so intimately interconnected with each other that any attempt to interpret social practices by exclusively reference to an isolated domain will eventually be dismissed.

Domain theory brings into focus three central elements involved in the nexus of social practices, namely social-institution, interaction order and the historical body. It affords researchers analytical power, together with clear epistemological viewpoints, to account for the causal processes underlying the patterned social practices operating at simultaneously different levels of social life.

However, it seems that domain theory, when applied in the field of applied linguistics where language acts as a central mediational means, may pay insufficient attention to the semiotic aspect of social practices (Sealey & Carter, 2004). This caveat may be partially explained by the fact that Layder is a sociologist but not a linguist and that he prioritizes the investigation of *why* social practices are enacted. As such, Layder has underexplored the issue of *how* social practices are enacted. For this reason, rather than a counterbalance to the thesis demonstrated in domain theory, this research argues here that in light of the tenets presented in domain theory, the semiotic aspect of social practices has their own properties and features that can be distinguishable from those of other domains.

The domain theory, as outlined above in Fig. 3.1, emphasizes the notion of power embodied in each domain stretched across time and space. Like Foucault's concept of capillary power (Foucault, 1980), Layder (2006) argues that the power resides in each domain that is highly interconnected with each other. Structural powers in the domains of social settings and contextual resources are reproduced features of social life, and represent the kind of power that has traversed varying spans of history. Structural powers may serve to explain why social reality remains relatively stable. By contrast, the power derived from the domains of situated activity and that of psychobiography situates within "this envelop of more encompassing power relations" (Layder, 2006, p. 284). Individual powers may serve to elucidate the possibility of social changes. Hence, social practices suggest a blend of powers derived from such multiple domains. While the vertical dimension in Fig. 3.1 (p. 34) demonstrates the ontological depth of social reality, the horizontal dimension illustrates the dynamics of social activity and social processes that are situated within these domains, which are interconnected through relations of power stretched across time and space.

3.4.2 Outlining the Ontology of Multiperspectival Approach

The MP approach empirically grows out of substantial research efforts of its initiators, Christopher Candlin and Jonathan Crichton in areas of applied linguistics as diverse as classroom settings, professional and organizational discourses (e.g. Candlin, 1997, 2006; Candlin & Crichton, 2011, 2013; Crichton, 2010), inter alia. Theoretically, it has inherited the legacies from the domain theory proposed by Layder (1993, 2006).

Central tenets of such a research program are that firstly any discursive practice is inevitably situated within a nexus of practice involving elements from different levels. Secondly, the interdiscursive nature of social practices makes necessary corresponding interdisciplinary methodologies, seeking to match their descriptive, interpretative and explanatory demands through connecting social-institutional practices and the interaction order with the distinctive properties of professional experiences of social actors. Thirdly, in line with the domain theory, the MP approach fosters a view upholding that these perspectives are dynamically and organically combined, without, a priori, subordinating, prioritizing or excluding any perspective.

The MP approach itself incorporates five perspectives: the analysts', participants', social practice, social-institutional, and semiotic perspectives. Before I elaborate on each perspective in the following, a key point needs to be highlighted here. That is, each perspective in the MP approach is equally necessary and mutually informing and at the same time is interconnected with each other. In this sense, each perspective, in tune with Layder's (1993, 2006) recommendation for social research, has its distinctive characteristics and properties, and thus merits close scrutiny in its own right. They converge at some critical moments or sites of engagement to enable social practices. There is however no primacy of one perspective over another. Rather, "entry points to the analysis will vary in relation to particular sites and their relevant focal themes (Roberts & Sarangi, 2005) and to the particular research questions that are being addressed" (Candlin & Crichton, 2013, p. 10). Social practices (e.g. journalistic stance) can only be fully appreciated by integrating affordances of all perspectives.

3.4.2.1 The Analysts' Perspective

The ecological validity (Cicourel, 2007) of the study on journalistic stance, or any social research in general, requires the examination of its social-institutional contexts, the involved interaction order and the practitioners' personal and professional experience. However, the analysts' account for such ecological validity is mirrored in and aligned with particular theoretical orientations, social-political positions, research concerns and their distinctive research background. Accordingly, balanced research requires an analyst to demonstrate explicitly their motivational relevancies (Sarangi & Candlin, 2001) and the practical relevance of the study in general (Roberts & Sarangi, 1999). Such a position suggests that the analysts' and participants' perspectives are mutually influencing. Likewise, the study of journalistic stance in this research, on one hand, demands explicit explanation of theoretical orientation and value positions, together with clearly outlined and articulately demonstrated research methodology, while on the other it requires the explanation of practical relevance of research results to the participants, issues that will be discussed in various sections of this book.

3.4.2.2 The Participants' Perspective: Identity and Habitus

The purpose of drawing on the participants' narrative account of their psychobiography is to retrieve participant's distinctive professional experience and to gain insight into understanding their habitus (Bourdieu, 1977b, 1984) stretched across time and space in social life. The associated methodology requires participants to describe and interpret their experience as influenced by social interaction with others and to suggest how their identities are enacted through participants positioning themselves vis-à-vis other social actors and the social contexts.

The MP approach recognizes the autonomy and independence of the individuality, without losing sight of its inextricable relation to the concerned social contexts. The unique identity associated with such distinctive psychobiographical experiences may lead participants to undertake stances that may seem incongruent with the social-institutional values that are currently operational. The degree of deviance however depends upon critical life events and their effects on psychological resilience. That is to say, social actors (e.g. journalism practitioners) could appropriate alternative stances against the constraints upon their intended stance taking, only if they intend to do so (Giddens, 1984). One potential risk of taking this viewpoint to the extreme point where participants' psychobiographies are over-emphasized is that it loses sight of social structural influences and individual variations such as social power, capacities, resources and resilience. This is as dangerous as under-estimating their contribution to the interpretation of discursive practices. It further underwrites the importance of jointly problematizing the discursive practices by the researchers and researched in that participants may become unaware of the influence of the interaction order, and social-cultural contexts in which their daily routine unfolds. Accordingly, the issues surrounding the intersubjective and objective aspects of discursive practice demand to be addressed in light of perspectives of social practice (Sect. 3.4.2.3) and social-institutional contexts (Sect. 3.4.2.4), respectively.

3.4.2.3 Social Practice Perspective: Interaction Order

As Goffman pointed out, "it is a fact of our human condition that, for most of us, our daily life is spent in the immediate presence of others; in other words, that whatever they are, our doings are likely to be, in the narrow sense, socially situated" (Goffman, 1983, p. 2). This is especially true in the case of journalists' daily practices which are primarily concerned with interaction with news sources, readers, in house editors and their superiors, among others. The interaction order, constituting a key element of journalists' social life, is "a substantive domain in its own right" (Goffman, 1983, p. 2). The social practice perspective is therefore proposed and integrated in the MP approach seeking to interpret how social actors contribute to social practices by means of participating into social interaction, the intersubjective dimension of social life. In contrast to the desire of preserving a more private self, as implied in the participants' perspective, each individual is also in need of a social self (Goffman, 1981) in order to sustain their social life. The social practices an individual undertakes bear with them constraints and enablement of the interaction order, which "protects itself from the self-interests of those involved by placing moral obligations on them to adhere to the ground rules of the interaction" (Layder, 2006, p. 242). The strategically ongoing performance involved in light of such interaction order serves to secure each person's "face" (Goffman, 1981). Since interaction and social self are by nature vulnerable to the perceptions of others, an individual accordingly needs to tactically draw on semiotic resources to convey their desirable "front" in Goffman's sense, and thus minimize the risks of revealing their real personal self in routine interaction. That is to say, interactions operate on the working consensus of encounters to save face, suggesting that the interaction order is negotiated between involved encounters "attending to and seeking to adjust to their best advantage the way they align themselves to others and frame what is going on" (Goffman, 1981, cited in Crichton, 2010, p. 40). The moral commitment of people to the maintenance of social transaction implied in the concept of interaction order requires mutual trust between encounters and their willingness to take on the responsibilities of engaging with others. As Giddens puts it succinctly, "people shore-up or repair the moral fabric of interaction, by displaying tact in what they say and do, by engaging in 'remedial practice' and helping others to save face" (Giddens, 1987, p. 113). Although Goffman envisages that the interaction order of daily interaction is loosely coupled with its associated institutional order, he "provides us with no analysis of power and domination, and no extensive analysis of institutions except insofar as they impinge on situated interaction" (Layder, 2006, p. 251). For this research, it is necessary to investigate the influence of broader social-cultural contexts in which social practices arise (Roberts & Sarangi, 1999).

3.4.2.4 Social-Institutional Perspective: Discourses in Place

The social-institutional perspective recognizes that all discourses are anchored in the physical spaces and real times of the material worlds (also see Scollon & Scollon, 2003). These worlds may constitute immediate institutional/organizational environment or more remote social-cultural context. Institutional contexts furnish local accumulation of reproduced social relations, positions and practices, and thus reproduce those conventions resulting from past social practices (Giddens, 1984; Layder, 2006). Institutions embody distinctive forms of power, which, in formal settings such as newsrooms, regulate clearly articulated and hierarchical social relationships and positions. Journalistic social interaction is defined accordingly through these positions and the associated reproduced practices. Journalists' social practices are therefore constrained and at the same time enabled by the rules and resources established in the institutions.

Such local aggregation of reproduced practices draws on the accumulation of resources including material resources and historically accumulated cultural resources such as knowledge (Layder, 2006, p. 281). Cultural resources constitute "the ultimate source of societal values (dominant, sub-cultural or counter cultural), which not only shape the cultural context of social settings, but also the consciousness of those individuals who are influenced by them" (Layder, 2006, p. 281). Cultural resources are influenced, though not determined, by material resources. As Layder (2006, p. 281) puts it eloquently, "cultural resources are unevenly allocated and aligned with groupings such as those based on class, ethnicity, age, gender, status and so on. These furnish the immediate socio-economic context of particular social settings and their effects are felt and experienced in social activities and the inner mental lives of individuals". It is in this way that social structures are interwoven with situated social actions (e.g. Perrin, 2013).

3.4.2.5 Semiotic Perspective

The primary aim of analyzing semiotic aspect of journalistic stance is not to investigate language itself, but to canvass the ways in which journalists undertake stances by means of semiotic resources. Hence, the semiotic perspective focuses on the description of semiotic resources drawn upon by journalists to create meaning in daily social life. Halliday (1978) views language as a social semiotic, and maintains that human beings construe experiences through language (Halliday & Matthiessen, 2014). Language is thus envisaged not so much as a set of rules, but as a system of resources for meaning making. In this research, I will adopt the APPRAISAL framework to systematically study the discursive aspect of journalistic stance in news texts. This research will focus on the linguistic aspects of journalistic stance and will ignore its multimodal aspect in the sense of Kress and Van Leeuwen (2001) and Norris (2012) for the sake of scope.

Of the semiotic perspective, the participants' perspective, the analysts' perspective, the social-institutional perspective and the social practice perspective, none of these incorporated in the MP approach comes new or is newly proposed. What is new, I believe, is the synthesis of the characteristics and affordances of these perspectives within a single and unified framework. It also advances a position holding that context does simply provide a background to the enactment of social practices (e.g. Crichton, 2010). Rather, context itself changes dynamically in interaction, and in this sense it coevolves with the dynamic social practices. Or put it in MDA's term, social practices are semiotic aggregates of a nexus of discourses (Scollon & Scollon, 2003). For this reason, news values that guide social practices of journalism practitioners (Chap. 6) and the exercise of symbolic power (9) should not be simply taken into consideration as a way of understanding journalistic stance better (also see Jones & Norris, 2005, p. 8). Rather, journalistic stance taking practices are semiotic aggregates of news values, the exercise of symbolic power and linguistic devices, inter alia.

Due to the intricate interconnectedness of the five perspectives in the MP approach, it is difficult to point out exactly how each perspective is operationalized in this book. Broadly, the analyst perspective has been explicated in Chap. 1, Sect. 3.5 of Chaps. 3, and 4. The semiotic perspective will be elaborated in Chaps. 5–8 in the form of corpus findings. Social-institutional and participants' perspective will be discussed in Chaps. 9 and 10 in relation to the examination of news values and symbolic power in the process of news production. The length and scope of the book would not have permitted a detailed analysis of interaction order (i.e. social practice perspective) to be undertaken, though this remains an intriguing possibility for future work.

3.5 Fieldwork and Ethnographic Data

The ontological and epistemological tenets being settled, this section will present the methods that have been adopted in collecting ethnographic data. The set of ethnographic data incorporates interviews with rank-and-file journalists, copy-editors, senior editors and some government people in the department of publicity, and more importantly it includes a two-month period of participant observation in a Chinese Party-affiliated newspaper. I will exclusively focus on the Chinese context because research on professional practices in Australian context, and more generally in the Western world, has been largely detailed elsewhere (e.g. Bell, 1991; Cotter, 2010; Cottle, 2007; Cottle & Ashton, 1999; Davis, 2000; Gans, 2004/1979; Jacobs, 2011; Machin & Niblock, 2006; Perrin, 2013; Van Hout, Pander Maat, & De Preter, 2011). In contrast, accesses to Chinese news institutions have been extremely limited due to press control in China, and as such we have as yet insufficient knowledge about the news production processes surrounding daily editorial meetings and journalistic social practices in the Chinese context. That said, my ethnographic work in a Chinese newspaper is broadly organized into three sequential stages in line with the general chronological sequences of the activities conducted (Blommaert & Dong, 2006; Scollon & Scollon, 2004). The first stage concerns the issues of preparation and documentation prior to fieldwork. The second stage mainly involves engaging and navigating the fields during fieldwork; and lastly analyzing data and writing up associated reports after fieldwork.

The methodological strengths and blind spots of ethnography in researching news production have been discussed in detail by other scholars (e.g. Cottle, 2007). This research does not intend to reiterate them here. My participant observation was conducted in one typical municipal-level Party-affiliated (the Communist Party of China, CPC) newspaper in China. This case study is able to reveal in-depth insights into understanding news production in Chinese context, since, as Small (2009, p. 26) puts it succinctly, "a well-executed single-case study can justifiably state that a particular process, phenomenon, mechanism, tendency, type, relationship, dynamic, or practice exists". Having secured this position, I now turn to present the methods adopted in collecting ethnographic data.

3.5.1 Preparation and Documentation

Several activities are required prior to conducting ethnographic work in field sites. Some central preparatory activities include the design of well-articulated research questions, an awareness of the necessity and potential contribution of ethnographic work to the overall project, valid research proposal and manageable work plan, among others. These are general preparation applicable to all sorts of similar research. The following sections will elaborate on issues concerning gaining access to the field, preparing software and developing interview questions to elicit journalists' account of professional experiences.

3.5.1.1 Gaining Access to the Field

Gaining access to the field is the first step to "understand and study the possible contexts in which your object will occur, micro as well as macro" (Blommaert & Dong, 2006, p. 19). This preparatory work assists to decide whether the field sites are researchable. Thus, I firstly tried to establish contacts with target Chinese journalists who might be willing to take part in my research; secondly, I attempted to gain access to the field—news institutions—for conducting participant observation of institutional and professional practices of journalism practitioners. In this process, I utilized several strategies to do so, including online carpet search and snowball strategy. By online carpet search, I mean I used *Weibo*, the Chinese version of *Twitter*, to find target journalists and sent them message requesting their approval to be involved in my research. By snowball strategy, I mean I made use of some "guanxi" (social network) to maneuver this process. I contacted friends who might refer to me their journalist friends who might agree to either be involved in my research or be willing to recommend other journalists. It turns out that the snowball strategy worked more efficiently than online carpet search.

Before I began to contact research participants, I obtained ethic approval from Macquarie University, where clearing such ethic issues has been a compulsory and mandatory requirement for any research involving human or animals. As my research topic is concerned with hard news reporting rather than soft news, I needed to recruit journalists working on hard news reporting to establish relevance to my research topic.

A more thorny issue was to gain access to the field site to conduct participant observation that involves following some journalists for a relatively long period, observing daily editorial meetings and recording journalists' copy-editing processes, etc. Considering the fact that all the news agencies in China are strictly controlled by the government, such accesses were extremely difficult to gain.

I was successful in interviewing ten rank-and-file journalists working on hard news reporting, two senior editors, three sub-editors, and one government person in the department of publicity who was responsible for reviewing all the local newspapers. All of them were clearly informed of the ethics. Informed consent was obtained before interviews. They were aware that they could quit the interview or refuse to answer any questions that they felt uncomfortable about at any time without giving any kind of notice to the interviewer. They were also aware that their names would be totally anonymous and their institutions would not be identified.

Basically, there are two types of newspapers in China, one being official newspaper of government department and the committees of the Communist Party of China (CPC) at different levels (i.e. Party-papers) while the other being called market newspaper. Both are controlled by the government, but it is not compulsory for market newspapers to report routine official activities of local or central authorities, unless such activities are of great importance to local citizens as perceived by journalists. My informants cover both types of newspapers, but the participant observation was conducted in a Party-affiliated newspaper in a city in the middle part of China. This newspaper was chosen for several reasons. The most obvious one was that this newspaper was one of the few available news institutions to which I could gain access. Secondly, it was a Party-paper that was considered in China as so-called "mainstream" newspaper, and thus could by and large represent the "mainstream" newspapers of the same kind. Thirdly, this newspaper was a daily newspaper that built its reputation on hard news reporting. Fourthly, since all newspapers published in Mainland China were subject to censorship of the government at different levels, market papers and Party papers only differ from each other in form but not in substance. Lastly, the Party paper under investigation had established a press conglomerate to commercialize itself (see Chap. 10), and as such it was able to show the most recent ways of journalistic professional practices in the Chinese context.

3.5.1.2 Formulating Interview Questions

The formulation of interview questions was guided by the social, institutional, the participants', and semiotic perspectives of the MP approach (Sect. 3.4, p. 33). The social perspective affords ways of drafting questions concerning the potential influence of such issues as law, financial income of the news agency, and ownership on journalists' stance taking. The institutional perspective invokes questions relating the power relations and interaction order within the institution. The participants' perspective invokes questions aiming to elicit journalists' perception of their professional identity, news values, and habitus. The semiotic perspective encourages questions about journalists' perception of selective use of stance makers.

A pilot version of interview questions was sent via email to one senior Chinese journalist, who was based in a Party-affiliated newspaper in Tianjin, to test its validity. Premised on his answers and suggestions, together with my further revision in line with theoretically informative work, the final version was produced and carried to the field sites (see Appendix A for a translated version of the questions). However, during the interviews, as the number of interviewees increased and as the researcher gained more in-depth understanding of the Chinese context of news production, this interview was constantly modified to elicit more insightful information.

3.5.2 *Navigating the Field*

Tacit knowledge was still not easily available to the researcher as an outsider of the journalistic community of practice. A more engaged position and a relatively detached position were thus required at the same time to achieve a balance between insiders' and outsiders' perspectives in understanding journalistic stance taking practices.

3.5.2.1 The Outsider Advantage and Avoiding Observer Effect

As an outsider, a fieldworker never presents him/herself in the field in a natural way as the informants do. There is always a potential bias involved in the process of data collection in natural settings with the presence of the fieldworker. This is known as the observer effect (Blommaert & Dong, 2006; N. Coupland et al., 2001) or the observer's paradox (Labov, 1970). Such an observer effect is particularly salient in the early stages of fieldwork when mutual trust between fieldworker and informants still remain weak, but it diminishes as this relationship gets stronger.

The presence of observer effect might also be caused by the instrument the ethnographers deploy to mine data. As some examples, if I had used video cameras in my fieldwork and moved around with a camera continually pointing at the journalists' face or at their superiors during the editorial meeting, this observer effect would have been immediately called into question. I believe the journalists, most of whom I met for the first time through the reference from a mutual friend, would have perceived me to be suspicious. Chances were very high that my participant observation in the editorial meeting room could be suspended. In view of this, I used a voice-recorder at a relatively remote distance, so this observer effect might be minimized. This however does not necessarily mean the observer effect disappeared.

Based on my experience, the closer the relationship between a fieldworker and the informants is, the more invisible and less relevant such an effect is. This is clearly exhibited in my fieldwork. My first interviewee C was a journalist working in a high-quality provincial-level market paper in the northwestern part of China. I was introduced to him through a friend of my former undergraduate classmate. Our first meeting took place on the second day after I arrived at his city when he was setting out for an investigative event involving a possible murder in a nearby rural village. The first few questions after greeting were concerned with my general research aims. Considering that I was an overseas researcher, he seemed worried about issues concerning my identity and my intentions to conduct such research, as could be evidenced by two of his half-joke questions: "Are you a spy?" and "Are you a member of the Communist Party of China?" To remove his suspicion, I clarified my research purposes and disclosed to him the ethics involved in my research. I spent two days following his investigative news report. I interviewed him on the second night after a late dinner in the hotel twin room I shared with him. He said he would try his best to answer my questions sincerely. After the interview he confirmed his anonymity. Although the observer effect was minimised, it still remained there, as he constantly looked at the voice recorder.

The second interviewee Q was my former undergraduate classmate who was working in a provincial-level official Party paper in the middle part of China. As we were fairly acquainted with each other, the observer effect was almost negligible. I interviewed her in a coffee shop where we had lunch together. I asked her whether I could record our talk. She said, "Yes, of course. Please do that, otherwise you cannot remember what I will say". The observer effect was minimized to a negligible level, as can be further evidenced by our casual talks, her use of taboo words, answering her private phones in the presence of me, and so on.

However, being an outsider, I was able to take the advantage of this role to ask questions that might seem silly and naive to those insiders. I entered the news agency where I conducted participant observation as an intern rather than a totally outside independent researcher. There were pains and gains in the first few days when my supervising journalist found it hard to define my role as it was her first time to come across one who conducted such kind of research (or any ethnographic research in a news agency). The first day I was following this journalist T, she asked me to write a news report based on the clues she just received, just the way she asked her other interns to do so. I had no background in news writing, but I was trying to follow her instructions for two reasons. On one hand, it was impolite to refuse her at that moment especially when she still considered me as an intern, while on the other hand, I took this as a good opportunity to understand what a journalist should do after obtaining a clue, and what the differences between my amateur writing and her professional news writing would be. This turned out to be very informative and useful in my later stage of ethnographic work, as it enriched my understanding of news structure Chinese journalists follow and major activities they conduct in writing a news report when they were not and would not be on site. After this first trial, I explicitly reiterated my research purposes to her, although I guess she was still confused, as shown in her kindness to put me as co-author in several of her news reports to which I almost contributed nothing more than taking few notes when following her to interview news sources.

3.5.2.2 Consolidating Critical Moments

A further positive effect of being an outsider was that I had experienced more 'strategic or critical moments' (Candlin, 1987) than insiders did. The primary thing to do in the field site was to find crucial social actors, who one might immediately think of journalists and editors. I slowly learned in the field site that journalists worked in a complex and iterative institutional process of news production. The first thing a journalist does every day is to consult news sources. Depending on the status of news sources (e.g. official or ordinary citizens), journalists needed to negotiate the news value of a news event or issue with their head of department before proceeding to do the report.

A very important part of their daily routine was to inform the head of their department of their progresses before 4.00 pm every day when they were on duty so that the head could produce a budget of news stories for review in the afternoon editorial meeting. The deadline for finalizing and submitting daily news reports was set at 8.00 pm when news reports were expected to be ready for review by editors.

In the writing of a news report, journalists sometimes needed to negotiate issues regarding their news at stake with their editors, or to conduct a complementary interview with their interviewee if they found some key questions were not previously raised. Editors did not set space or words limit to journalists regarding a news report, however experienced journalists had internalized this and had in their mind how many words a news report may be worthy of, depending on their news values. The editors then edited the news reports based on their professional knowledge and their negotiation with their superior on duty, because every news report must be signed off by this superior before editors could retrieve them from their system for editing. After editing, the editor sent in the edited news reports to the superior again for review, before the copy editor and art editor could retrieve them through their system.

3.5.3 Data Storage and Transcription

A range of datasets were collected on field sites, including (1) audio-recordings of editorial meetings and interviews with journalists; (2) field notes I took when following journalists in the field; (3) several policy documents in the news institution under investigation; and (4) some photos of news room, editorial meeting room, field sites, and their notice board. However, due to ethics requirements and the request of my interviewees and the involved news institutions, I am disallowed to show the photos and the policy documents here.

The interviews with journalists were conducted in mandarin Chinese and were consequently transcribed by the researcher according to the minimum transcription requirements of conversation analysis. However, the editorial meetings were conducted in a local dialect that I cannot fully understand. This was totally unexpected considering that there were journalists from other areas of China who did not speak such a dialect. This set of data was transcribed by a research assistant recruited specifically for this job. The research assistant was notified of the ethics requirements to do such a job and was paid at an acceptable rate. I have translated the transcribed data into English by myself.

3.6 Summary

In this chapter, I have outlined several points of consensus among approaches towards the study of language in social life, on which I ground my research on journalistic stance. I have also presented the research map of the multiperspectival approach, aiming at achieving a fuller description, interpretation and explanation of journalistic stance. The MP approach necessarily requires the examination of the psychobiographical experience of social actors, its associated social-institutional contexts, the involved interaction order, and the semiotic resources social actors adopted to enact social practice. However, each perspective is independent from but at the same time intimately interconnected with the other. While each perspective merits careful investigation in its own right, such investigation is likely to lose insight without considering other perspectives. It is also important for researchers to explicate their motivational relevancies, coupled with the practical relevance of research to the researched. This chapter has presented the ethnographic research methods adopted to reify and consolidate the ontological and epistemological tenets afforded by the MP approach in the study of journalistic stance. The next chapter continues to present the research methodology adopted to study stance, but the focus will be on the linguistic identification of journalistic stance markers in the Chinese and Australian corpora.

References

Bednarek, M. (2006). *Evaluation in media discourse: Analysis of a newspaper corpus*. London/New York: Continuum.

Bell, A. (1991). *The language of news media*. Oxford/Cambridge MA: Blackwell.

Bhatia, V., Flowerdew, J., & Jones, R. H. (2008). *Advances in discourse studies*. New York: Routledge.

Blommaert, J. (2005). *Discourse: A critical introduction*. Cambridge: Cambridge University Press.

Blommaert, J. (2009). Ethnography and democracy: Hymes's political theory of language. *Text & Talk, 29*(3), 257–276.

Blommaert, J., & Dong, J. (2006). *Ethnographic fieldwork: A beginner's guide*. New York: Multilingual Matters.

Bourdieu, P. (1977). *Outline of a theory of practice*. Cambridge: Cambridge University Press.

Bourdieu, P. (1984). *Distinction: A social critique of the judgement of taste*. Cambridge, MA: Harvard University Press.

Bourdieu, P. (1986). The forms of capital. In J. Richardson (Ed.), *Handbook of theory and research for the sociology of education* (pp. 241–258). New York: Greenwood.

Bourdieu, P. (1991). *Language and symbolic power*. Cambridge, MA: Harvard University Press.

Candlin, C. N. (1987). Explaining moments of conflict in discourse. In R. Steele & T. Treadgold (Eds.), *Language topics: Essays in honour of Michael Halliday* (pp. 413–429). Amsterdam: John Benjamins.

Candlin, C. N. (1997). General editor's preface. In *The construction of professional discourse* (pp. ix–xiv). London: Longman.

Candlin, C. N. (2006). Accounting for interdiscursivity: Challenges to professional expertise. In M. Gotti & D. S. Giannoni (Eds.), *New trends in specialized discourse analysis* (pp. 21–45). Bern: Peter Lang.

Candlin, C. N., & Crichton, J. (2011). Introduction. In C. N. Candlin & J. Crichton (Eds.), *Discourses of deficit* (pp. 1–22). Basingstoke: Palgrave Macmillan.

Candlin, C. N., & Crichton, J. (2013). From ontology to methodology: Exploring the discursive landscape of trust. In C. N. Candlin & J. Crichton (Eds.), *Discourses of trust* (pp. 1–20). Basingstoke: Palgrave Macmillan.

Candlin, C. N., & Sarangi, S. (2004). Making applied linguistics matter [Editorial]. *Journal of Applied Linguistics, 1*(1), 1–8.

Carter, B., & New, C. (Eds.). (2004). *Making realism work: Realist social theory and empirical research*. London/New York: Routledge.

Carter, B., & Sealey, A. (2000). Language, structure and agency: What can realist social theory offer to sociolinguistics? *Journal of Sociolinguistics, 4*(1), 3–20.

Cicourel, A. V. (1992). The interpenetration of communicative contexts: examples from medical encounters. In A. Duranti & C. Goodwin (Eds.), *Rethinking context: Language as an interactive phenomenon* (pp. 291–310). Cambridge: Cambridge University Press.

Cicourel, A. V. (2007). A personal, retrospective view of ecological validity. *Text & Talk, 27*(5–6), 735–752.

Cotter, C. (2010). *News talk: Investigating the language of journalism*. Cambridge: Cambridge University Press.

Cottle, S. (2007). Ethnography and news production: New(s) developments in the field. *Sociology Compass, 1*(1), 1–16.

Cottle, S., & Ashton, M. (1999). From BBC newsroom to BBC newscentre: On changing technology and journalist practices. *Convergence: The International Journal of Research into New Media Technologies, 5*(3), 22–43.

Coupland, N., Sarangi, S., & Candlin, C. N. (2001). *Sociolinguistics and social theory*. London: Longman.

Crichton, J. (2010). *The discourse of commercialization: A multi-perspectived analysis*. Palgrave Macmillan.

Davis, A. (2000). Public relations, news production and changing patterns of source access in the British national media. *Media, Culture and Society, 22*(1), 39–59.

Fairclough, N. (1992). *Discourse and social change* (Vol. 73). Polity press Cambridge.

Fairclough, N. (2009). A dialectical-relational approach to critical discourse analysis in social research. In R. Wodak & M. Meyer (Eds.), *Methods of critical discourse analysis* (2nd ed., pp. 162–187). London: Sage.

Fairclough, N. (2010). *Critical discourse analysis: The critical study of language*. Harlow: Pearson Education Limited.

Fairclough, N. (2014). *Language and power* (3rd ed.). London: Longman.

Foucault, M. (1980). Power/knowledge: Selected interviews and other writings, 1972–1977. In C. Gorden (Ed.). New York: Pantheon.

Gans, H. J. (2004/1979). *Deciding what's news: A study of CBS evening news, NBC nightly news, newsweek, and time*. Illinois: Northwestern University Press.

Geertz, C. (1983). *Local knowledge: Further essays in interpretive anthropology*. New York: Basic books.

Giddens, A. (1984). *The constitution of society: Outline of the theory of structuration*. Cambridge: Polity Press.

Giddens, A. (1987). *A contemporary critique of historical materialism: The nation-state and violence*. Berkeley: University of California Press.

Goffman, E. (1981). *Forms of talk*. Philadelphia: University of Pennsylvania Press.

Goffman, E. (1983). The interaction order. *American Sociological Review*, 1–17.

Halliday, M. A. K. (1978). *Language as social semiotic*. Maryland: University Park Press.

Halliday, M. A. K., & Matthiessen, C. M. (2014). *An introduction to functional grammar* (4th ed.). New York: Routledge.

Hymes, D. (1980). What is ethnography? In D. Hymes (Ed.), *Language in education: Ethnolinguistic essays* (pp. 88–103). Washington, DC: Center for Applied Linguistics.

Jacobs, G. (2011). Press conferences on the internet: Technology, mediation and access in the news. *Journal of Pragmatics, 43*(7), 1900–1911.

Jones, R. H., & Norris, S. (Eds.). (2005). *Discourse In Action: Introducing Mediated Discourse Analysis*. New York: Routledge.

Kress, G., & Van Leeuwen, T. (2001). *Multimodal discourse*. London: Arnold.

Labov, W. (1970). The study of language in its social context. *Studium Generale, 23*, 30–87.

Lave, J. (1998). *Communities of practice*. New York: Cambridge University Press.

Lave, J., & Wenger, E. (1991). *Situated learning: Legitimate peripheral participation*. Cambridge: Cambridge University Press.

Layder, D. (1993). *New strategies in social research: An introduction and guide*. Cambridge: Polity Press.
Layder, D. (2006). *Understanding social theory* (2nd ed.). London: Sage.
Machin, D., & Niblock, S. (2006). *News production: Theory and practice*. London: Routledge.
Norris, S. (2012). *Multimodality in practice: Investigating theory-in-practice-through-methodology*. New York: Routledge.
Perrin, D. (2013). *The linguistics of newswriting*. Amsterdam: John Benjamins Publishing.
Rampton, B. (2007). Neo-hymesian linguistic ethnography in the United Kingdom. *Journal of Sociolinguistics, 11*(5), 584–607.
Rampton, B., Tusting, K., Maybin, J., Barwell, R., Creese, A., & Lytra, V. (2004). *Linguistic ethnography: A discussion paper*. http://www.ling-ethnog.org.uk.
Reisigi, M., & Wodak, R. (2009). The discourse-historical approach. In R. Wodak & M. Meyer (Eds.), *Methods of critical discourse analysis* (2nd ed., pp. 87–121). London: Sage.
Roberts, C., & Sarangi, S. (1999). Hybridity in gatekeeping discourse: Issues of practical relevance for the researcher. In S. Sarangi & C. Roberts (Eds.), *Talk, work and institutional order: Discourse in medical, mediation and management settings* (pp. 473–503). Berlin: Mouton de Gruyter.
Roberts, C., & Sarangi, S. (2005). Theme-oriented discourse analysis of medical encounters. *Medical Education, 39*(6), 632–640.
Sarangi, S. (2008). The conditions and consequences of professional discourse studies. *Journal of Applied Linguistics and Professional Practice, 2*(3), 371–394.
Sarangi, S., & Candlin, C. N. (2001). Motivational relevancies: Some methodological reflections on social theoretical and sociolinguistic practice. *Sociolinguistics and Social Theory*, 350–388.
Sarangi, S., & Candlin, C. N. (2003). Introduction: Trading between reflexivity and relevance: New challenges for applied linguistics. *Applied Linguistics, 24*(3), 271–285.
Sarangi, S., & Candlin, C. N. (2007). Making methodology matter. *Journal of Applied Linguistics and Professional Practice, 1*(2), 101–106.
Schegloff, E. (1987). Between micro and macro: Contexts and other connections. In J. C. Alexander, B. Giensen, R. Munch, & N. J. Smelser (Eds.), *The micro-macro link* (pp. 207–234). Berkely/Los Angeles/London: University of California Press.
Scollon, R. (1998). *Mediated discourse as social interaction: A study of news discourse*. New York: Routledge.
Scollon, R. (2001). *Mediated discourse: The nexus of practice*. London: Routledge.
Scollon, R., & Scollon, S. W. (2003). *Discourses in place: Language in the material world*. London: Routledge.
Scollon, R., & Scollon, S. W. (2004). *Nexus analysis: Discourse and the emerging internet*. London: Routledge.
Scollon, R., & Scollon, S. W. (2007). Nexus analysis: Refocusing ethnography on action. *Journal of Sociolinguistics, 11*(5), 608–625.
Sealey, A., & Carter, B. (2004). *Applied linguistics as social science*. Edinburgh: A&C Black.
Small, M. L. (2009). 'How many cases do I need?': On science and the logic of case selection in field-based research. *Ethnography, 10*(1), 5–38. https://doi.org/10.1177/1466138108099586.
Smart, G. (2006). Ethnographic-based discourse analysis: uses, issues and prospects. In V. Bhatia, J. Flowerdew, & R. H. Jones (Eds.), *Advances in discourse studies* (pp. 56–66). New York: Routledge.
Van Dijk, T. A. (1993). Principles of critical discourse analysis. *Discourse & Society, 4*(2), 249–283.
Van Dijk, T. A. (2007). *Discourse studies* (Vol. 5). London: Sage.
Van Hout, T., Pander Maat, H., & De Preter, W. (2011). Writing from news sources: The case of Apple TV. *Journal of Pragmatics, 43*(7), 1876–1889.

Van Leeuwen, T., & Wodak, R. (1999). Legitimizing immigration control: A discourse-historical analysis. *Discourse Studies, 1*(1), 83–118.
Wodak, R. (1999). Critical discourse analysis at the end of the 20th century. *Research on Language & Social Interaction, 32*(1–2), 185–193.
Wodak, R., & Busch, B. (2004). Approaches to media texts. In *The SAGE handbook of media studies*. Thousand Oaks, CA: SAGE Publications, Inc.
Wodak, R., & Meyer, M. (2009). Critical discourse analysis: History, agenda, theory and methodology. In R. Wodak & M. Meyer (Eds.), *Methods for critical discourse analysis* (2nd ed., pp. 1–33). London: Sage.

Chapter 4
Corpus Construction and Annotation

4.1 Introduction

The primary aim of this chapter is to present in detail the procedures that I have adopted in the construction of specialized comparable corpora of Chinese and Australian hard news reporting to investigate the discursive aspect of journalistic stance. The corpus-based study of journalistic stance in this research, though far from being capable of addressing my overall research concern as outlined in the previous chapter, constitutes the first step in this regard.

The existing literature on APPRAISAL analysis seems to focus primarily on reporting results drawing on a small amount of manually analysed texts, despite few attempts to conduct corpus-based studies (e.g. Bednarek, 2008, 2009a; Haarman & Lombardo, 2009; Pounds, 2010). Despite the large body of work on stance in English, particularly in written academic genres (e.g. Biber, 2006; Hyland & Guinda, 2012; Precht, 2000), the study of journalistic stance in Chinese news discourse has been glaringly absent. In addition, some methodological issues of how to construct a specialized comparable corpus for comparing Chinese journalistic stance with that in other languages remain unclear. The writing system of Chinese differs considerably from Roman languages such as English, and requires different technological considerations in the corpus construction. Hence, the other aim of this chapter is to address this issue and to stimulate more debates in this regard.

4.2 Determining the Nature of the Corpus

The nature of a corpus exerts considerable influence on the kind of data to be collected. It is crucial for determining the nature of a corpus because different types of corpus tend to have different criteria for selecting candidate data.

C. Huan, *Journalistic Stance in Chinese and Australian Hard News*,
https://doi.org/10.1007/978-981-13-0791-1_4

There are various ways to categorize corpora in accord with different criteria. Based on an examination of the classification of publically available corpora (e.g. McEnery, Xiao, & Tono, 2006, p. 59), I generally describe my corpora as *synchronic written comparable bilingual corpora involving simplified Chinese and English in hard news reporting in relation to discourses of Risk*. The corpus is synchronic, as opposed to a diachronic (also named historical) or monitor corpus. In this sense, no further texts are planned, at least for the present research, to be added on a regular basis to construct a monitor corpus such as the Bank of English (BoE) corpus. The period of the data to be collected is confined to a short-term 'brachychrony' (Mair, 1997; Renouf, 2002) beginning from 2004 to 2013. It is a written corpus in that no spoken English or Chinese data is involved in the corpus. It is a comparable rather than a parallel corpus. A comparable corpus is composed of "original texts in two or more languages matched by criteria such as genre, time of publication, etc." (Johansson, 2007, p. 9), whereas a parallel corpus is composed of source texts and their translations into one or more different languages (Baker, 1995; McEnery et al., 2006). The topics of data to be collected in the corpus focus on print media hard news reports in relation to discourses of Risk.

4.3 Contouring the Frame of Corpus Data

This research operationalizes hard news into a manageable concept as news items that cover political, economic and social issues, that focus on the societal consequences of the events, and that are reported in a detached instead of sensational or interpretative fashions. Accordingly, news items will be excluded from my corpus if their topics concern infotainment news events, if their focuses fall on individual consequences of political, economic and social events, or if the styles allude to emotional, subjective or sensational presentation despite of the topics and focus of the news reporting.

The topic of corpus data is further confined to that of discourses of Risk, focusing on risk events in local regions of China and Australia. To be specific, this research focuses on food safety (e.g. food recall) and bushfire issues in Australian hard news and food safety and earthquake issues in the Chinese context. Such a narrowed focus, together with a clearly articulated definition of hard news, anchors the concept to a manageable data frame in service of corpus construction.

The news texts in discourses of Risk surrounding the issues of food safety, bushfire and earthquake are selected in light of the significance of these topics in people's daily life in China and Australia. To be specific, the issues of earthquake and bushfire concern most people residing in China and Australia, respectively, as evidenced by the disaster of earthquake in Sichuan, China, in 2008 where approximately 90,000 people died and/or lost, and by the terrifying death toll caused by bush fires annually in Australia nationwide. The issue of food safety is the most frequently reported news events in newspapers in both countries, although the focus of the events or the real risks involved differs in these two contexts.

In addition, the issue of food safety constitutes one of the eleven top concerns for humanitarian affairs by the United Nations. It then goes without saying that this thematic issue concerns the whole population worldwide.

4.4 Corpus Preparation

Before embarking on the corpus construction, I engaged in exploring currently available corpora that may satisfy addressing my research concerns. However, the survey of existing corpora presented no available corpus ready to be used for my research purposes, and as such it was necessary to build one from scratch.

4.4.1 Size of Corpora

The size of corpus constitutes a central issue to the corpus creation, but scholars are far from reaching a consensus on how large a corpus should be. Generally speaking, the larger the corpus size, the better it is (e.g. Sinclair, 1991, 2002). However, the measurement for the size of corpora varies across types of corpora. For instance, any spoken corpus, according to O'Keeffe, McCarthy, and Carter (2007, p. 4), is considered large with over one million words, whereas written corpora with less than five million words are quite small. Flowerdew holds a slightly different viewpoint arguing that small corpora contain up to 250,000 words (Flowerdew, 2004, p. 19). Again, no consensus has yet been reached in terms of how many words a small/large corpus should include. There is no ceiling for corpus size, but the minimum size of a corpus mainly depends on two factors: (1) the kind of research concerns that are to be addressed by users; (2) the methodology that is to be adopted to examine the data (Sinclair, 1991). These criteria primarily apply, however, to general corpora designed for lexico-grammatical studies, they do not necessarily hold good for other kinds of corpus (e.g. Koester, 2010), specialized corpora for instance.

That said, the overall size of a corpus is not all-important (Leech, 1991; cited in McEnery et al., 2006, p. 72). It "can be secondary to the need for adequate sampling" (Nelson, 2010, p. 56), since "small corpora can be very useful, providing they can offer a balanced and representative picture of a specified area of the language" (Nelson, 2010, p. 55).

In addition to the research questions as a potential factor limiting the size of corpus, the present corpus takes into account two further considerations: pragmatic and historical. "Practical considerations must always play a part in corpus creation and the larger lexicographical corpora such as the BNC and COBUILD that run into hundreds of millions of words were not a feasible option for one lone researcher to undertake" (Nelson, 2010, p. 56). It is always important to weigh human, material and financial resources over the size of corpus. "The availability of machine-readable data is often the main limiting [material] factor in corpus-building" (McEnery et al., 2006, p. 72). Three ways are identified for converting documents into file formats (txt file in most cases) that can be processed by corpus extraction tools (Nelson, 2010, p. 62; Sinclair, 1991, p. 14). The best option obtains data from available websites or other ready copy resources, and then saves them as plain text format. Another way employs OCR tools (Optical Character Recognition) as a facilitator to do so. The OCR-recognized texts in most cases need to be manually checked for accuracy. The last and the most time-consuming method is to key texts in, but such a method may sometimes prove to be preferable than utilising OCR to achieve a higher rate of accuracy, depending on the amount and quality of original texts.

The size of the present corpus incorporates 272,505 Chinese words and 117,146 English tokens (12,662 types). A detailed summary of Chinese and Australian corpora will be provided in Sect. 4.4.6 below. I have considered "historical reasons" (Nelson, 2010, p. 56) to reach this amount of data, by examining the size of several specialised corpora constructed by other researchers in their studies of evaluative language in different discourses. To be specific, the 70,300-word-token corpus created by Bednarek (2006) produced 5158 individual evaluators, equivalent to my discursive stance markers, for her investigation of evaluation in British broadsheets and tabloids. Charles (2003) explored the construction of stance through nouns in two corpora with each containing 200,000 words in M.Phil. theses of social sciences and 300,000 words in Ph.D. theses of sciences. Pounds (2011) constructed a 24,796 words corpus to examine APPRAISAL resources in the discourse of online property advertising. Pounds (2010) built a small corpus consisting of English (6728 words in total) and Italian (6624) hard news reporting to explore the reporter voice in selected newspapers. Haarman and Lombardo (2009) collected news related to the Iraq War in four TV programs during a period of one month from 20 March to 9 April 2003. The number of words for each corpus amounts to 103,806 (for BBC One), 59,045 (for CBS), 89,808 (for RAI Uno), and 108,330 (for Canale 5), totalling at 360,989 words. The larger size of my corpus has generated a substantial number of stance markers (see Chap. 5 for attitudinal profiling).

4.4.2 Representativeness of Corpora

The issue of representativeness of corpora constitutes another essential consideration in corpus design. It means "the extent to which a sample includes the full range of variability in a population" (Biber, 1993, p. 243). The operationalization of this concept is not as simple as its definition may indicate, since different meanings of representativeness are assigned to different types of corpora. For instance, the general corpus BNC is generally considered as representative because a wide spectrum of texts has been included (Meyer, 2002), but even such carefully constructed corpus as BNC is challenged by the issue of representativeness (e.g. Burnard, 2002; Mitton, Hardcastle, & Pedler, 2007). The texts in written component of the BNC were selected in line with three external or situational criteria (Biber, 1993): domain (content type of texts, e.g. science, social science, or fictions), time (period of text production) and medium (types of text publication, e.g. books, magazines, or journal articles). For specialized corpora, these criteria do not apply, because most specialized corpora have already focused on special domain, time, and medium of the data. As far as the present corpus is concerned, it focuses on hard news (i.e. domain) in Chinese and Australian print broadsheets (i.e. medium) over a period of one decade from 2004 to 2013 (i.e. time). This does not automatically endow a specialized corpus with representativeness, since a specialized corpus is often considered to represent the population when the lexical features (or other linguistic features depending on research questions) are "subject to very limited variation beyond a certain point" (McEnery et al., 2006, p. 16). Such a measurement does not go without criticism as it involves examining the "linguistic variability" of a corpus (Biber, 1993, p. 243) at the expense of the "situational variability". Scholars tend to agree that "the samples collected for the corpus should reflect both kinds of criterion, but situational criteria must be used first, as there is no way of establishing that the corpus is linguistically representative without first having established that it is situationally representative" (Koester, 2010, p. 69, also see Biber, 1993). Linguistic criterion can serve to check the skewedness of a corpus collected in tune with situational criterion. The representativeness of a corpus is hardly possible to be evaluated objectively (Tognini-Bonelli, 2001), and it relates to the notion of balance.

4.4.3 Balance

The issue of balance is as important as the size and representativeness of a corpus. Simply put, "the proportions of different kinds of text it contains should correspond with informed and intuitive judgements" (Sinclair, 1991). However, there has been no reliable scientific measure of corpus balance as yet, and any claim of corpus balance is largely an act of faith rather than a statement of fact as (Hunston, 2002, pp. 28–30; McEnery et al., 2006, p. 16). As far as the balance of the present corpus is concerned, the news texts were selected according to the selected topics in discourses of Risk, and their frequency of occurrences in newspapers. For example, readers might experience twice as much food safety issues in newspapers as bush fire, according to a rough research result in the Sydney Morning Herald.

The balance of a corpus is secondary to the concept of good practice (Douglas, 2003). A good practice in corpus creation demands that the corpus allows the research questions to be adequately addressed, and that "corpus builders make publicly available documentation of the methodologies underlying their corpora" (Douglas, 2003, p. 34). This is why detailed produces in corpus construction are documented here.

4.4.4 Copyright

The issue of copyright underlies the whole process in corpus construction, since the construction of a corpus is legally prohibited if using its texts infringes copyright.

To clear the copyright issues in light of common practice of other practitioners in corpus-based studies, I checked the copyright laws in each country, with special focus on the fair dealing provisions. It turned out that the fair dealing provision (43c, added by the Copyright Amendment Act 2006) of Australian copyright law has provided a range of exceptions for "fair dealing" that enable the exercise of certain copyrights without infringing copyrights. These exceptions include using copyright materials for the following purposes: "research or study; criticism or review; the reporting of news; judicial proceedings or professional legal advice; parody or satire". It is later added to the Copyright Amendment Act, 2006 that a copy of a literary work, magazine, or newspaper article for private use can be made without constituting copyright infringement. Same conditions of use can also be found in the corresponding Chinese fair use provision (provision 22) of the copyright law, which clearly states that no infringement of copyrights is constituted by using published materials for private studies or research. In such cases, no permissions need to be sought from or payment to be made to copyright holders, providing the name(s) of authors and the title of the intellectual materials are properly acknowledged.

4.4.5 Corpus Software

The construction of a corpus demands its builders to be aware of and consequently master a range of corpus software. The development of corpus linguistics has made available a growing number of such corpus tools tailored for addressing different purposes. These corpus tools can be generally categorized into six major types in line with the processes of corpus construction and data extracting.

The first type of software is used to retrieve data from online resources. For instance, the WebGetter function of WordSmith[1] can be deployed to extract texts from websites according to pre-determined search conditions. There may be other software that can be adopted to serve a similar purpose, but the present research utilizes Chinese free software of this kind—the Intelligent Software (www.zdexe.com)—to facilitate mining all data about hard news reporting in Australian newspapers. Basically, I have separately searched two keywords—food safety and bushfire—in the websites of the four selected Australian newspapers (i.e. the Age, the Australian, Canberra Times and Sydney Morning Herald), and then copy the URLs of each searched result to the Intelligent Software. The software then downloaded all searched results from these websites and stored each news report in

[1]http://www.lexically.net/wordsmith/index.html.

one text file with the character code of UTF-8. Subsequently, I read each single news item to eliminate those that are inconsistent with my selection criteria for corpus data (see Sect. 4.4.6 for detailed sampling procedures).

The second type of corpus tool mainly serves to clean up or format written texts or transcribed spoken texts (e.g. PowerGREP for English texts, 文本整理器 [text cleaning tool] for Chinese texts), or to facilitate transcribing spoken data (e.g. Nvivo, Sitman PC) before the raw corpus is built up. The present research adopts the above two mentioned tools for written texts. It is also necessary to check duplication among files. I have adopted NLPIR (Natural Language Processing and Information Retrieval, http://www.nlpir.org/) to filter out those duplicated files.

The third type of corpus software is adopted to convert all files into plain text format. As the document format of several Chinese news reports includes word and pdf documents, I have adopted the tool of All Office Platinum to convert these files to the format of plain text. Other tools such as NCH Dixillion Document Converter, Word2text, and OCR may also be used for this purpose. With the assistance of the software of Rename-it, I have coded metadata regarding language, source and topic of corpus data in filenames. An example of the filename is "OZSMHFS01", in which 'OZ' means Australian news reports, 'SMH' represents the newspaper of Sydney Morning Herald, 'FS' suggests that the topic of this news text concerns food safety issue, and '01' indicates the number of the text.

The fourth type of corpus tools serves to assign part-of-speech (POS) tags or word classes to the raw texts to afford more sophisticated queries of the tagged texts (e.g. using regular expressing or wild cards). The Australian dataset was POS tagged by employing CLAWS 4 with an accuracy rate reliably achieving 96–98%. The Chinese corpus is POS tagged by using ICTCLAS (Institute of Computing Technology, Chinese Lexical Analysis System, http://ictclas.org/), a tagger with a precision rate of more than 97% (Zhang & Liu, 2002).

The fifth type of corpus tool is employed to assign semantic or pragmatic tags to the data. I have deployed Filemaker Pro® (http://www.filemaker.com/) to categorize stance markers in line with the APPRAISAL framework (Martin & White, 2005), since it on one hand allows designers and users to freely create and modify the coding scheme at any stage of the coding process, while on the other, it affords processing files in bulk. W-Matrix (http://ucrel.lancs.ac.uk/wmatrix/) has been adopted to automatically assign USAS semantic tags (http://ucrel.lancs.ac.uk/usas/) to the Australian data. The Chinese data was not semantically tagged of the kind carried out in the Australian corpus due to the lack of reliable semantic taggers.

The last type of corpus tools mainly serves to extract data for exploring issues surrounding the frequency, concordances, collocations and keywords, etc. To do so, the present research adopts the SysConc (C. Wu, 2009), and WordSmith (5.0).

4.4.6 Sampling Procedures

In selecting candidate data for the Chinese corpus, I relied on two sources: one is a Chinese news database, the *Chinese Database for Key Newspapers* (中国重要报纸数据库, *zhōngguó zhòngyào bàozhǐ shùjùkù*) and the other is a website (www.zccw.info) focusing specifically on listing all the food safety news stories covered by the Chinese press from 2004. Sources of Chinese and Australian newspapers were limited to broadsheet newspapers, rather than tabloids, the reason for which was twofold. On one hand, there were significant differences between broadsheets and tabloids in terms of linguistic features, especially stance markers (e.g. Bednarek, 2006). On the other hand, all the selected Chinese sources were broadsheets, and as such, the choice of corresponding Australian newspapers was limited to four sources: the *Australian*, the *Age* (Melbourne), the *Canberra Times* and the *Sydney Morning Herald.* Chinese sources and newspapers refer to those published in the Mainland China only. Newspapers published in Hong Kong, Marco, Taiwan, or other Chinese-speaking countries/areas were excluded from the present corpora. The language of Chinese data was accordingly simplified Chinese.

Consequently, 258 news stories about bushfire events were collected from the Age, 130 from the Australia, 296 from Sydney Morning Herald and none from Canberra Times. The initial bushfire reports collected with the assistance of the Intelligent Software amounted to 684 news stories. A number of 234 news stories about food safety issues or events were collected from the Age, 70 from the Australian, 66 from Canberra Times and 290 from Sydney Morning Herald, totalling at 660 news stories.

A number of 509 news stories about earthquake reports were collected from the Chinese Database of Key Newspapers, and 1221 news stories about food safety events were collected from the website mentioned previously. A summary of each corpus will be provided in Table 4.1.

In line with the previously defined hard news, I excluded tips or workshops regarding food safety. Briefs were also excluded because most of their content was

Table 4.1 Summary of Chinese and Australian corpora

Corpus	Topics	News texts (Original)	News texts (Final)	Word count (Final)	Total word count
Australian	Bush fire	684	158	63,996 (tokens) 6051 (types)	117,146 (tokens) (12,662 types)
	Food safety	660	118	53,150 (tokens) 6611 (types)	
Chinese	Food safety	1221	485	215,433 (tokens) (13,197 types)	272,505 (tokens) (70,269 types)
	Earthquake	509	129	57,072 (tokens) (6601 types)	

Note Word count of the Australian corpus was calculated based on WordSmith (Version 5.0), and word count of the Chinese corpus was done based on MyZiCiFreq. Tool irrelevant to the target topics. News in other news genres, such as editorials, features, comments and opinions, photo news, letters, and government alters, etc., were excluded as well for similar reasons. In short, only those news reports conforming to the concept of hard news as defined in this research were incorporated in the corpus. Additionally, to use hard news as a criterion in selecting corpus data could satisfy an important principle in corpus design—to use language external or non-linguistic criteria in corpus construction, and therefore avoid circularity of findings. Eventually, only 158 news stories about bushfire events and 118 news stories about food safety issues were retained in the Australian corpus. A number of 129 news stories about earthquake events and 485 reports about food safety events were included in the Chinese corpus. All these news stories are full texts rather than extracts of a longer story.

Other factors considered as potential factors limiting the number of sample texts and the size of the corpus included time, area and sources of news events under investigation. The present corpus is a synchronic one, focusing on news language in a short term period, in order to "provide an accurate view of contemporary English [Chinese, as well] undisturbed by language change" (Meyer, 2002, p. 45). Language may change subtly in a relatively short period of time (Mair, 1995), suggesting that a purely synchronic corpus is hardly achievable. However, research indicated that the time frame "does not need to be as narrow as the one-year frame in Brown and LOB, a time-frame of five to ten years seems reasonable" (Meyer, 2002, p. 46). Accordingly, the period of the data included in my corpus was limited to duration of time between 01 January 2004 and 31 December 2013. The other reason for such a consideration was because of the time frame covered by the food safety database, which had listed news reports on food safety events since 2004. The areas where news events occurred were strictly confined to those in Australia reported by Australian newspapers written in English and those in China covered by Chinese newspapers in Chinese. For instance, a food safety crisis happened in the U.S. was excluded for candidature, and a news event reported in an Australian newspaper but sourced to Chinese newspapers/news agencies was disqualified as well. Consequently, the final corpus incorporated 614 Chinese news reports and 276 Australian ones. Table 4.1 summarizes the news texts collected and those finally selected in each corpus, together with word count of the final corpora.

4.4.7 *Organizing Corpus Data*

The above issues surrounding sample procedures, representativeness, balance and size of the corpus being settled, the task that follows in corpus creation is to organize data into machine-readable format for storage and retrieval. Such kind of organization of data involves data entry, file naming and data mark-up.

File names that clearly index the content of the file allows easy retrieval of data through corpus tools. A researcher may choose to rename all files manually if the corpus at issue embraces a relatively small amount of files. Otherwise, the

"Rename-it" software may serve to complete such a task in an automatic and instant fashion (Mac users can use AppleScripts to do so).

"Corpus mark-up is a system of standard codes inserted into a document stored in electronic form to provide information about the text itself and govern formatting, printing or other processing" (McEnery et al., 2006, p. 22). It provides extra-linguistic information about the data, allowing users and researchers to contextualize the data. It is separate from the body of text and can compensate the losses of such information in the file names. "Mark-up adds value to a corpus and allows for a broader range of research questions to be addressed as a result" (McEnery et al., 2006, p. 23; Reppen, 2010, p. 35). McEnery et al. (2006, pp. 23–26) present an overview of available mark-up schemes for corpus linguistics. Corpus tools such as "metadata encoder" may facilitate researchers to mark up the corpus, but the corpora in this research were not marked up for two reasons. The first one is that my research focuses on the main body of news texts, therefore, all other information such as title, author, and publication date have been deleted. The deleted metadata may be necessary for the interpretation of corpus findings for other research purposes, but they are unnecessary for addressing my research concerns. The other reason is that the metadata concerning the topics, language and sources of news reports have been coded in the filenames.

4.4.8 Character Encoding

Character encoding seldom forms a question for alphabetical languages such as English, which uses ASCII characters by default (McEnery & Xiao, 2005). It constitutes however an important issue for any multilingual corpora containing data in a different writing system from Roman alphabets, such as Chinese, Thai, or Japanese. The language for the Chinese data in my corpus is simplified Chinese, and that for Australian data is English. As such, the UTF-8 (Unicode Transformation Format) character encoding standard has been adopted to standardize language data into a single character set (McEnery & Wilson, 2001; Xiao, McEnery, Baker, & Hardie, 2004). There are three major encoding systems for Chinese characters: GB2312 for simplified Chinese, Big 5 for traditional Chinese, and Unicode (McEnery, Xiao, & Mo, 2003, p. 365). However, only Unicode can accommodate Chinese, along with English, characters, and ensure the compatibility between Chinese character and all the Unicode-compliant XML processing tools, WordSmith Tools version 4.0, for instance, (X. Hu, McLaughlin, & Williamson, 2007, p. 423; X. Hu, Williamson, & McLaughlin, 2005, p. 289; McEnery et al., 2003, p. 365). This research has used "Multi-Lingual Corpus Toolkit" (MLCT), developed by Richard Xiao at Lancaster University to convert my Chinese encoding from GB2312 to UTF-8, a task that can also be performed by "NLPIR".

4.5 Corpus Annotation

The corpus in this research has been annotated with POS and semantic tags. For the Chinese corpus, a further segmentation/tokenization is applied. In computational linguistics, word tokens of alphabetic language, such as English, are relatively easily discernible with white spaces delimiting one word token, except for multi-words (e.g. so that), merger (e.g. can't) and variably spelt compounds (e.g. noticeboard, notice-board, notice board) (Xiao, Rayson, & McEnery, 2009, p. 3). As a naturally occurring Chinese sentence is composed of unseparated running strings of characters, segmenting words therefore constitutes an essential task in the process of corpus annotation for Chinese data (McEnery et al., 2003, p. 366). Segmentation at word level (i.e. tokenization) refers to the process of splitting running text strings into individual meaningful units. Such a kind of annotation can avoid meaningless corpus retrieval and resolve ambiguity in Chinese texts (see McEnery et al., 2003 for detailed comments on this). It is prerequisite for all Chinese texts in a corpus to be segmented into legitimate meaning word units, prior to any serious linguistic analysis being undertaken (Feng, 2001; McEnery et al., 2003). This will also significantly impact subsequent search results, as unsegmented data will produce fewer concordance lines than will do segmented data.

There are three major segmentation tools available to process Chinese texts. The first and most reliable one is the NLPIR (http://ictclas.nlpir.org) developed by Pinghua Zhang (Zhang & Liu, 2002; Zhang, Liu, Zhang, & Cheng, 2002) at the Institute of Computing Technology, Chinese Academy of Sciences. Another one is the Stanford Chinese word segmenter, developed by Huihsin Tseng and his colleagues (Tseng, Chang, Andrew, Jurafsky, & Manning, 2005). The last one is the tokenizer (for English) and segmenter (for Chinese) developed by Liang, Li, and Xu (2010) at BFSU, China. This research has adopted the NLPIR to segment my corpus chiefly for two reasons. Firstly, the system itself was trained using news texts and performed "exceptionally" well on such a genre (Zhang et al., 2002). Considering that my corpus is entirely composed of news texts, this system is therefore expected to perform equally well on my corpus. Secondly, this system can achieve a precision rate of 97.58% with a recall rate as high as 99.94% (Zhang & Liu, 2002), while the Stanford segmenter reaches an accuracy rate of 94.44%.

4.5.1 *Part-of-Speech Tagging*

Another layer of annotation added to the corpus is POS tagging, which refers to the process of assigning a part-of-speech mnemonic, a POS tag, to individual word in a corpus (McEnery et al., 2006, p. 34). It is the most common and widely used annotation in a corpus affording a wide range of linguistic queries and forming the basis of further forms of analysis such as semantic and pragmatic annotations. The development of computational linguistics has provided a handful of POS taggers allowing reliable automatic POS tag for many languages with the precision rate of more than 97%. The CLAWS4 (http://ucrel.lancs.ac.uk/claws/) and the ICTCLAS have been employed to assign POS tags to English and Chinese data in my corpus respectively. Both tagging systems can achieve an exceptionally high precision rate, and have been successfully applied in many linguistic studies.

4.5.2 Semantic Annotation of Stance Markers

The corpora being constructed and marked up, the next crucial task in examining journalistic stance is to compile a comprehensive list of both Chinese and English lexical stance markers to be incorporated in the analysis.

This research has drawn on a wide range of sources in line with the semantic features of evaluative language as presented in the APPRAISAL framework. The list of English affect lexis has been produced by relying on Bednarek's (2008) list of 1060 potential 'affect' terms. This list of 'affect' markers has been generated based on her thorough survey of relevant literature on emotion terms, as well as some dictionaries and thesauri, and therefore it is "more comprehensive than many other lists" (Bednarek, 2008, p. 22). The primary source used by Bednarek (2008) is the Encarta Thesaurus, one growing out of corpus-based studies (Bednarek, 2008, p. 20). Moreover, her study of emotion terms was also based on the 'affect' sub-system of the APPRAISAL framework, and in this sense, her list excludes those 'judgement' and 'appreciation' markers which have been included in my research by drawing on two sources. The first one is a list of stance markers by Precht (2000) and the other is sentiment lexis produced by the HowNet Knowledge Databases released on 22 July 2007. The latter list derives from corpus-based studies of sentiment. Although it is not grounded in the APPRAISAL framework, the large amount of evaluative lexis provided in this list still is of considerable usefulness to my corpus-based study of stance markers.

As for the list of Chinese attitudinal markers, in addition to the list of Chinese sentiment lexis provided by the HowNet Knowledge Databases, I also draw on a list of Chinese attitudinal terms by Xu and Tao (2003), a list based on semantic analysis of all emotion terms in a corpus. The following examples illustrate some journalistic ATTITUDE markers concerning 'affect', 'judgement' and 'appreciation' that are identified in Chinese and Australian hard news, with the stance markers in bold font.

(1) We all **love** the Australian bush … (Positive affect in the Australian corpus)
(2) Too many people **ignore** the most critical part of a fire plan. (Negative judgement in the Australian corpus)
(3) The rest of south-east Australia is also gearing up for a **horror** weekend of extreme heat and bushfires. (Negative reaction in the Australian corpus)
(4) 这一切,充分体现了总书记对灾区人民的深切挂念…

All these have sufficiently shown the General Secretary's **heart-felt caring** of those in disaster areas. (Positive affect in the Chinese corpus)

(5) 黑心老板X已被警方拘留...
X, the **black-hearted** boss, has been arrested by police. (Negative judgement in the Chinese corpus)

(6) 一组触目惊心的图片在南通市"X论坛"上受到网友的强烈关注。

A group of **shocking** photos has caused net citizens' great concerns in the X online forum. (Negative reaction in the Chinese corpus)

In addition to the investigation of journalistic ATTITUDE, this book also concerns the examination of the ways journalists engage with sources of information. The markers that are adopted to index ENGAGEMENT are named intersubjective journalistic stance markers. Intersubjective stances are interrogated in line with the ENGAGEMENT system of the APPRAISAL framework. I draw exclusively on two resources to extract a list of English items for such stance markers. One is Coffin's (2006) *Historical Discourse*, and the other is the *Collins COBUILD English Grammar* (third edition). When it comes to the Chinese lexis of intersubjective stance markers, I draw entirely on Hsieh's (2008) study of evidentiality in Chinese newspaper reports, and the *Dictionary of Chinese Verb Usages* compiled by Cong Men and his colleagues from which 95 reporting verbs were selected. Due to space limitations, I provide below some stance markers identified in the Australian corpus and the corresponding ENGAGEMENT features they express:

(7) A police spokesman on Wednesday **said** the officer … had probably taken time out to reflect on things. ('said' denotes 'acknowledge')

(8) The study also **found** a marked increase in the quality of hygiene standards in kitchens once inspection results were public. ('found' suggests journalists' 'endorsement' of the proposition)

The list of stance markers being settled, the next step in the analysis of journalistic stance is to determine the relevance of the senses of these items to the concept of stance as defined in the book. This issue concerns the problem of polysemy and homonymy, which is a central issue to the annotation of a sense-sensitive corpus. As there is no reliable or indeed available software serving to recognize different senses of a word, corpus concordance tools will instead list all occurrences of a queried word form, regardless of its meaning. To do so will require considerable amount of human efforts to check manually the senses of each word in order to determine its relevance to stance meaning. Dr. Canzhong Wu and I have designed a coding scheme using the Filemaker to facilitate stance coding (see Fig. 4.1 for a snapshot of the interface). It was also used to extract frequencies (e.g. count of each stance marker and each appraisal feature in question).

For each stance marker (e.g. 'satisfied' as shown in this snapshot), the coding scheme will present its context in use (e.g. the sentence in which it occurs) and the ATTITUDE feature it realizes (i.e. affect), polarity orientations (i.e. positive), non/mediated (i.e. mediated), emoter (i.e. officials), local grammatical pattern (i.e. n be ADJ that-clause). It also shows other information such as its word class (i.e. JJ—

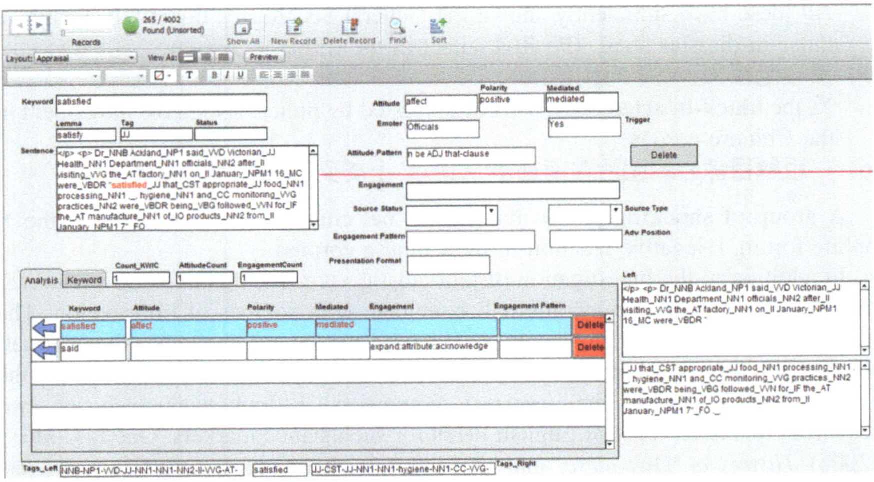

Fig. 4.1 Snapshot of the interface for coding stance markers

general adjective), its lemma (i.e. SATISFY), the total counts of ATTITUDE and ENGAGEMENT markers in this sentence. At the bottom, this file automatically recognizes all word classes of the surrounding words. But, as we may find that in the 'Tags_Right' column, there is a mistake—the word 'hygiene' is not expected to appear, suggesting that this automatic tagging needs to be further developed. This program can also show the source file each stance marker is embedded in, depending on the custom setting. In short, this tool affords researchers flexible ways of creating and modifying the coding scheme. One problem that may frustrate researcher from using this tool is that users need to design their own coding scheme, which is not an easy task as it sounds, even though there are some training tutorials available online for beginners. But once this technique is mastered, users can manoeuvre its functions such as managing scripts, and custom functions, among others, to facilitate subsequent processes surrounding building lexical-grammatical stance patterns and data analysis.

In an attempt to categorize news actors, Bell (1991, p. 194) argues that most news actors fall into one of the following categories: political figure, official, celebrity (e.g. film or music star), sportsperson, professional or other public figure (e.g. lawyer), criminal or accused, human interest figure, and participant (e.g. victim or witness). Premised on this categorisation and also on the news actors actually identified in my corpus (e.g. celebrity and sportsperson are irrelevant to our study), I broadly divided news actors into two groups: the powerful (i.e. social elites, including political and professional figures) and the powerless (i.e. citizens or consumers, and risk makers). Risk makers are those individuals or institutions (e.g. food producers) who produce food that threatens others' health or life. In the coding process, I also noticed the presence of journalists' explicit reference to themselves (e.g. 记者仔细察看—reporters carefully examine…), although the occurrence was rare (5 occ. in total). For those news actors that are unknown or implicit, I coded them as unspecific.

In general, the coding was conducted on the basis of the semantics of the stance item (appraisal item) in its co-text. In cases of clashes, I consult native speakers of English to elicit their understanding of the ambiguous meanings of an appraisal item. For general appraisal items (e.g. good, bad, great), their attitudinal meanings (i.e. affect, judgement, appreciation), were decided on the premise of their actual meaning in co-text. For instance, 'good' in 'a good man' is a judgement marker but it is a marker of appreciation in 'that's a good way of knowing the truth'. In some cases, one APPRAISAL item actually realizes another category. For instance, "假冒" (faked) in 假冒酱油 (faked soy source) evaluates the quality of the soy source, but it actually realizes JUDGEMENT of negative 'propriety' in its embedded phrase "某人生产假冒酱油" (Someone produces faked soy source). Cases of such target-value mismatches are called "Russian dolls" (Thompson, 2014, p. 47), meaning that "an expression of one category of attitude may function as a token (an indirect expression) of a different category; and that token may itself function as an indirect expression of yet another category, and so on". In coding cases of this kind, I assigned JUDGEMENT feature to their 'value' (actual ATTITUDINAL meaning). In short, the appraisal meaning of a stance item was assigned on the basis of their actual meaning in its co-text.

The considerable human efforts devoted into this process in fact means that "the analysis is less easily replicable than a computationally straightforward, automated corpus study, and retains some elements of subjectivity in the interpretation of the meaning of emotion terms" (Bednarek, 2008, p. 23). This research acknowledges this unavoidable subjectivity, and meanwhile maintains that the manual analysis further improves the accuracy of stance marker identification.

4.5.3 Annotating Local Patterns of Attitude

In discussion of the local grammatical patterns and emotional meanings, Bednarek (2008) identifies three categories of affect. The first category is **unemoted affect** wherein emotion items are employed to describe an entity rather than deployed to "evaluate emoters or triggers" (Bednarek, 2008, p. 73). For instance, the stance item "*the joys of political hate*" in "*Books: The sorrows of love and* ***the joys of political hate*** *(BNC)*" (cited in Bednarek, 2008, p. 72) is used to describe the book at issue rather than to evaluate any stance takers or stance triggers. As such this type of emotional pattern appears weak in exercising evaluative power and "it is perhaps best not to consider such unemoted instances as affect in a strict sense" (Bednarek, 2008, p. 73). In my annotated corpora examples of this kind have been eliminated from analysis because I am more concerned with how journalists in the news texts undertake certain stances to an event or an entity, rather than with the ways stance is expressed or realized in news reporting in general. Consequently, the following analyses of journalistic stance patterns will concentrate on those involving stance

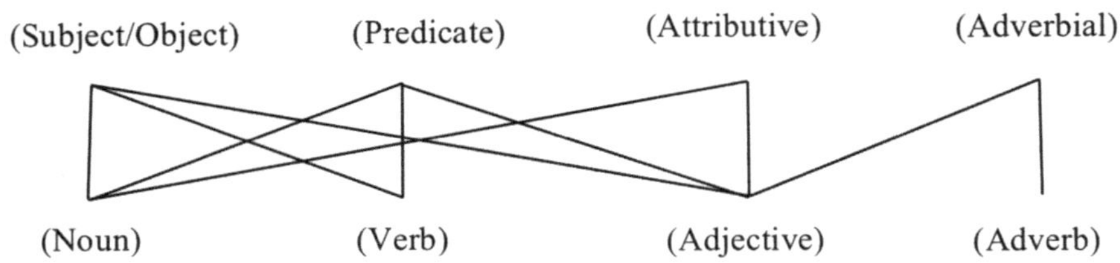

Fig. 4.2 Correspondence between word class and syntactic roles of a Chinese word (after J. Lu, 2003, p. 10)

takers (i.e. sources of ATTITUDE) or stance triggers or targets. Patterns that do not specify triggers are categorized as "**undirected stance patterns**", whereas "**directed stance patterns**" refers to those explicating stance triggers.

Before presenting these patterns, it is necessary to briefly introduce the unique nature of Chinese grammar especially its word class and local phrasal/syntactic patterns. There is a general one-to-one correspondence between the word class of a word and its syntactic role in Indo-European system of languages such as English and Russian. For instance, 'nouns' often function as 'subject' or 'object', 'verbs' as 'predicate', 'adjectives' as 'attributive', and 'adverbs' as 'adverbial'. By contrast, the Chinese language lacks inflectional variations and thus does not present a clear one-to-one correspondence. Instead, the relationship is that of one-to-many (Fig. 4.2).

This one-to-many relationship has caused a thorny issue to assign word classes to Chinese words (J. Lu, 2003) in that the word class of a Chinese word is not determined by its grammatical meaning (e.g. nouns refer entities or human beings; verbs refer to material or mental activities) or the syntactic roles it may perform in a clause. Instead, it is determined by the form-meaning consistence. That is to say, different forms of a type of word are categorized into one single word class only if they have same pronunciation and same lexical meaning. The same word may have the same form and meaning but perform rather different grammatical functions in a clause. There are controversies among Chinese grammarians as to how to categorize the word class of these words, but J. Lu (2003) has treated them as the same word class. Since this situation only occurs rarely in stance markers, I have followed Lu's (2003) argument for practical reasons. One example may suffice to reify his point. "劳动" (láodòng, work/labour) in the following four examples is categorized as a verb, although it may appear to be a noun and/or a verb in examples *b*, *c* and *d* (Table 4.2). They are tagged as a verb because they are pronounced in the same way as "láodòng", and all denote some kind of labour or actions in a general sense.

Despite the one-to-many correspondence between syntactic roles and a Chinese word class, there is a strict coupling of local grammatical patterns. To be specific, a subject always precedes a predicate, an object always follows a predicate verb and a modifier always comes before a head noun/adjective/verb, and a complement always comes after a head noun/verb/adjective. The order of different elements in a

Table 4.2 "劳动" (láodòng) and its word class (modified from J. Lu, 2003, p. 46)

N	Chinese	Pinyin	English	Functions
a	他劳动	tā láodòng	He works	predicate
b	劳动光荣	láodòng guāngróng	(To) work is glorious	subject
c	他爱劳动	tā ài láodòng	He loves (to) work	object
d	要关心劳动人民	yào guānxīn láodòng rénmín	(We) should care working people	attributive

Table 4.3 An example of the relationship between word order and patterns in Chinese (modified J. Lu, 2003, p. 12)

N	Examples	Gram. relations		Examples	Gram. relations
a	眼睛大大的 eyes big	[Zhu-Wei] subject - predicate	≠	大大的眼睛 big eyes	[Pian-Zheng: attributive + head noun]
b	吃饭了 eat dinner	[Shu-Bin] verb - object	≠	饭吃了 dinner has been eaten	[Zhu-Wei] subject + predicate
c	客人来了 guests have come	[Zhu-Wei] subject - predicate	≠	来客人了 there come guests	[Shu-Bin] verb - object
d	来早了 come early	[Zhong-Bu] verb - adverbial	≠	早来了 already came	[Pian-Zheng: adverbial + head verb]

Table 4.4 Local phraseological patterns of JUDGEMENT markers in Chinese

No.	Local patterns	Glosses	English glosses
1	Zhuwei	subject + predicate	n V
2	Shubin	verb + object	V n
3	Zhongbu	head + complement	V adv.
4	Zhuangzhong	adverbial + head	ADV v
5	Dingzhong	attributive + head	ADJ n

phrase plays an important role in Chinese. A change of order will lead to parallel changes of local patterns and the corresponding semantics. Let us take the first example in Table 4.3 to illustrate such a point. '大大的' (dàdà de, *big*) functions as a predicate when it follows the noun '眼睛' (yǎnjīng, eyes), while it takes the attributive role when it comes before the noun '眼睛'. In English 'big' is a predicative adjective in the former case, whereas it is an attributive adjective in the latter.

Since the identification of local patterns in Chinese and English follow different rules, I will not compare the patterns of journalistic stance in Chinese and

Australian corpora. That said, I have identified five major patterns of JUDGEMENT markers in Chinese for the purposes of this study (see Table 4.4).

I have identified two variations of the pattern of 'Pian-Zheng': 'Ding-Zhong' (attributive + head noun) and 'Zhuang-Zhong' (adverbial + head adjective/verb). Depending on the functions that complements perform (e.g. result, extent, number, time and place, etc.), 'Zhong-Bu' may have many variations in pattern, but this research has reduced the complexity to the general pattern of 'Zhong-Bu'. The last two patterns are unique in Chinese grammar.

To emphasize my point in discussing local grammatical patterns in Chinese in the above, these patterns are not meant to be directly comparable across Chinese and Australian hard news corpora, but they will be compared within Chinese corpus across different ATTITUDE features. For space limitations, analysis of local grammatical patterns will be confined to JUDGEMENT, and readers can refer to Huan (2015) for more detailed analysis of local grammatical patterns of 'affect' and 'appreciation' across corpora.

4.6 Summary

This chapter has documented detailed processes of corpus creation, issues surrounding the delineation of the nature of corpora, the preparation of corpus tools, the determination of the sampling procedures, and the annotation of the corpora. The presentation of such detailed procedures is essential for two reasons. On one hand, it stands in line with "good practice" in corpus-informed studies, while on the other, it is consistent with the call for explicating the analysts' motivational relevancies (Sarangi & Candlin, 2001) in (corpus informed) discourse analysis. This chapter has also provided methodological insights into filling the research gap left in the literature regarding the investigation of journalistic stance across Chinese and Australian hard news. As for the construction of the corpus per se, this chapter indicates that the articulation of research questions constitutes a guiding principle in the whole process of corpus construction. The corpus is finally assessed according to its affordances to address the research concerns. To do so, the research issues need to be operationalized into a manageable data frame, in line with which the corpus is built.

References

Baker, M. (1995). Corpora in translation studies: An overview and some suggestions for future research. *Target, 7*(2), 223–243.

Bednarek, M. (2006). *Evaluation in media discourse: Analysis of a newspaper corpus*. London/New York: Continuum.

Bednarek, M. (2008). *Emotion talk across corpora*. Basingstoke/New York: Palgrave Macmillan.

Bednarek, M. (2009). Language patterns and ATTITUDE. *Functions of Language, 16*(2), 165–192.

Bell, A. (1991). *The language of news media*. Oxford/Cambridge MA: Blackwell.
Biber, D. (1993). Representativeness in corpus design. *Literary and Linguistic Computing, 8*(4), 243–257.
Biber, D. (2006). Stance in spoken and written university registers. *Journal of English for Academic Purposes, 5*(2), 97–116.
Burnard, L. (2002). Where did we go wrong? A retrospective look at the British National Corpus. In B. Kettemann & G. Marko (Eds.), *Language and computers, teaching and learning by doing corpus analysis. Proceedings of the Fourth International Conference on Teaching and Language Corpora* (pp. 51–70). Amsterdam: Rodopi.
Charles, M. (2003). 'This mystery…': A corpus-based study of the use of nouns to construct stance in theses from two contrasting disciplines. *Journal of English for Academic Purposes, 2* (4), 313–326.
Coffin, C. (2006). *Historical discourse: The language of time, cause and evaluation*. London/New York: Continuum.
Douglas, F. M. (2003). The Scottish corpus of texts and speech: Problems of corpus design. *Literary and Linguistic Computing, 18*(1), 23–37.
Feng, Z. W. (2001). Hybrid approaches for automatic segmentation and annotation of a Chinese text corpus. *International Journal of Corpus Linguistics, 6*(Special Issue), 35–42.
Flowerdew, L. (2004). The argument for using English specialized corpora to understand academic and professional language. In U. Connor & T. Upton (Eds.), *Discourse in the professions: Perspectives from corpus linguistics* (pp. 11–33). Amesterdam: John Benjamins.
Haarman, L., & Lombardo, L. (2009). Introduction. In L. Haarman & L. Lombardo (Eds.), *Evaluation and stance in war news: A linguistic analysis of American, British and Italian television news reporting of the 2003 Iraqi War* (pp. 1–26). London/New York: Continuum.
Hsieh, C.-L. (2008). Evidentiality in Chinese newspaper reports: Subjectivity/objectivity as a factor. *Discourse Studies, 10*(2), 205–229.
Hu, X., McLaughlin, J., & Williamson, N. (2007). Syntactic positions of prepositional phrases in the history of Chinese: Using the developing Sheffield Corpus of Chinese for diachronic linguistic studies. *Literary and Linguistic Computing, 22*(4), 419–434.
Hu, X., Williamson, N., & McLaughlin, J. (2005). Sheffield Corpus of Chinese for diachronic linguistic study. *Literary and Linguistic Computing, 20*(3), 281–293.
Huan, C. (2015). *Journalistic stance in Chinese and Australian hard news* (Doctoral thesis), Macquarie University, Sydney.
Hunston, S. (2002). *Corpora in applied linguistics*. Cambridge: Cambridge University Press.
Hyland, K., & Guinda, C. S. (2012). *Stance and voice in written academic genres*. Basingstoke: Palgrave Macmillan.
Johansson, S. (2007). *Seeing through multilingual corpora: On the use of corpora in contrastive studies*. Amsterdam: John Benjamins.
Koester, A. (2010). Building small specialised corpora. In M. McCarthy & A. O'Keeffe (Eds.), *The Routledge handbook of corpus linguistics* (pp. 66–79). London/New York: Routledge.
Leech, G. N. (1991). The state of the art in corpus linguistics. In K. Aijmer & B. Altenberg (Eds.), *English corpus linguistics* (pp. 8–29). London: Longman.
Liang, M., Li, W., & Xu, J. (2010). *Using corpora: A practical coursebook*. Beijing: Foreign Language Teaching and Research Press.
Lu, J. (2003). *Studies on contemporary Chinese grammar (现代汉语语法研究)*. Beijing: Pekin University Press.
Mair, C. (1995). Changing patterns of complementation, and concomitant grammaticalisation, of the verb help in present-day British English. In B. Aarts & C. Meyer (Eds.), *The verb in contemporary English: Theory and description*. Cambridge: Cambridge University Press.
Mair, C. (1997). Parallel corpora: A real-time approach to the study of language change in progress. In M. Ljung (Ed.), *Corpus-based studies in English: Papers from the Seventeenth International Conference on English Language Research on Computerized Corpora (ICAME 17)* (pp. 195–209). Amsterdam: Rodopi.

Martin, J. R., & White, P. R. R. (2005). *The language of evaluation*. Basingstoke: Palgrave Macmillan.
McEnery, T., & Wilson, A. (2001). *Corpus linguistics* (2nd ed.). Edinburgh: Edinburgh University Press.
McEnery, T., & Xiao, R. (2005). Character encoding in corpus construction. In M. Wynne (Ed.), *Guide to good practice* (pp. 1–11). Oxford: AHDS.
McEnery, T., Xiao, R., & Mo, L. (2003). Aspect marking in English and Chinese: Using the lancaster corpus of Mandarin Chinese for contrastive language study. *Literary and Linguistic Computing, 18*(4), 361–378.
McEnery, T., Xiao, R., & Tono, Y. (2006). *Corpus-based language studies*. London: Routledge.
Meyer, C. F. (2002). *English corpus linguistics: An introduction*. Cambridge: Cambridge University Press.
Mitton, R., Hardcastle, D., & Pedler, J. (2007). *BNC! Handle with care! Spelling and tagging errors in the BNC*. Paper presented at *the Fourth Corpus Linguistics Conference*, Birmingham, U.K. (downloaded at http://eprints.bbk.ac.uk).
Nelson, M. (2010). Building a written corpus. In M. McCarthy & A. O'Keeffe (Eds.), *The Routledge handbook of corpus linguistics* (pp. 53–64). London/New York: Routledge.
O'Keeffe, A., McCarthy, M., & Carter, R. (2007). *From corpus to classroom: Language use and language teaching*. Cambridge: Cambridge University Press.
Pounds, G. (2010). Attitude and subjectivity in Italian and British hard-news reporting: The construction of a culture-specific 'reporter' voice. *Discourse Studies, 12*(1), 106–137.
Pounds, G. (2011). "This property offers much character and charm": Evaluation in the discourse of online property advertising. *Text & Talk, 31*(2), 195–220.
Precht, K. (2000). *Patterns of stance in English* (Unpublished Ph.D. thesis). Northern Arizona University, Arizona.
Renouf, A. (2002). The time dimension in modern English corpus linguistics. *Language and Computers, 42*(1), 27–41.
Reppen, R. (2010). Building a corpus: What are the key considerations? In M. McCarthy & A. O'Keeffe (Eds.), *The Routledge handbook of corpus linguistics* (pp. 31–37). London/New York: Routledge.
Sarangi, S., & Candlin, C. N. (2001). Motivational relevancies: Some methodological reflections on social theoretical and sociolinguistic practice. *Sociolinguistics and Social Theory*, 350–388.
Sinclair, J. (1991). *Corpus, concordance, collocation*. Oxford: Oxford University Press.
Sinclair, J. (2002). Introduction. In M. Ghadessy (Ed.), *Small corpus studies and ELT: Theory and practice* (pp. xvii–xxiii). Philadelphia, PA: John Benjamins.
Thompson, G. (2014). Affect and emotion, target-value mismatches, and Russian dolls. In G. Thompson & L. Alba-Juez (Eds.), *Evaluation in context* (pp. 47–66). Amsterdam: John Benjamins.
Tognini-Bonelli, E. (2001). *Corpus linguistics at work*. Amsterdam: John Benjamins.
Tseng, H., Chang, P., Andrew, G., Jurafsky, D., & Manning, C. (2005). A conditional random field word segmenter for sighan bakeoff 2005. In *Proceedings of the fourth SIGHAN Workshop on Chinese Language Processing* (pp. 168–171).
Wu, C. (2009). Corpus-based research. In M. A. K. Halliday & J. Webster (Eds.), *Continuum companion to systemic functional linguistics* (pp. 128–142). London: Continuum.
Xiao, R., McEnery, T., Baker, P., & Hardie, A. (2004). Developing Asian language corpora: Standards and practice. In *Proceedings of the 4th Workshop on Asian Language Resources* (pp. 1–8).
Xiao, R., Rayson, P., & McEnery, T. (2009). *A frequency dictionary of Mandarin Chinese: Core vocabulary for learners*. London/New York: Routledge.
Xu, X., & Tao, J. X. (2003). A study of affect in Chinese. In *Proceedings of the 1st Chinese Conference on Affective Computing and Intelligent Interaction*, 199–205.

Zhang, H. P., & Liu, Q. (2002). Model of Chinese words rough segmentation based on NYShortestYPaths method. *Journal of Chinese Information Processing, 16*(5), 1–7.

Zhang, H. P., Liu, Q., Zhang, H., & Cheng, X. Q. (2002). Automatic recognition of Chinese unknown words based on roles tagging. In B. Tseo, O. Kwong, & T. Lai (Eds.), *Proceedings of the First SIGHAN Workshop on Chinese Language Processing, COLING 2002* (Vol. 18, pp. 71–77).

Chapter 5
Attitude Profiling

5.1 Introduction

This chapter contours ATTITUDE profiles of the corpora with respect to lexical, part-of-speech (POS), and semantic variation concerning attitudinal markers. Such ATTITUDE profiling constitutes the departure point for understanding journalistic discursive practices of stance taking. This is because linguistic choices are social semiotics and mainly motivated by function.

5.2 Frequent Lemmas Across Corpora

This section reports the frequency distribution of ATTITUDE lemma in the Chinese and Australian corpora. To do so, I follow two steps. The first step concerns the presentation of some most frequent ATTITUDE lemma identified in the corpora. The second step relates to the interrogation of the polarity orientations of ATTITUDE (i.e. whether the ATTITUDE is positive or negative in orientation). The corpus was lemmatized in the Filemaker Pro and all instances of stance lemmas were carefully examined in the co-text.

Before presenting the top ten most frequent lemmas of ATTITUDE in each corpus in Tables 5.1 and 5.2, I need to point out that the tentative categorization of these frequent attitudinal lemmas into ATTITUDE features (e.g. affect, judgement and appreciation) is imprecise, as some of them (e.g. concern, 假冒—jiǎmào) can realize different attitudinal meanings in different patterns and contexts. In this sense, the assignment of an ATTITUDE feature to each lemma in these two tables is not definitive but rather preliminary. The results of carefully coded ATTITUDE markers in each corpus will be presented in Tables 5.3 and 5.4 in this section, along with a discussion of their distribution across polarity.

C. Huan, *Journalistic Stance in Chinese and Australian Hard News*,
https://doi.org/10.1007/978-981-13-0791-1_5

Table 5.1 shows that potential ‘appreciation’ lemmas (i.e. DANGEROUS, THREATEN, BAD, IMPORTANT, SIGNIFICANT, BETTER, GREAT), amounting to 24.36% of all ATTITUDE lemmas identified in the Australian corpus, prevail in the distribution of those frequent ATTITUDE lemmas. By all attitudinal markers, I mean all the ATTITUDE markers as based on the lists, and it is possible that there are ATTITUDE markers that occur in the corpus but are not in the lists and hence not captured in the analysis. That said, possible ‘affect’ lemmas (i.e. CONCERN, HOPE, FEAR), amounting to 15.94% of all lemmas of ATTITUDE in the Australian corpus, occur less frequently whereas there is no ‘judgement’ lemma in this list. Broadly, this finding suggests that Australian journalists prefer to evaluate risk events or entities per se, rather than to invoke subjective emotions or to judge human behaviours. The order of ATTITUDE features in the Australian corpus in terms of their frequency seems to be ‘appreciation’, ‘affect’ and ‘judgement’.

Despite the manifold meanings of some ATTITUDE markers, the ten most frequent ATTITUDE markers in the Chinese corpus (Table 5.2) display a similar trend to prioritizing ‘appreciation’ (i.e. hégé, yánzhòng, jiǎ, zhòngyào, yǒudú, yǒuhài), with

Table 5.1 The ten most frequent lemmas of ATTITUDE (Australian corpus)

N.	ATTITUDE markers	Freq.	%
1	CONCERN	79	10.08
2	DANGEROUS	36	4.59
3	THREATEN	32	4.08
4	BAD	32	4.08
5	IMPORTANT	27	3.44
6	SIGNIFICANT	24	3.06
7	HOPE	23	2.93
8	FEAR	23	2.93
9	GOOD	22	2.81
10	GREAT	18	2.30

Note English lemmas in corpus linguistics are often presented in small caps. This convention has been followed in this research

Table 5.2 The ten most frequent ATTITUDE markers (Chinese corpus)

N.	Keyword	Pinyin	Trans.	Freq.	%
1	合格	hégé	Up to standard	548	13.13
2	严重	yánzhòng	Severe	235	5.63
3	假	jiǎ	Fake	212	5.08
4	黑	hēi	Black/Illegal	115	2.76
5	正常	zhèngcháng	Normal	89	2.13
6	假冒	jiǎmào	Counterfeit	83	1.99
7	重要	zhòngyào	Important	80	1.92
8	非法	fēifǎ	Illegal	76	1.82
9	有毒	yǒudú	Poisonous	66	1.58
10	有害	yǒuhài	Harmful	63	1.51

Table 5.3 Distribution of ATTITUDE across polarity orientations (Australian corpus)

	Positive		Negative		Neutral		Mediated		Non-med.		Total	
	No.	%	No.	%	No.	%	No.	%	No.	%	No.	%
Affect	94	35	149	56	22	8	211	80	54	20	265	34
Judgement	29	41	31	44	11	15	53	75	17	24	71	9
Social esteem	24	42	22	39	11	19	41	72	16	28	57	7
Social sanction	5	36	9	64	0	0	12	86	1	7	14	2
Appreciation	124	35	211	59	22	6	259	73	98	27	357	46
Reaction	13	14	76	84	2	2	74	81	17	19	91	12
Total	260	33	467	60	57	7	597	76	186	24	784	100

Note Social esteem and social sanction are two subcategories of judgement, I have shown them separately in this table for ease of comparison and explanation. The number of judgement markers is always the sum of social esteem and social sanction markers, and therefore in the total counts judgement markers are only counted once. Reaction is a sub-category of appreciation and has been singled out from appreciation for the same reason, but the number of appreciation excludes that of reaction. As such appreciation and reaction markers have been counted separately. This rule applies to Tables 5.3, 5.4, 5.5 and 5.6 as well

Table 5.4 Distribution of ATTITUDE in the Chinese corpus

	Positive		Negative		Neutral		Mediated		Non-med.		Total	
	No.	%	No.	%	No.	%	No.	%	No.	%	No.	%
Affect	163	54	130	43	8	3	162	54	139	46	301	7
Judgement	427	52	371	45	19	2	561	69	256	31	817	20
Social esteem	379	76	99	20	19	4	356	72	141	28	497	12
Social sanction	48	15	272	85	0	0	205	64	115	36	320	8
Appreciation	1041	35	1865	64	31	1	2474	84	463	16	2937	70
Reaction	29	24	71	60	19	16	60	50	59	50	119	3
Total	1660	40	2437	58	77	2	3257	78	917	22	4174	100

potential 'appreciation' markers amounting to 28.85% of all ATTITUDE markers in the Chinese corpus. However, possible 'judgement' markers (i.e. hēi, jiǎmào, fēifǎ) seem to be more salient than 'affect' markers in the Chinese corpus, since there is no 'affect' marker in this list. The order of ATTITUDE features in the Chinese corpus in terms of their frequency seems to be 'appreciation', 'judgement' and 'affect'.

However, this is not to suggest that Chinese corpus presents no 'affect' at all, or Australian corpus records no 'judgement'. The key insight provided by the frequency list is the rough picture of ATTITUDE rather than the exact figure of individual ATTITUDE feature (e.g. 'affect', 'judgement' and 'appreciation'). Judging from the meaning of the lemmas of ATTITUDE in Tables 5.1 and 5.2, it seems that both corpora prioritize the 'appreciation' of entities or things involved in risk events. However, the Chinese corpus seems to highlight the judgement of human behaviours in mediating risk communication, whereas the Australian corpus appears to emphasize human emotions and marginalize ‘judgement’. Without examining these markers/ lemmas in their arising context, this finding is rather tentative. The point here however is to propose such a hypothesis or to draw a tentative finding informed by the frequency of ATTITUDE lemmas and then to either confirm or reject this hypothesis with further evidence in the following.

The examination of all ATTITUDE markers identified in the Australian corpus (Table 5.3) shows that in general the Australian corpus favors ‘appreciation’ (46% + 12%) over ‘affect’ (34%) and ‘judgement’ (9%), a finding ascertaining the above hypothesis proposed in light of the frequency list (appreciation > affect > judgement).

Prior to the discussion of the distribution of ATTITUDE features across polarity, I have to make it clear that this research does not distinguish negative feelings from positive feelings that are grammatically negated, a distinction that has been drawn by Martin and White (2005, p. 73). As such, examples such as ‘not happy’ and ‘unhappy’ have been coded as the same—negative ‘affect’—in these two cases. The same criterion applies to the Chinese data as well. For instance, in Chinese news texts this research has not drawn a distinction between ‘无害’ (wú hài—harmless) and ‘没有害’ (méiyǒu hài—no harm).

In terms of polarity of ATTITUDE, Table 5.3 shows that negative ATTITUDE is more likely to be invoked in risk communication by Australian journalists, with the number of negative ATTITUDE markers (60%) almost doubling the positive (33%). Negative ATTITUDE markers occur more frequently than positive and neutral markers across each ATTITUDE category (negative > positive > neutral) in the Australian news corpus, except that there are two more positive markers of ‘social esteem’ than the negative.

As for the sources mediated (e.g. quoted speech) by Australian journalists, Table 5.3 shows that the number of mediated ATTITUDE markers (76%) considerably exceeds that of non-mediated markers (24%) and this is also true across each ATTITUDE category. This indicates that in risk communication Australian journalists favour invoking attitudes of the quoted sources over explicating their own subjective emotions.

Table 5.4 shows the Chinese corpus prioritizes ‘appreciation’ (70%) over ‘judgement’ (20%) over ‘affect’ (7%). This finding affirms the above assumption about the frequency order of ATTITUDE features (i.e. appreciation > judgement > affect) as deduced from the frequency list in the Chinese corpus. The frequency list of stance markers/lemmas (see Tables 5.1 and 5.2) thus seems to be able to predict the overall distribution of ATTITUDE markers.

Overall, the Chinese corpus (Table 5.4) orients towards negative ATTITUDE (58%). While negative ‘appreciation’ and negative ‘reaction’ outnumber their positive equivalents, the Chinese corpus exhibits more positive than negative ‘affect’ and ‘judgement’ in general. However, it is noteworthy that positive ‘social esteem’ markers (379 occ.) occur far more frequently than the negative markers

(99 occ.), whereas the reverse is true for 'social sanction', a finding that suggests that those who are judged against 'social esteem' in the Chinese corpus are more likely to be cast in a positive light but those who are judged by reference to 'social sanction' often receive a negative value (see Chap. 7 for detailed descriptions).

When it comes to the sources mediated by Chinese journalists, Table 5.4 shows that the Chinese corpus, resembling the Australian corpus, displays a preference of mediated ATTITUDE (78%). However, this difference is not marked between mediated affect markers (54%) and those non-mediated (46%), or between mediated 'reaction' (50%) and non-mediated 'reaction' markers (50%). This finding suggests that Chinese journalists often intrude in texts and impose their own emotions and emotional reaction to risk events whereas Australian journalists are less likely to do so (see Chap. 6 for more details).

Bednarek (2008, p. 50) reported a preference of negative emotions over the positive across all sub-corpora of the BNC (i.e. news reportage, academic discourse, fiction, and conversation corpus) and provided a threefold explanation. Firstly, there are more negative ATTITUDE markers than positive ones in the language system (Nöth, 1992, p. 82). Secondly, negative ATTITUDE markers are "psychologically salient emotion words to which an individual has immediate access to when asked to make a list of emotion words" (Schrauf & Sanchez, 2004, p. 270, cited in Bednarek, 2008, p. 50). Lastly, human beings seem to focus on negative experience more than they do the positive.

However, the above findings concerning the polarity of ATTITUDE in the Chinese corpus have demonstrated that in the realization of some ATTITUDE features (e.g. 'affect', 'social esteem') positive markers may well override negative markers, indicating that the expression of ATTITUDE varies across cultures. In this sense, the above threefold explanation provided by Bednarek (2008) may be insufficient to explain such a cultural deviation. In order to better explain such cultural differences in the adoption of ATTITUDE, it seems useful to probe more fully into the social-institutional context which gives rise to such ATTITUDE. This issue will be elaborated on in Chaps. 6 and 7.

5.3 Part-of-Speech Variation Across Corpora

This section will problematize the projecting of ATTITUDE features and their associated polarity orientations on each word class—nouns, verbs, adjectives, adverbs—with a view to understanding the relationship between ATTITUDE and the lexical properties. It is worth mentioning here that the list of stance markers may not include an equal amount of instances from each word class and thus may run the risk of deriving the findings from the methods. In this sense, the following discussion on the distribution of ATTITUDE should not be considered as conclusive.

5.3.1 *Overall Distribution of* ATTITUDE *Across POS*

Table 5.5 demonstrates that the Australian corpus clearly favors an overall style of adjectival ATTITUDE (52%). In Bednarek's (2008, p. 35) discussion of the most frequent emotion terms in the news sub-corpus of BNC, it is the nominal 'affect' (e.g. 'affect' realized in nominal forms) that is the most salient style, but my Australian news corpus shows a preference of a verbal-nominal 'affect' style and an adjectival-nominal 'reaction' style. My Australian corpus inclines to a style of adjectival-adverbial 'judgement', but a clear style of adjectival 'appreciation' is recorded. The prevailing 'appreciation' markers have directed the whole corpus to an overall style of adjectival ATTITUDE.

In a similar vein, the Chinese corpus (Table 5.6) displays a style of adjectival ATTITUDE (87%). In comparison, verbal ATTITUDE markers (7%) appear infrequently in the Chinese corpus, and adverbial (3%) and nominal ATTITUDE (3%) are rather marginal.

Comparing the distribution of ATTITUDE markers across word classes in the Australian corpus (Table 5.3) with that in the Chinese corpus (Table 5.6), I find that they both orient to an overall style of adjectival ATTITUDE. However, the Australian

Table 5.5 Distribution of ATTITUDE across POS in the Australian corpus

	Adjectives		Nouns		Verbs		Adverbs		Total	
	No.	%	No.	%	No.	%	No.	%	No.	%
Affect	61	23	90	34	97	37	17	6	265	34
Judgement	34	48	3	4	8	11	26	37	71	9
Social esteem	23	40	2	4	7	12	25	44	57	7
Social sanction	11	79	1	7	1	7	1	7	14	2
Appreciation	266	75	10	3	38	11	43	12	357	46
Reaction	46	51	37	41	4	4	4	4	91	12
Total	407	52	140	18	147	19	90	11	784	100

Table 5.6 Distribution of ATTITUDE features across POS in the Chinese corpus

	Adjectives		Nouns		Verbs		Adverbs		Total	
	No.	%	No.	%	No.	%	No.	%	No.	%
Affect	105	35	1	0	191	63	4	1	301	7
Judgement	660	81	20	2	61	7	76	9	817	20
Social esteem	432	87	7	1	41	8	17	3	497	12
Social sanction	228	71	13	4	20	6	59	18	320	8
Appreciation	2783	95	93	3	14	0	47	2	2937	70
Reaction	77	65	0	0	42	35	0	0	119	3
Total	3625	87	114	3	308	7	127	3	4174	100

Table 5.7 Summary of ATTITUDE patterns in relation to word classes

	Chinese	Australian
Affect	Verbal-adjectival	Verbal-nominal
Judgement	Adjectival	Adjectival-adverbial
Appreciation	Adjectival	
Reaction	Adjectival-verbal	Adjectival
Overall	Adjectival	

news corpus exhibits a verbal-nominal affect style, while Chinese news corpus displays a verbal-adjectival affect style. An adjectival reaction style is documented in the Australian corpus, but an adjectival-verbal reaction style is recorded in the Chinese corpus. The Australian corpus inclines to an adjectival-adverbial judgement, whereas the Chinese corpus orients towards a clear adjectival judgement style. An adjectival appreciation style prevails in both Chinese and Australian corpora. A summary of ATTITUDE patterns in relation to word classes is tabulated in Table 5.7.

5.3.2 Distribution of ATTITUDE *Across POS*

In the following sections (Sects. 5.3.2.1–5.3.2.4), for the sake of convenience I will place together nominal ATTITUDE features and their respective polarity orientation in both Chinese and Australian corpora, as shown in Table 5.8. Tables of the same kind will be available for verbal, adverbial and adjectival forms of ATTITUDE as well. It should be noted that the figures presented in Table 5.8, and Table 5.11, Table 5.14 and Table 5.17 alike are raw frequency only. In this sense, I intend to avoid directly comparing these figures. Normalized percentage of the variation of ATTITUDE across word classes will be summarized and compared in Sect. 5.4 in this chapter.

Rather than exhausting the list of all lemmas of ATTITUDE identified in each corpus, I have decided to put them in a table with a focus on those frequent ones in

Table 5.8 Nominal ATTITUDE and the polarity (Chinese and Australian corpora)

Noun (Raw frequency)	Positive		Negative		Neutral		Total	
	CN	OZ	CN	OZ	CN	OZ	CN	OZ
Affect	1	18	/	68	/	4	1	80
Reaction	/	4	/	32	/	1	0	37
Social esteem	7	2	/	/	/	/	7	2
Social sanction	10	/	3	1	/	/	13	1
Appreciation	23	6	65	4	5	/	93	10

Note "/" for no occurrence

Table 5.9 List of nominal lemmas of ATTITUDE (Australian corpus)

Affect	Reaction	Social esteem	Social sanction	Appreciation
CONCERN (34)	CONCERN (22)	DETERMINATION (1)	RESPECT (1)	IMPORTANCE (4)
FEAR (10)	HORROR (4)	COMPASSION (1)		HAZARD (5)
COMPLAINT (7)	TENSION (1)			IDEAL (1)
HOPE (5)	SURPRISE (1)			
GRIEF (4)	SHOCK (1)			
PANIC (4)	REGARD (1)			
PREFERENCE (3)	PITY (1)			
EXPECTATION (3)	PANIC (1)			
WORRY (2)	MADNESS (1)			
SYMPATHY (2)	GRIEF (1)			
FRUSTRATION (2)	CONFUSION (1)			
	COMPLAINT (1)			
	ANGUISH (1)			

each category. However, since ATTITUDE lemmas are distributed unevenly across their semantic features and word classes, I will not list all lemmas of ATTITUDE, especially those with infrequent occurrence. For instance, in Table 5.9, I have shown all stance items identified in realizing 'social esteem', 'social sanction' and 'appreciation', although most of them occur once only. But I have excluded those with one occurrence in the realization of 'affect' to avoid producing a rather tedious list. This practice has been followed consistently in this section (i.e. Sect. 5.3.2).

In short, the primary aim of this section (Sect. 5.3.2) is to describe the relation between ATTITUDE and its word classes and polarity orientations. The issue of how ATTITUDE co-selects certain polarity orientation, semantic features and news actors will be discussed in Chap. 6 through examining patterns of ATTITUDE.

5.3.2.1 Nouns

Table 5.5 has shown that nominal ATTITUDE markers in the Australian corpus account for 18% of all ATTITUDE markers. These nominal markers are primarily adopted to realize reaction (41%) and affect (34%) in the Australian corpus while judgement (4%) and appreciation (3%) are seldom realized by nouns. Likewise, nominal ATTITUDE markers in the Chinese corpus are marginal (3%) with 119 occurrences as illustrated in Table 5.6. There is only one marker of affect and no marker of reaction in the Chinese corpus in the nominal form. Nominal markers of judgement (2%) and appreciation (3%) are rather marginal as well.

Table 5.8 has summarized the raw frequency of nominal ATTITUDE identified in each corpus. The realization of ATTITUDE in each cell in this table (e.g. positive affect, negative reaction) will be presented in detail below.

The Australian corpus has recorded 90 occurrences of **nominal affect** lemmas with 11 of them occurring more than once as illustrated in Table 5.9. There are 18 positive nominal affect markers, four neutral and 68 negative. Overall, **nominal affect** orients to **negativity** in my Australian corpus.

Amid the 37 **nominal reaction** markers found in the Australian corpus (Table 5.9), two lemmas—CONCERN (22 occ.) and HORROR (4 occ.)—occur more than once, while others occur once only. Most of them (32 occ.) orient to negativity and only one (i.e. SURPRISE) expresses a neutral value. The only one positive reaction lemma (i.e. CONCERN) acquires the positive value through negating its negative value (e.g. *There was no cause of* ***concern*** *for infants who…*). In short, **nominal reaction** orients to the **negative** value in the Australian corpus.

The Australian corpus only presents three **nominal judgement** lemmas with each occurring once only (Table 5.9). The lemma of 'RESPECT' in the phrase of 'lack of respect' realizes **negative social sanction**, whereas 'DETERMINATION' and 'COMPASSION' realize **positive social esteem**. The infrequent occurrence of these nominal judgement lemmas, resembling that of **nominal appreciation** lemmas, shows no preference of polarity.

As shown in Table 5.10, there is only one **nominal affect** marker in the Chinese corpus—深情 (passion). My Chinese corpus presents **no nominal reaction** markers. It seems that nouns are seldom deployed to realize human emotions in Chinese hard news, at least this is the case in my Chinese corpus. By contrast, nouns are frequently adopted to express human emotions in the Australian corpus.

Amid the 20 **nominal judgement** markers (2%), **seven** are adopted to realize **social esteem**, with one—困难 (difficulty) often in the structure of 'somebody overcomes difficulties to-infinitive' occurring five times with each of the rest occurring once. The rest 13 nominal judgement markers—爱心 (love, 10 occ.), 道德 (morality, 2 occ.), and 贼 (stealer, 1 occ.)—realize **social sanction**. All **nominal social esteem** markers orient to the **positive** value and there are more markers of **positive nominal social sanction** (10 occ.) than the **negative** (3 occ.).

Resembling the low frequency of **nominal appreciation** markers in the Australian corpus, these markers occur rather infrequently in the Chinese corpus

Table 5.10 List of nominal lemmas of ATTITUDE (Chinese corpus)

Affect	Reaction	Social esteem	Social sanction	Appreciation
深情 (passion, 1)	/	困难 (difficulty, 5) 艰难险阻 (difficulty, 1) 热血 (enthusiasm, 1)	爱心 (love, 10) 道德 (morality, 2) 贼 (stealer, 1)	破坏性 (destroy, 12) 臭味 (stink, 11) 名牌 (top brand, 8) 毒 (poison, 7) 弹性 (flexibility, 7) 关键 (crucial, 6) 清香 (faint scent, 5) 困难 (difficulty, 4) 自然 (normal, 4) 脏乱差 (dirty, messy & bad conditions, 3) 光鲜 (brightness, 3) 污秽 (dirty, 2) 光亮 (shininess, 2)

(93 occ.) accounting for 3% of all appreciation markers. In comparison, the Australian corpus prioritizes the appreciation of importance of involved issues, whereas the Chinese corpus primarily assesses the quality (e.g. toxin) of reported things. There are 65 negative appreciation markers, 23 positive and five neutral markers, suggesting **nominal appreciation** in Chinese corpus orients to a **negative** value.

5.3.2.2 Verbs

The number of verbal ATTITUDE (19%) only slightly overtakes that of its nominal markers (18%) in the Australian corpus, and this is also the case in the Chinese corpus with verbal markers of ATTITUDE (7%) slightly overriding the nominal markers (3%). Again the point of presenting the distribution of ATTITUDE markers in their verbal forms is not to simply list these verbal markers but to discern a pattern of coupling between ATTITUDE, polarity orientations and the verbal forms. For instance, the challenge is to find whether ATTITUDE and the associated polarity orientations are distributed evenly in the verbal forms, and which ATTITUDE markers are frequently adopted.

Table 5.11 summarizes verbal ATTITUDE identified in each corpus. Broadly, Chinese corpus registers more positive verbal affect and social esteem markers than those negative, and the reverse is the true for verbal reaction, social sanction and appreciation markers. In the Australian corpus, verbal reaction, social esteem and social sanction markers are rather marginal. There are slightly more positive verbal affect markers than the negative, but verbal appreciation is dominated by negativity in the Australian corpus.

In the Australian corpus, **verbal affect** markers (97 occ.) account for 37% of all affect markers. There are slightly more positive verbal affect markers (42 occ.) than those negative (39 occ.). Neutral verbal affect markers (16 occ.) often express people's intention or expectation (i.e. EXPECT, PLAN, INTEND in Table 5.12). Overall **verbal affect** shows no preference of **negativity** or **positivity**.

Judgement and reaction are seldom realized by verbs in the Australian corpus (Table 5.12). **Verbal reaction** markers are extremely marginal with only four lemmas and each occurs once. There are only **eight verbal judgement** markers.

Table 5.11 Verbal ATTITUDE and the polarity orientations

Verb (Raw frequency)	Positive		Negative		Neutral		Total	
	CN	OZ	CN	OZ	CN	OZ	CN	OZ
Affect	118	42	65	39	8	16	191	97
Reaction	8	1	16	2	18	1	42	4
Social esteem	31	1	10	6	/	/	41	7
Social sanction	8	1	12	/	/	/	20	1
Appreciation	4	1	10	37	/	/	14	38

Table 5.12 List of verbal lemmas of ATTITUDE (Australian corpus)

Affect	Reaction	Social esteem	Social sanction	Appreciation
HOPE (18)	SURPRISE (1)	IGNORE (4)	HONOUR (1)	THREATEN (28)
FEAR (13)	SHOCK (1)	TRAUMATISED (1)		DEVASTATE (3)
WORRY (9)	SATISFY (1)	TRUST (1)		WORSEN (3)
LOVE (9)	DEVASTATE (1)	APPRECIATE (1)		TORMENT (1)
EXPECT (8)				IGNORE (1)
PLAN (5)				HURT (1)
CONCERN (5)				CARE (1)
INTEND (4)				
GRIEVE (4)				
WISH (2)				
REGRET (2)				
PREPARE (2)				
PANIC (2)				
COMPLAIN (2)				

Six of them realize **negative social esteem** with only one being positive (i.e. TRUST). One verbal social sanction marker is found and it takes a positive value.

Verbal appreciation markers in the Australian corpus (38 occ.) occupy 11% of all appreciation markers. Only three verbal appreciation lemmas occurring more than twice have been identified in the Australian corpus, while others only appear once. One verbal appreciation marker (i.e. CARE) orients to the positive value, and all the rest **verbal appreciation** markers show a **negative** value.

In the Chinese corpus, verbs are the chief word class in realizing **affect** (191 occ.) accounting for 63% of all word classes of affect. Amid all **verbal affect** markers, almost two thirds (118 occ.) are **positive**. Negative (65 occ.) and neutral (8 occ.) verbal affect markers together constitute the other one third. This is in sharp contrast with verbal affect in the Australian corpus where neither positive nor negative affect dominates the other.

Dissimilar from the marginal portion of verbal reaction in the Australian corpus (4%), Chinese corpus presents a substantial number of **verbal reaction** markers (35%). Among all verbal reaction in the Chinese corpus (42 occ.), 18 are neutral, 16 negative and 8 positive. It seems that in risk communication in Chinese hard news, **verbal reaction** markers are more likely to express **neutral** and **negative** values.

Akin to the Australian corpus, the Chinese corpus records few **verbal judgement** markers (7%) with 61 occurrences, as illustrated in Table 5.13. These markers are scattered across social esteem (41 occ.) and social sanction (20 occ.). Overall, **positive verbal judgement markers** (39 occ.) outnumber those **negative** (22 occ.). There are more markers of **negative verbal social sanction** (12 occ.) than the positive equivalents (8 occ.) whereas the opposite is true in verbal realizations of **social esteem** (31 positive vs. 10 negative). This finding suggests that those who are judged by reference to social esteem in verbal forms are more likely to receive a positive value while the case is reversed when they are judged by reference to social sanction (see Chap. 7 for details).

Table 5.13 List of verbal markers of ATTITUDE (Chinese corpus)

Affect	Reaction	Social esteem	Social sanction	Appreciation
喜欢 (like, 24)	关注 (concern, 19)	完善 (to perfect, 14)	假冒 (fake, 5)	假冒 (counterfeit, 3)
担心 (worry, 22)	担心 (worry, 6)	了解 (to know, 6)	守法 (law-abiding, 3)	因地制宜 (to take actions that suit local circumstances, 2)
关注 (concern, 15)	放心 (reassure, 5)	疏忽 (ignore, 4)	伪造 (fake, 3)	
尊重 (respect, 14)	喜爱 (love, 5)	规范 (regulate, 2)	至上 (to be supreme, 2)	
关心 (care, 12)	担忧 (worry, 2)	小心 (to be cautious, 2)	在乎 (care)	
悼念 (grieve, 10)		安然无恙 (to be safe, 2)		
投入 (devoted, 9)		信任 (trust, 2)		
放心 (reassured, 8)				
感谢 (thank, 7)				
关怀 (care, 6)				
牵挂 (care, 5)				
奇怪 (strange, 5)				
震惊 (shock, 4)				
担忧 (worry, 4)				
感慨 (to lament, 4)				
怕 (be afraid of, 4)				
关爱 (care, 4)				
疑惑 (puzzle, 3)				

Verbal appreciation markers in the Chinese corpus are almost negligible (14 occ.), occupying less than 1% of all appreciation markers. Only two verbal appreciation markers appear more than once (Table 5.13). The infrequent verbal appreciation in the Chinese corpus however orients to a negative value (10 occ.).

5.3.2.3 Adverbs

Adverbs overall constitute the least frequent word class in the realization of ATTITUDE. The adverbial ATTITUDE markers in each corpus are summarized in Table 5.14.

The raw frequency of adverbial markers in corpora in Table 5.14 shows that there are more adverbial markers of affect, reaction and social esteem in the Australian corpus than those in the Chinese corpus, while adverbial social sanction markers are far more frequent in the Chinese corpus.

The difference between adverbial appreciation markers in each corpus is not considerable in terms of their raw frequency. However, it should be noted that the size of corpus is not balanced, and such direct comparison of raw frequency may be misleading without examining the normalized percentage of each category (see Sect. 5.4 for more details in this regard).

There are only 17 **adverbial affect** markers in the Australian corpus (Table 5.15), with 10 realizing positive affect and seven negative. However, only three lemmas occur relatively frequently, while others are rather marginal (Table 5.15). **Adverbial reaction** markers also occur rather infrequently with each of the four lemmas occurring once, all being negative.

Adverbial judgement (26 occ.) are predominantly adopted to realize social esteem (25 occ.), as illustrated in Table 5.15. Amid the 25 social esteem markers,

Table 5.14 Distribution of adverbial ATTITUDE across polarity

Adverb (Raw frequency)	Positive		Negative		Neutral		Total	
	CN	OZ	CN	OZ	CN	OZ	CN	OZ
Affect	/	10	4	7	/	/	4	17
Reaction	/	/	/	4	/	/	0	4
Social esteem	12	11	5	10	/	4	17	25
Social sanction	1	/	58	1	/	/	59	1
Appreciation	9	22	38	16	/	5	47	53

Table 5.15 List of adverbial lemmas of ATTITUDE (Australian corpus)

Affect	Reaction	Social esteem	Social sanction	Appreciation
UNFORTUNATELY (6) FORTUNATELY (4) HOPEFULLY (2) SURPRISINGLY (1) RIGHTLY (1) NERVOUSLY (1) INTERESTINGLY (1) HAPPILY (1)	SURPRISINGLY (1) HOPELESSLY (1) AWFULLY (1) ALARMINGLY (1)	WELL (7) INTENTIONALLY (5) CAREFULLY (4) IMPROPERLY (3) CORRECTLY (2)	MALICIOUSLY (1)	BETTER (8) SIGNIFICANTLY (6) WELL (6) BADLY (6) OFFICIALLY (5) DANGEROUSLY (3) BEST (3) BAD (2)

Table 5.16 List of adverbial lemmas of ATTITUDE (Chinese corpus)

Affect	Reaction	Social esteem	Social sanction	Appreciation
无奈 (helplessly, 4)	–	千方百计 (effortlessly, 3) 从重 (severely, 3) 牢牢 (firmly, 2)	非法 (illegally, 40) 私自 (without explicit/official approval, 5) 大肆 (fearlessly, 3) 偷偷 (illegally, 3) 全心全意 (whole-heartedly, 2) 明目张胆 (brazenly, 2)	难以 (hardly, 19) 非法 (illegally, 11) 快 (quickly, 8) 堂而皇之 (abruptly 4)

11 are positive, 10 negative and four neutral. The only adverbial social sanction marker (i.e. MALICIOUSLY) judges the involved person in a negative manner.

Among the 43 markers of **adverbial appreciation**, 22 of them are positive and 16 are negative. There are only eight adverbial affect markers occurring more than twice, while the rest appear once each (i.e. WRONG, RATIONALLY, INCORRECTLY and IMPORTANTLY in Table 5.15).

In the Chinese corpus, there is only one **adverbial affect** marker (i.e. 无奈, helplessly, in Table 5.16) occurring four times, while no **adverbial reaction** marker is recorded therein. Adverbial appreciation markers (47 occ.) account for 2% of all appreciation markers in the Chinese corpus. Among them, 38 orient to a negative value, whereas the rest nine incline towards positivity.

Amid all **adverbial judgement** markers (76 occ.), the overwhelming number of them realizes social sanction (59 occ.) while only 17 adverbial social esteem markers are recorded in the Chinese corpus, a finding standing in sharp contrast with the priority of adverbial social esteem in the Australian corpus. The Australian corpus presents nearly equal amount of positive and negative adverbial social esteem, whereas the Chinese corpus registers more positive **social esteem** (12 positive vs. 5 negative) but shows more negative adverbial **social sanction** (58 negative vs. 1 positive).

5.3.2.4 Adjectives

ATTITUDE markers are predominantly realized in adjectival forms in each corpus. This section will examine the distribution of adjectival ATTITUDE in relation to polarity.

An overview of the distribution of adjectival forms of ATTITUDE in each corpus across polarity orientations (Table 5.17) shows that adjectival affect, reaction, social sanction and appreciation in each corpus favour negativity over positivity and neutrality. The Chinese corpus records far more positive adjectival social esteem markers whereas the difference of social esteem between polarity orientations is not significant in the Australian corpus.

In the Australian corpus, **adjectival affect** markers (61 occ.) amount to 23% of all affect markers, as illustrated in Table 5.18. Overall **adjectival affect** favours a **negative** value (35 occ.) over positive (24 occ.) or neutral (2 occ.) values. Likewise, **adjectival reaction** (46 occ.) presents a similar orientation of polarity, as indicated

Table 5.17 Distribution of adjectival ATTITUDE across polarity

Adjective (Raw frequency)	Positive		Negative		Neutral		Total	
	CN	OZ	CN	OZ	CN	OZ	CN	OZ
Affect	44	24	61	35	/	2	105	61
Reaction	21	8	55	38	1	/	56	46
Social esteem	329	10	84	6	19	7	432	23
Social sanction	29	4	199	7	/	/	228	11
Appreciation	1005	95	1752	154	26	17	3011	1864

Table 5.18 List of adjectival lemmas of ATTITUDE (Australian corpus)

Affect	Reaction	Social esteem	Social sanction	Appreciation
CONCERN (18) PROUD (4) SATISFY (3) OUTRAGED (3) NERVOUS (3) LOVE (3) SURPRISE (2) SICK (2) HORRIFY (2) HOPEFUL (2) HAPPY (2)	WORRY (5) TERRIBLE (4) APPAL (4) SAD (3) INTEREST (3) ALARM (3) INCREDIBLE (2) FRIGHTEN (2) DEVASTATE (2) AWFUL (2)	CAREFUL (7) WELL-KNOWN (2) DEDICATE (2)	RIGHT (4) MALICIOUS (4) GUILTY (2)	DANGEROUS (36) BAD (30) IMPORTANT (27) SIGNIFICANT (24) GREAT (18) BETTER (13) CRITICAL (12) DEVASTATE (10) BEST (10) OFFICIAL (9) SUBSTANTIAL (7) RISKY (5) HAZARDOUS (5) ESSENTIAL (5) TRAGIC (4) THREATEN (4) GRIM (4) DESPERATE (4) PERFECT (3) INCORRECT (3) DREADFUL (3) CHERISH (3) WRONG (2) TROUBLESOME (2) STAGGER (2) RIGHT (2), GUT (2)

Table 5.19 List of adjectival lemmas of ATTITUDE (Chinese corpus)

Affect	Reaction	Social esteem	Social sanction	Appreciation
热情 (enthusiastic, 8) 惊讶 (astonishing, 6) 吃惊 (surprised, 6) 满意 (satisfied, 5) 无奈 (helpless, 5) 放心 (reassuring, 5) 高兴 (happy, 3) 稳定 (stable, 3) 恐慌 (fearful, 3)	可疑 (suspicious, 9) 恶心 (disgusting, 8) 放心 (reassuring, 7) 触目惊心 (terrifying, 6) 诱人 (tempting, 5) 可怕 (terrible, 4) 惊人 (surprising, 3)	积极 (active, 46) 仔细 (careful, 29) 坚决 (determined, 24) 认真 (careful, 23) 主动 (initiative, 18) 严肃 (serious, 15) 详细 (careful, 14) 妥善 (proper, 13) 谨慎 (cautious, 13) 坚强 (courageous, 13) 随意 (random, 11) 有效 (effective, 11) 合理 (reasonable, 10) 不当 (improper, 10) 科学 (scientific, 8)	黑 (black, metaphorically means illegal, 55) 地下 (underground, metaphorically means illegal, 28) 不法 (unlawful, 25) 假 (fake, 23) 假冒 (counterfeit, 21) 黑心 (black-hearted, 16) 非法 (illegal, 13)	合格 (up to the standard, 548) 严重 (severe, 232) 假 (fake, 189) 正常 (normal, 87) 重要 (important, 80) 有毒 (poisonous, 66) 有害 (harmful, 63) 安全 (safe, 61) 黑 (black, often meaning a shame list, 60) 假冒 (counterfeit, 54) 科学 (scientific, 42) 有效 (effective, 37) 差 (bad, 36) 新鲜 (fresh, 35) 知名 (well-known, 32) 毒 (poisonous, 30)

by the most frequent lemmas. Amid all **adjectival reaction** markers, 38 of them express a **negative** value while the rest show a positive value.

Adjectival judgement markers in the Australian corpus (34 occ.) account for 48% of all judgement markers (71 occ.), as illustrated in Table 5.18. However, there are only few adjectival judgement lemmas occurring more than once. Adjectival judgement in the Australian corpus records more social esteem (23 occ.) than social sanction markers (11 occ.). There are slightly more positive adjectival markers of social esteem (10 occ.) than those neutral (7 occ.) and negative (6 occ.). In contrast, markers of positive adjectival social sanction (4 occ.) occur less frequently than those negative (7 occ.). Despite this, adjectival social sanction markers (11 occ.) occupy 79% of all social sanction markers.

Adjectival appreciation markers (75%) in the Australian corpus with 266 occurrences dominate the word classes of appreciation, as illustrated in Table 5.18. Amid all adjectival appreciation markers in the Australian corpus, the negative orientation (154 occ.) stands out whereas positive (95 occ.) and neutral markers (17 occ.) are less prominent.

In the Chinese corpus, although there are 105 occurrences of **adjectival affect** markers, only few of them appear more than twice (see Table 5.19). The **negative adjective affect** markers (61 occ.) in the Chinese corpus outnumber those positive (44 occ.). Negative values often concern emotions such as 'ASTONISHING', 'SURPRISE' and 'HELPLESS', whereas positive values relate to emotion such as 'ENTHUSIASTIC', 'HAPPY' and 'SATISFYING'.

In a similar vein, **negative adjectival reaction** markers (55 occ.) rather than those positive (21 occ.) or neutral (1 occ.) dominate the polarity orientation of adjectival reaction in the Chinese corpus (78 occ.), as illustrated in Table 5.19.

There are overall more **positive adjectival judgement** markers (52%) than those negative (45%). Positive adjectival **social esteem** (76%) outnumbers those negative (20%) whereas the reverse is the case for **social sanction** (85% negative vs. 15% positive). Among all adjectival judgement markers (660 occ.), 358 of them are positive, while 283 are negative. Adjectival social esteem markers (432 occ.) appear more frequently than do adjectival social sanction markers (228 occ.). The gap between the negative and positive values of judgement is much bigger in the adjectival realization of social esteem (329 positive vs. 84 negative) than it is in the expression of social sanction (29 positive vs. 199 negative). Negative social sanction mainly concerns illegally operating firms in China, while negative social esteem chiefly relates to the incompetency of individuals or institutions in dealing with risks.

Adjectival appreciation markers (95%) prevail in the Chinese corpus in the construal of ATTITUDE. The adjectival appreciation markers in the Chinese corpus are characterized with negativity (1752 occ.) rather than positivity (1005 occ.) or neutrality (26 occ.). These most frequent markers suggest that adjectival appreciation in the Chinese corpus chiefly concerns the quality of things or products in the event of food risks and the severity of risk situations in the event of earthquake risks.

5.4 Summary

Collating the above findings shown in Sect. 5.3.2, I find that the polarity orientation of ATTITUDE is projected unevenly across word classes in Chinese and Australian corpora.

For the sake of convenience and in order to examine the distribution of ATTITUDE from a different angle, Tables 5.20 and 5.21 have summarized the variation of

Table 5.20 Distribution of ATTITUDE across word classes and polarity (Australian corpus)

Australian corpus		Positive		Negative		Neutral		Total	
		Freq.	%	Freq.	%	Freq.	%	Freq.	%
Affect	Noun	18	7	68	26	4	2	90	34
	Verb	42	16	39	15	16	6	97	37
	Adverb	10	4	7	3	0	0	17	6
	Adjective	24	9	35	13	2	1	61	23
	Subtotal	94	35	149	56	22	8	265	100
Reaction	Noun	4	4	32	35	1	1	37	41
	Verb	1	1	2	2	1	1	4	4
	Adverb	0	0	4	4	0	0	4	0
	Adjective	8	9	38	42	0	0	46	51
	Subtotal	13	14	76	84	2	2	91	100
Social esteem	Noun	2	4	0	0	0	0	2	4
	Verb	1	2	6	11	0	0	7	12
	Adverb	11	19	10	18	4	7	25	44
	Adjective	10	18	6	11	7	12	23	40
	Subtotal	24	42	22	39	11	19	57	100
Social sanction	Noun	0	0	1	7	0	0	1	7
	Verb	1	7	0	0	0	0	1	7
	Adverb	0	0	1	7	0	0	1	7
	Adjective	4	29	7	50	0	0	11	79
	Subtotal	5	36	9	64	0	0	14	100
Appreciation	Noun	6	2	4	1	0	0	10	3
	Verb	1	0	37	10	0	0	38	11
	Adverb	22	6	16	4	5	1	43	12
	Adjective	95	27	154	43	17	5	266	75
	Subtotal	124	35	211	59	22	6	357	100
Total		260	33	467	60	57	7	784	100

Note In Tables 5.20 and 5.21, the percentage is calculated by dividing the figure of raw frequency of each cell (e.g. positive nominal affect—18) by the subtotal of marker in each ATTITUDE category. For instance, positive nominal affect in the Australian corpus (Table 5.20) accounts for 7%, and this is calculated by dividing the raw frequency (i.e. 18) by the subtotal of all affect markers in the Australian corpus (i.e. 265). In a similar vein, the percentage of subtotal of each category (e.g. subtotal of positive affect (i.e. 94) or subtotal of nominal affect (i.e. 90) in Table 5.20) is calculated by dividing its raw frequency by the subtotal of the same subtotal of markers in each attitudinal category. For instance, positive affect in Table 5.20 accounts for 35% of all affect markers in the Australian corpus, and this percentage is obtained by dividing 94 (i.e. the number of raw frequency) by 265 (i.e. subtotal of all affect markers in the Australian corpus)

ATTITUDE across word classes in line with ATTITUDE features—affect, reaction, social esteem, social sanction and appreciation. To avoid making each table too dense, I have shown the distribution of ATTITUDE in relation to polarity and word classes in the Australian corpus in Table 5.20 and present that in the Chinese corpus in

Table 5.21 Distribution of ATTITUDE across word classes and polarity (Chinese corpus)

Chinese corpus		Positive		Negative		Neutral		Total	
		Freq.	%	Freq.	%	Freq.	%	Freq.	%
Affect	Noun	1	0	0	0	0	0	1	0
	Verb	118	39	65	22	8	3	191	63
	Adverb	0	0	4	1	0	0	4	1
	Adjective	44	15	61	20	0	0	105	35
	Subtotal	163	54	130	43	8	3	301	100
Reaction	Noun	0	0	0	0	0	0	0	0
	Verb	8	7	16	13	18	15	42	35
	Adverb	0	0	0	0	0	0	0	0
	Adjective	21	18	55	46	1	1	77	65
	Subtotal	29	24	71	60	19	16	119	100
Social esteem	Noun	7	1	0	0	0	0	7	1
	Verb	31	6	10	2	0	0	41	8
	Adverb	12	2	5	1	0	0	17	3
	Adjective	329	66	84	17	19	4	432	87
	Subtotal	379	76	99	20	19	4	497	100
Social sanction	Noun	10	3	3	1	0	0	13	4
	Verb	8	3	12	4	0	0	20	6
	Adverb	1	0	58	18	0	0	59	18
	Adjective	29	9	199	62	0	0	228	71
	Subtotal	48	15	272	85	0	0	320	100
Appreciation	Noun	23	1	65	2	5	0	93	3
	Verb	4	0	10	0	0	0	14	0
	Adverb	9	0	38	1	0	0	47	2
	Adjective	1005	34	1752	60	26	1	2783	95
	Subtotal	1041	35	1865	64	31	1	2937	100
Total		1660	40	2437	58	77	2	4174	100

Table 5.21. Other visual graphs (e.g. pie chart, line chart or bar chart) would be useful to show the relationship among ATTITUDE, word classes and polarity orientations across corpora, but to include all these in a graph would have made the graph too dense which turns out to be not a good practice. Hence this decision to present them in two tables for each corpus.

Negative **affect** (56%) overrides positive affect (35%) in the **Australian** corpus, and this is particularly true when affect markers are realized in their nominal and adjectival forms. In contrast, the difference between positive and negative affect is not marked in their verbal and adverbial forms. Positive **affect** (54%) exceeds negative affect (43%) in the **Chinese** corpus, but this is only the case when they are realized in verbal forms. While adjectival affect orients towards a negative value, there are hardly any nominal and adverbial affect markers.

Reaction is seldom realized in verbal (4 occ.) and adverbial forms (4 occ.) in the **Australian** corpus, but its nominal and adjectival forms show a clear negative orientation in the same way as it does in general. The **Chinese** corpus presents a tendency to negative **reaction** (60%) as well, and exhibits no nominal and adverbial reaction markers. In those verbal and adjectival forms of reaction, the negative tendency prevails, and neutral verbal reaction markers (18 occ.) slightly overtake those negative (16 occ.).

In the **Australian** corpus, there are nearly as many positive judgement markers (41%) as those negative (44%). Negative **social sanction** markers (9 occ.) occur slightly more often than those positive (5 occ.) but social sanction inclines to a positive orientation when realized in adjectival forms. Positive **social esteem** markers (24 occ.) appear slightly more often than those negative (22 occ.), and this is particularly true when realized by adverbials (11 positive vs. 10 negative). However, verbal social sanction shows a tendency to positivity, and adjectival social sanction is characterized with positive and neutral values in the Australian corpus.

In the **Chinese** corpus, positive **judgement** markers (52%) appear slightly more often than those negative (45%). **Social esteem** subscribes to a clear positive orientation (76%) whereas negativity prevails in the expression of **social sanction** (85%). This tendency is viable across verbal, adjectival and adverbial forms of social esteem and social sanction, but their nominal forms orient to the positive value. While social esteem overall exceeds social sanction in the Chinese corpus, there are more social sanction markers than social esteem markers when they are realized in nominal and adverbial forms.

Generally, negative **appreciation** markers overtake those positive in both **Chinese** and **Australian** corpora. This tendency is found true across all word classes of ATTITUDE markers in the Chinese corpus and across verbal and adjectival forms in the Australian corpus. However, the Australian corpus records one more positive nominal appreciation marker and six more positive adverbial appreciation markers than those negative.

The findings presented in this chapter contour the profile of ATTITUDE in relation to frequent lemmas, polarity orientations, part-of-speech, and appraisal meanings. Despite the insights afforded by these findings, this chapter has largely isolated the analysis of ATTITUDE out of the arising contexts. As such, limited knowledge has as yet been obtained regarding the issues surrounding whose ATTITUDE is mediated in each corpus and mapped onto different appraisal meanings. To address these issues, it is necessary to examine the ATTITUDE markers in their co-text. This is the central task of the next two chapters with a focus on the relation between ATTITUDE and news actors.

Prior to the discussion of patterns of ATTITUDE and ENGAGEMENT in the corpus, I have to point out that the investigation of stance markers in this book has been confined to those inscribed (e.g. explicit) in news texts at the expense of implicit ones. This caveat is relevant to the corpus investigation techniques adopted in this book. As Hunston (2011, p. 168) put it succinctly, "searching the corpus in a way that does not prioritise the integrity of each constituent text but instead makes quantitative generalisations across texts can answer specific questions about evaluative language…but cannot identify or quantify all of it". That said, compared to manual qualitative analysis of all stance markers in each single text, my analysis of stance markers cannot claim comprehensiveness. In other words, there might be ATTITUDE and/or ENGAGEMENT markers that occur in the corpus but are not in the lists and hence not captured in the analysis. However, corpus-informed studies of stance markers or evaluative language can offer insights into the mechanism of these markers (e.g. permit interrogation of the mapping of evaluative meanings onto lexico-grammatical structures where these coincide consistently) that are not easily achievable by manual analysis.

References

Bednarek, M. (2008). *Emotion talk across corpora*. Basingstoke/New York: Palgrave Macmillan.

Hunston, S. (2011). *Corpus approaches to evaluation: Phraseology and evaluative language*. New York: Routledge.

Martin, J. R., & White, P. R. R. (2005). *The language of evaluation*. Basingstoke: Palgrave Macmillan.

Nöth, W. (1992). Symmetries and asymmetries between positive and negative emotion words. In W. G. Busse (Ed.), *Anglistentag 1991* (pp. 72–88). Tübingen: Niemeyer.

Schrauf, R. W., & Sanchez, J. (2004). The preponderance of negative emotion words in the emotion lexicon: A cross-generational and cross-linguistic study. *Journal of Multilingual and Multicultural Development, 25*(2–3), 266–284.

Chapter 6
The Strategic Ritual of Emotionality

6.1 Introduction

The strategic rituals of emotionality constitute central part of journalistic stance taking in news discourse. Emotions will be analyzed in accordance with the 'affect' system in appraisal as presented in Chap. 2. Thus, emotion and 'affect' will be used interchangeably in this chapter. As stated in Chap. 2, in comparison with other approaches to the study of emotion talk (see Bednarek, 2008, pp. 7–10, for an overview), Hunston (2011, p. 49) puts it, 'the appraisal framework is more successful in accounting for news discourse than other approaches'. Additionally, the appraisal framework focuses on language in social life, rather than on language in the mind, and one of its sub-systems (i.e. affect) deals specifically with emotions (Bednarek, 2008). In line with discourse studies (Blommaert, 2005; Fairclough, 2010; Gee, 2014; Scollon, 1998; Van Dijk, 1988; Wodak & Meyer, 2009) and anthropological approach to emotions (e.g. Abu-Lughod & Lutz, 1990), I delineate emotions in news discourse as discursive practices of journalism practitioners in organizing solidarity.

This chapter sets out to investigate the ways in which Chinese and Australian strategically mobilize and mediate emotions in hard news reporting on risk events that disturb social order. Corpus findings will concentrate on the central role of journalistic strategic ritual of emotionality in (re)constructing social values in the face of risk events. The interpretation and explanation of corpus findings will be discussed in relation to Chinese and Australian contexts of news production, with a particular view on press conditions such as tightening media budget, increasing press competition, and rising broadloidization.

C. Huan, *Journalistic Stance in Chinese and Australian Hard News*,
https://doi.org/10.1007/978-981-13-0791-1_6

6.2 A Brief Review of Emotion Studies

It is a traditional belief in journalism studies that objectivity constitutes a cornerstone of journalism practices (Bell, 1991; Chalaby, 1998; Mindich, 1998; Schudson, 1978, 2001; Schudson & Anderson, 2009; Tuchman, 1972; Van Dijk, 1988; Wahl-Jorgensen, 2013a; White, 1998). Tuchman (1972, p. 660) considers journalists' ritual of objectivity as a 'survival mechanism' and a strategy to avoid professional risks (e.g. libel suits). By analogy with the ritual of objectivity, Wahl-Jorgensen (2013a, p. 130) argues that there is also a strategic ritual of emotionality in journalism, which is delineated as 'an institutionalized and systematic practice of journalists narrating and infusing their reporting with emotion'. However, journalists' emotions are often considered to be at odds with objectivity (Franklin, 1997), and their mere presence in news discourse signals decaying, unprincipled and flawed journalism (Chalaby, 1998; Mindich, 1998; Molek-Kozakowska, 2013; Peters, 2011; Schudson & Anderson, 2009; Wahl-Jorgensen, 2013a). This assumption rests largely on 'Cartesian dualism of emotion and rationality when discussing "quality" journalism' (Peters, 2011, p. 299). Objective news shapes public rationality and occupies a central place in sustaining democracy in late modern social life (Hartley, 1996; McNair, 2011; Wahl-Jorgensen, 2013a), whereas emotionality is typically conflated with commercialization, tabloidization, sensationalism, bias of journalism, and the like (Franklin, 1997; Harrington, 2008; McNair, 1999; Pantti, 2010; Peters, 2011; Sparks, 1998; Stenvall, 2008).

However, following a number of important recent publications on emotionality in journalism studies (Bednarek, 2006, 2008; Kitch, 2000, 2003; Martin, 2004; Pantti, 2010; Pantti & Husslage, 2009; Pantti & Sumiala, 2009; Pantti & Van Zoonen, 2006; Pantti & Wieten, 2005; Peters, 2011; Stenvall, 2008, 2014; Wahl-Jorgensen, 2013a, 2013b), our understanding of emotionality in news discourse has shifted away from an old and rather simplistic opposition between emotion and reason, and relatedly between emotionality and objectivity, to a new view that brings into focus their complementarity. As Wahl-Jorgensen (2013a, p. 130) puts it succinctly 'the strategic ritual of emotionality does not call on journalists to express their own emotions. Rather, emotional expression is heavily policed and disciplined' (see also Stenvall, 2014; Thomson, White, and Kitley 2008). That is to say, emotionality does not necessarily run counter to objectivity but may operate alongside.

This view has been articulately explained in the concept of 'bonding' in the field of systemic functional linguistics, a concept that is concerned with 'ways of building togetherness, inclusiveness and affiliation' (Stenglin, 2004, p. 402) through infusing values with (journalistic) field. On this view, we can reasonably argue that in journalism practices, emotionality bonds dynamically with objectivity. As Martin (2004, p. 327) puts it, 'ideologically a text unfolds as rationality—a quest for "truth"; axiologically it unfolds rhetorically—an invitation to community'.

A growing body of research in this line has demonstrated how journalists of different cultures adopted the rituals of emotionality strategically in constructing social solidarity and inclusiveness and how emotions assist to reconstruct centres of social values in face of risk events that disturb social order (see Telle & Pfister, 2016 for an overview). In Finnish context of news reporting on risk events, Pantti and Sumiala (2009) take a severe traffic accident in Finland as an example to illustrate that there is one common theme to be found in media reporting of mourning rituals, the theme being social inclusiveness. In Dutch society, Pantti and Wieten (2005) demonstrate how Dutch Television news reporting of the death of controversial right-wing politician Pim Fortuyn constructs a shared nationwide feeling community through the representation of mourning and grief. In American culture, similar findings have been documented by Kitch (2000) in her study of the public mourning for famous people in American newsmagazines. Wahl-Jorgensen (2013a, p. 141) draws on Pulitzer Prize-winning news articles and demonstrates that emotional storytelling is 'the driving force behind award-winning journalism, with the aim of drawing the audience's attention to complex topics of social and political import'. In Hong Kong context of news reporting on the 9/11 event, Martin (2004) focuses on the rhetorical power of evaluative language (feeling in particular) and outlines the ways a Hong Kong lifestyle magazine editor negotiates solidarity with readers and naturalizes diverse reading positions in the wake of the 9/11 event. Likewise, Kitch (2003) also finds that in media coverage of the 9/11 event emotions of shock and fear were replaced by inspiration, patriotic pride and heroism as part of a grand cultural narrative of American resilience and progress. In Australian and Haitian print media reporting on natural disasters, Yell (2012) finds that 'affect' functions to position readers and also to shape local and global publics. For domestic disasters, readers are positioned to share more intense emotions with the local readers for an extended period of time, whereas for foreign disasters readers are positioned to feel for, and thus distance from, the disaster-affected community.

Broadly, those studies have provided insights into understanding the significance of mediated emotions as journalistic stance in news discourse, especially the role of emotions in positioning readers to belong to the same imagined feeling community, in eliciting pro-social behaviour, and in constructing, sustaining and negotiating social bonds and inclusiveness.

Yet, scholarly attention has been particularly scarce in the study of how emotions assist to reconstruct centres of social values in the face of risk events that disturb social order in Chinese hard news reporting. Additionally, our understanding has been insufficient in relation to issues such as how the rituals of emotionality are strategically adopted by journalists across different cultures. In view of this, this chapter focuses on a comparative study of the ways emotions of different news actors are presented and represented across Chinese and Australian hard news reporting in relation to risk events.

6.3 Overview of Affect Patterns

This section provides an overview of the distribution of 'affect' features across corpora. Figure 6.1 shows that the Australian corpus exhibits significantly more markers of 'inclination' (13% in the Australian corpus vs. 0% in the Chinese corpus), 'insecurity' (40% vs. 24%), neutral 'inclination' (8% vs. 3%) and 'dissatisfaction' (9% vs. 7%) than does the Chinese corpus, whereas the reverse is true in relation to the realization of 'happiness' (31% in the Chinese corpus vs. 7% in the Australian corpus), 'unhappiness' (10% vs. 9%), 'satisfaction' (12% vs. 5%) and 'security' (13% vs. 9%). The most prominent 'affect' feature in the Australian corpus is that of 'insecurity' (40%), whereas that in the Chinese corpus is 'happiness' (31%). These findings suggest that 'affect' features are mapped differently onto a comparable corpus comprising data on similar topics in different socio-cultural contexts of hard news reporting on risk events. Such a preference for distinctive attitudinal meanings provides significant analytical insights into understanding social values in each context of hard news reporting on risk events (see Discussion in this chapter). Given the low frequency of 'dis/inclination' markers in the Chinese corpus (3%), we are unable to compare patterns of 'dis/inclination' across corpora and hence a comparable analysis of 'dis/inclination' is excluded from this research.

Let us now turn to the relationship between 'affect' features and emoters (see Fig. 6.2). Elites and citizens are the two most frequently represented emoters in both corpora. However, the Australian corpus shows more occurrences of elites and unspecified emoters (i.e. 'non' in Fig. 6.2) than the Chinese corpus does, whereas the latter corpus overtakes the former in relation to such emoters as citizens and risk makers. Despite the relatively high frequency in the Australian corpus, unspecified emoters inform us of nothing about emoters, and hence they are excluded from analysis in this chapter. That said, given the frequency of occurrence in both

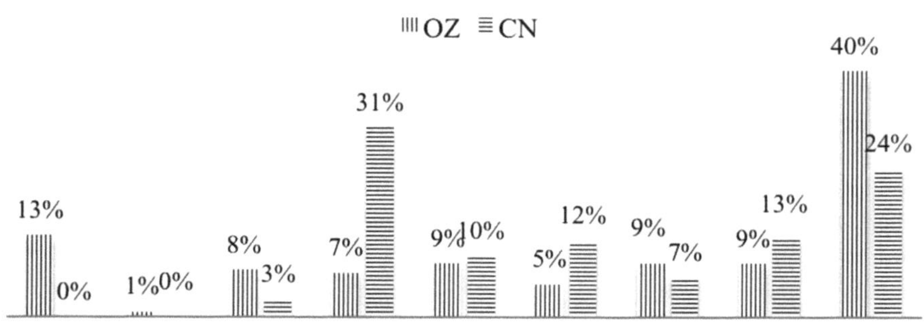

Fig. 6.1 Distribution of 'affect' across corpora. The symbol of "+" signals positive values, "–" negative, and "=" neutral. The total number of 'affect' markers in the Australian corpus is 264, and that in the Chinese corpus is 274

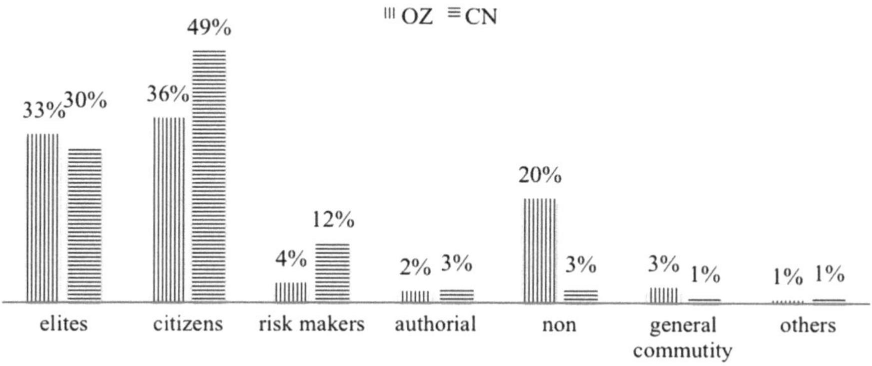

Fig. 6.2 Distribution of 'affect' across emoters in both corpora

corpora, this chapter will centre on emotions of elites, citizens and risk makers, and discuss those of journalists themselves where relevant.

Collating corpus findings in this section, we have noticed that 'affect' features are culture-sensitive in the similar vein as their valences are, and that emoters are not represented equally across cultures. In view of these findings, let us now explore deeper into who expressed what emotions and how emotions are interconnected with social statuses of news actors across corpora. The relation between emotions and social statuses of news actors will inform us of the way centres of social values are constructed in each context of hard news reporting.

6.4 Affect Patterns in Chinese and Australian Hard News

6.4.1 Patterns of 'Un/Happiness' in the Australian Corpus

Overall, occurrences of 'un/happiness' in the Australian corpus seem to be rather small. Markers of 'un/happiness' of citizens are far more frequent than those of other emoters. We will focus on 'happiness' of citizens, since it is the more popular of the two alternatives. Citizens' 'happiness' is chiefly related to their *love* of (living in) an Australian place (see example (1)), or to comforting bushfire victims who were deeply loved by victims' families (see example (2)). In the former case, citizens' *love* of a place is contrasted with the devastating consequences of bushfires, hence inviting sympathy with emoters; whereas in the latter case, the same rhetorical effect is achieved through foregrounding the loss of beloved family members.

(1) Karina Morris, Weetangera Celebrate citizens, I **love** living in Canberra …
(2) … victims' families were anxious to retrieve the bodies of their **loved** ones but …

Like 'happiness' of citizens, that of elites primarily relates to experts *loving* Australian places/bushes (e.g. *We all love the Australian bush, but our houses are not equipped to withstand eucalypt fireballs.*); and elites' love of the Australian bush is brought to contrast with horrible bushfires as well. Elites' 'unhappiness' is often triggered by the loss of bushfire victims (e.g. *The AWU Victorian Branch last night said it was* ***grieving*** *the loss of two DSE firefighters …*).

Markers of authorial 'un/happiness' explicitly inscribe journalists' stance in news reporting. Among them, three markers are positive referring to journalists' love of an Australian place in the event of bushfires (see example (3)). Again, a contrast is established between authors' *love* of Australia and the appalling bushfires. Readers are therefore invited to share sympathy with journalists but share hatred towards bushfires. The only marker of 'unhappiness' expresses journalists' *grief* over bushfire victims (e.g. … *we* ***grieve*** *for those who didn't [survive]*). It is noteworthy that when inscribing authorial 'un/happiness' Australian journalists always incorporate readers as emoters through adopting an inclusive we. As such, Australian journalists construct solidarity with readers as if they share the same emotions together.

(3) Yet we still **love** this impossible land, even when appalling bushfires strike every few years …

The Australian corpus exhibits only two instances (i.e. regret) of 'un/happiness' of risk makers, both expressing 'unhappiness'. Risk makers are represented in risk events as those who regret their wrongdoings (e.g. *Siddiq said he* ***regretted*** *the breaches…*).

To collate corpus findings in this section, 'happiness' of citizens, elites, and journalists is related to their *love* of an Australian place in the event of bushfires and their 'happiness' is often contrasted with horrible and appalling bushfires that claim causalities. This contrast achieves two rhetorical effects. One is to invite sympathy with those who suffer from bushfires, and the other is to establish solidarity between emoters and readers. 'Unhappiness' of these emoters in the Australian corpus is concerned with their grief over bushfires victims. Such a negative emotion invites sympathy with families of victims and eventually establishes an alignment between these emoters and readers. By contrast, risk makers are represented solely in relation to 'unhappiness' in the context of food safety, which is often concerned with their regret of breaching laws. Thus, risk makers are emotionally isolated as 'Others' who are distant from 'Us'.

6.4.2 Patterns of 'Un/Happiness' in the Chinese Corpus

The Chinese corpus displays more markers of 'un/happiness' of elites than those of other emoters. Markers of 'un/happiness' of Chinese citizens are predominantly positive. 'Happiness' of citizens in the Chinese corpus also relates to their *love* (see example (4)), but the triggers are often risk food. In the Australian corpus, Australian citizens' *love* tends to be triggered by an Australian place and contrasts with appalling bushfires, and thus their *love* invites sympathy in the event of bushfires; by contrast, Chinese citizens' *love* regarding risk food seems to invite nothing more than negative judgement upon their ignorance and incapacity to safeguard their food security. Government officials should have taken the responsibility of overseeing local food markets for citizens. But to foreground Chinese citizens' *love* regarding risk food leaves the responsibilities of consuming risk food solely with Chinese citizens themselves. Negative judgement upon local government is thus avoided. In short, 'happiness' of Chinese citizens eschews negative judgement of 'capacity' upon power elites. In some cases, markers of citizens' 'happiness' can invoke positive judgement of 'propriety' (ethic behaviour) and 'capacity' of power elites (see example (5)).

(4) 以前,我们家**喜欢**用金浩茶油,茶油嘛,比较健康,现在居然传出含有致癌物质,我们肯定就不吃了,改吃别的茶油了。
Previously, our family **liked to** use Jinhao tea-seed cooking oil, which is relatively healthy. But now the rumour is that it contains cancerogenic substance, and we definitely abandon it and change to other alternative brands.
(5) 淳朴的尕玛松保**激动地**说,有党和政府的帮助,吃的喝的都没问题了。
Gamasongbao, honest and simple, said **excitedly** that with the help of the Communist Party and government there is no survival problem.

Markers of elites' 'un/happiness' favour positivity over negativity. Unlike 'happiness' of elites in the Australian corpus, that in the Chinese corpus is primarily related to their *caring* of earthquake victims (see example (6)). In short, 'happiness' of elites in the Chinese corpus invokes positive judgement upon their ethical behaviour, achieved through their *caring* of earthquake victims.

(6) 党和政府十分**关心**灾区群众的过冬问题。
The Party and government very much **care about** the issue of how people in disaster-affected areas could survive the winter.

Like the case in the Australian corpus, 'unhappiness' of elites is concerned with their *grieving over* earthquake victims. Through shared sorrow, elites are positioned to establish a close emotional bond with families of the victims and with other citizens who sympathize with victims (see example (7)).

(7) 中国国务院决定今日举行全国哀悼活动,**悼念**青海玉树地震死难者 …
The State Council decided to hold national memorial activities today to **grieve over** victims of the Yushu earthquake.

Contrary to our expectation, 'happiness' of risk makers (see example (8)) is far more frequently enacted than 'unhappiness'. The only marker of 'unhappiness' relates to regret of risk makers for creating confusion to consumers, which is also envisaged in the Australian corpus. However, the Australian corpus has recorded no markers of 'happiness' of risk makers.

(8) 误以为记者是新开张的烧烤店主，店铺的售货员**热情地**介绍 …
Mistakenly considered the reporter [the reporter who was on site reporting the event and who wrote the news report at issue] as new barbeque storekeeper, the shop assistant **passionately** introduce …

However, a close scrutiny of markers of risk makers' 'happiness' reveals that their 'happiness' actually invokes negative ethical judgement of their trading habits (see example (8)). Using 'happiness' of risk makers to invoke negative judgement upon them stands in marked contrast to our previous observation that 'unhappiness' of elites invokes positive judgement. This finding underwrites one of our principal arguments that news actors tend to be represented in relation to certain 'affect' features and their valences. Additionally, risk makers are represented in the Chinese corpus in the similar manner as Chinese citizens are. That is to say, Chinese journalists tend to align with power elites as 'Us' but distance from citizens and risk makers as 'Others'.

In short, Chinese journalists manipulate citizens' 'happiness' to invoke negative judgement upon citizens and at the same time avoid negative judgement upon elites who should have taken responsibility for their inaptitude in overseeing local food markets. Citizens' 'happiness' (often in adjectival forms) is also utilized to invoke positive judgement of capacity upon power elites in dealing with risks. 'Happiness' of elites invokes positive judgement of 'propriety' upon elites, whereas 'unhappiness' of elites establishes intimate emotional bonds between elites and the public through shared grief over earthquake victims. 'Happiness' of risk makers invokes nothing more than negative judgement. Broadly, a social distance between Chinese power elites and the powerless is created and sustained by Chinese journalists in covering risk events in connection with 'un/happiness'.

6.4.3 Patterns of 'Dis/Satisfaction' in the Australian Corpus

The Australian corpus shows more markers of 'dis/satisfaction' of citizens than those of other emoters. A great majority of these are negative. Markers of citizens' 'satisfaction' relate to their pleasure with Australian food or an Australian place (e.g. We are satisfied with the product.). 'Dissatisfaction' of citizens is often related to citizens' anger at or complaint of a risk place or situation (see example (9)).

(9) The investigation came after three customers independently **complained of** finding cock- roaches in their food.

Markers of 'dis/satisfaction' of elites are mostly positive, dealing with their pleasure in learning of improved risk situations (see example (10)). In terms of 'dissatisfaction', elites do not complain about risk situations, but instead they often feel disappointed or frustrated (see example (11)).

(10) The order was lifted after two days when authorities were **satisfied with** the state of the premises.

(11) Asked for his thoughts on RFS members who have so far been charged, Koperberg says: 'I am not surprised by it, but I am **disappointed**'.

In short, Australian citizens and elites are satisfied and dissatisfied for various reasons, but the triggers are risk events or situations.

6.4.4 Patterns of 'Dis/Satisfaction' in the Chinese Corpus

The Chinese corpus presents identical amount of markers of 'dis/satisfaction' of elites and citizens, but those of other emoters are rather infrequent. Markers of citizens' 'dis/satisfaction' favour negativity over positivity. 'Satisfaction' of citizens is primarily related to their gratitude to and satisfaction with elites or elites' efforts in restoring order in the event of an earthquake (see example (12)). By presenting how elites or their efforts trigger 'satisfaction' of citizens, positive judgement of power elites' 'capacity' is invoked. 'Dissatisfaction' of citizens is mainly related to consumers' anger towards risk makers (see example (13)).

(12) 王玉虎代表玉树 35 万各族群众**感谢**党中央、国务院, 省委、省政府以及全国各族人民对玉树的大力支持和无私援助。
Wang Yuhu, on behalf of the 350,000 people in Yushu, **expressed gratitude to** the selfless support provided by the Central Committee of the Party, the State Council, provincial Committee of the Party, provincial government and all nations of Chinese people.
(13) 房东赵先生回答: "我就是**看不惯**他造假酱油害人。
Landlord Zhao said 'it is only because I am **dissatisfied with** the way he faked soy source to harm others'.

All but one markers of 'dis/satisfaction' in relation to elites are positive, dealing with elites' respect of people's willingness (see example (14)). Lower-rank elites' 'satisfaction' is often triggered by assistance provided by higher-rank power elites. Broadly, 'satisfaction' of elites often invokes positive judgement of 'propriety' upon power elites in the Chinese context (see example (15)).

(14) 青海省在充分**尊重**捐赠人意愿的基础上 …
Qinghai province fully **respects** the willingness of donators …
(15) 都江堰市市委书记刘俊林还代表都江堰市, 对成都军区首长、机关和全体官兵对都江堰人民的深厚情谊表示衷心**感谢**。
Liu Junlin, secretary of Dujiangyan municipal Party committee, **expressed sincere thanks to** commanders of the Chengdu military district, military units and all officers and soldiers for their friendliness to Dujiangyan citizens.

The only marker of 'dissatisfaction' of elites relates to the fact that local policemen had no choice but stay at the place where risk food was produced in order to guard the food from being otherwise transported by risk makers. It is unethical behaviour of risk makers that triggers 'dissatisfaction' of elites, and thus positive judgement upon elites is implied.

Again, contrary to what we expected, risk makers in the Chinese corpus are represented more often positively than negatively. However, risk makers are institutions in the presentation of 'dis/satisfaction' (see example (16)) and are not individuals, which was the case in 'un/happiness'. Another marked difference between 'happiness' and 'satisfaction' of risk makers is that the former invokes negative judgement of 'propriety' upon individual risk makers, whereas the latter invokes positive judgement upon institutional risk makers. One speculation to account for this difference is that institutions are capable of mobilizing economic resources to manipulate public relations to minimize adverse effects of their risk products, but this is hardly affordable by individual risk makers. The other explanation could be that negative representation of individual risk makers enhances the news value of negativity (i.e. negative aspects of news events or actors) (e.g. Bednarek & Caple, 2014), a prominent value that is able to attract a larger readership in newspaper's pursuit of economic profits (see Sect. 6.5 for discussion).

(16) 可口可乐公司还表示，他们**尊重**山西省质量技术监督局对该厂生产管理方面做出的处理意见 …

The Coca-Cola Company said they **respect** the investigation results in relation to their operation and management given by Shanxi provincial Administration of Quality and Technology Supervision.

To collate corpus findings in this section, we find that triggers of 'satisfaction' of citizens are often power elites, whereas those of 'dissatisfaction' of citizens are often risk makers. In either case, the triggers are human beings rather than risk events (as we have envisaged in the Australian corpus). That is to say, elites are always represented positively in relation to 'dis/satisfaction' regardless of the valences; positive judgement upon elites is also invoked through 'satisfaction' of citizens. Additionally, institutional risk makers are more likely to be represented positively in relation to 'dis/satisfaction', whereas individual risk makers and Chinese citizens are represented negatively.

6.4.5 Patterns of 'In/Security' in the Australian Corpus

The Australian corpus shows more markers of 'in/security' of elites and citizens than those of other emoters. Markers of 'in/security' of elites are predominantly negative. 'Security' of elites mainly relates to panic, surprise or concerns that are grammatically negated (e.g. *We are not* ***concerned*** *about that.*). The insecurity of elites most often relates to their surprise in finding a risk situation, or to their concern about the possible worsening of risk situations (see examples (17) and (18)).

(17) She was **surprised** to find more than one in 10 children had a substantial reaction to foods often linked to allergies…

(18) He is especially **concerned** now about the cervical cancer vaccine being given to girls and young women…

Markers of citizens' 'in/security' are primarily negative. 'Security' of citizens (often parents) is mainly concerned with feelings (i.e. concerns and worries) that are grammatically negated as well (e.g. *Health authorities say there is no need for parents to be worried because…*). In comparison with 'insecurity' experienced by elites, 'insecurity' of citizens tends to more varied, including feelings of nervousness, worry and panic (see example (19)).

(19) Mallacoota caravan park owner Mark Rogers was **nervous about** the fuel loads near his property.

In addition, 'security' of citizens and elites that is not grammatically negated is related to their confidence in improved risk situations (e.g. *Australian consumers can have the utmost confidence in the disease-free status of Australian pork.*), and their pride in being an Australian (see example (20)).

(20) 'It just makes me **feel proud** to be an Australian.'

Broadly, 'security' of elites and citizens is often realized by negated 'insecurity' markers, but Australian citizens tend to experience more kinds of 'insecurity' than elites do in the face of risk events.

6.4.6 Patterns of 'In/Security' in the Chinese Corpus

The Chinese corpus displays far more markers of 'in/security' of citizens than those of other emoters. Most of these are markers of citizens' 'insecurity'. 'Security' of citizens is often assured by elites and markers of 'security' of citizens often collocate left with modal verbs to alleviate their concerns with food risk (see example (21)). 'Security' of citizens in both Australian and Chinese corpus is often warranted by experts or power elites.

(21) 这些海鲜丸的确是仿生海洋食品，但消费者不用担心安全性。
These seafood balls are indeed counterfeit seafood, but consumers **do not need to worry about** the safety.

Additionally, unlike 'security' of citizens in the Australian corpus where citizens' alignment with an Australian identity has been enacted, 'security' of citizens in the Chinese corpus is often related to their calmness, especially in the event of earthquakes (see example (22)). Such an emotional strategy adopted by Chinese journalists conforms to the political requirements of social stability in contemporary China (稳定压倒一切), but this runs counter to our normal expectation that citizens could really stay calm facing frequent aftershocks.

(22) 汶川地震余震频发广安**人心稳定**社会秩序良好。
Aftershocks happening frequently after the Wenchuan earthquake, people in Guangan are **calm** and social order is normal.

In addition to citizens' surprise with discovering food risks, markers of 'insecurity' also express citizens' worries about food risk and the associated adverse effects (see example (23)).

(23) "吃了有老鼠的粥,我们很**担心**会被传染疾病 ..."

'Having eaten porridge with a mouse inside, we are **anxious about** being affected by the diseases.'

Markers of 'security' in relation to elites are mainly concerned with their confidence in helping residents out of earthquakes. Markers of 'insecurity' deal with elites' surprise with discovering food risk situations (see example (24)).

(24) 科长张忠华看着这几枚疑似"橡皮蛋", 也颇感**惊讶**。

Zhang Zhonghua, division chief, looking at these seemingly 'rubber eggs', was **surprised**.

All instances of 'in/security' in relation to risk makers are negative. 'Insecurity' of risk makers is mainly concerned with their panic or impatience with journalists' inquiries (see example (25)).

(25) 大个子男子**很不耐烦地**回答说。

That tall man replied very **impatiently**.

In short, Chinese citizens, elites, and risk makers experience different kinds of 'in/security'. 'Insecurity' experienced by citizens and elites (e.g. being surprised by risk situations) is more or less similar, whereas that of risk makers is totally different. 'Security' of elites tends to invoke positive judgement of 'capacity' upon them in dealing with risks. 'Security' of citizens in the event of earthquakes is more likely to be presented to reproduce political values than to sustain news factuality. However, such a way of presenting 'security' of citizens does not necessarily invoke positive judgement of 'capacity' upon Chinese elites. Rather it undermines public confidence in journalists' professional credibility because it is impossible for citizens to feel secure in the immediate aftermath of earthquakes even with elites' support. That is, such reports run counter to our expectation or to the real situation.

6.5 Discussion

To briefly summarize the corpus findings presented in this chapter, I have found both cultural resemblances and variability in the way emotions are manipulated by Chinese and Australian journalists. To be specific, 'unhappiness' in both corpora is chiefly concerned with grief of news actors over bushfires victims (in the Australian context) or grief over earthquake victims (in the Chinese context). Australian and

Chinese journalists also resemble each other in presenting and representing 'in/security' of ordinary citizens and elites through foregrounding their concerns and worries about risks at issue.

However, corpus findings have recorded remarkable disparity in the ways Chinese and Australian journalists mobilize resources of 'happiness' and 'dis/satisfaction'. 'Happiness' in the Australian corpus is concerned with love of ordinary citizens, power elites and journalists themselves towards an Australian place in the event of bushfires. As such, a social bond has been built up between the powerful (e.g. power elites) and the powerless (e.g. ordinary citizens and risk victims) through shared emotions. By contrast, 'happiness' in the Chinese corpus is mainly related to citizens' love of risk food. In this way, negative judgement is invoked upon their purchase habits and at the same time negative judgement upon power elites is avoided. Resources of 'happiness' in the Chinese corpus separate the powerful (as Us) from the powerless (as Others).

As to 'dissatisfaction', Australian journalists tend to present citizens' emotion towards risk food, while Chinese journalists tend to present citizens' emotion towards risk makers. In the Australian corpus, citizens' 'satisfaction' is often related to their pleasure with Australian food, whereas in the Chinese corpus, citizens' 'satisfaction' is more often than not triggered by elites (and/or their efforts). 'Dis/satisfaction' of elites in the Australian corpus mainly relates to their pleasure with improved risk situations or disappointment with the current risk situations. By contrast, elites in the Chinese corpus always show their respect of people's willingness.

These findings strongly support the statement that 'there is some evidence of an increasing emotionalization of journalistic narratives' (Wahl-Jorgensen, 2013a, p. 142). However, the increasing emotionalization or emotionality does not suggest that news has become emotional. Rather, it signals more explicit journalistic involvement with readers in news discourse (Peters, 2011). Both authorial and non-authorial 'affect' has been documented in Australian and Chinese print media coverage of risk events. This finding suggests that emotions have not only become 'increasingly central in western societies' (Pantti, 2010, p. 168), but it is also the case in the Chinese context. For journalism practitioners in China and Australia, the strategic ritual of emotionality constitutes an indispensable professional skill, albeit rarely discussed or made explicit in journalism practices or in newsroom socialization (Wahl-Jorgensen, 2013a). Such professional skills are essential strategies in the context of tightening media budget and increasing press competition in Chinese and Australian contexts of news production (Huang, 2016; Tiffen, 2006a, 2006b; Zhao, 2008). This is because rituals of emotionality are strategically utilized in service of engaging with a broader readership and therefore accruing economic benefits. Additionally, emotionality is relevant to the rising broadloidization in news industry worldwide. Broadloidization refers to 'a growing tendency of broadsheet newspapers to adopt the stories and styles of tabloid reporting' (Franklin, 1997, 2005, p. 28; cited in Huang, 2016, p. 653).

Corpus findings have also pointed to the ways Chinese and Australian journalists undertake divergent stances through mediating emotions of news actors of different social statuses. Broadly, Chinese journalists tend to align with power elites through enacting positive appraisal of elites and avoiding negative judgement upon them, whereas Australian journalists do not take a skewed stance towards power elites. Such stances are relevant to the sociological aspect of emotions (Berezin, 2001, 2002; Clark, 1997; Stets & Turner, 2006; Tudor, 2003). That is, linguistic resources for construing emotions in news discourse are necessarily conditioned by socio-cultural, institutional, and professional contexts of news production, which give arise to these emotions. Emotions in news discourse bear ideological and social consequences. There is growing evidence to suggest that emotions play a vital role in eliciting pro-social behaviours, affirming dominant social values, and legitimizing the existing social order (see Telle & Pfister, 2016 for an overview). Risk events disturb social order and present a direct threat to people's emotional well being. Corpus findings show that both Australian and Chinese journalists endeavour to restore social order in the face of disorder and risk situations through manoeuvring emotions of news actors.

To be specific, in the context of earthquakes in China and bushfires in Australia, grieving constitutes a transitional healing period for survivors and bereaved families, reunites survivors and readers, and augments a sense of social belonging. Private and personal emotions of news actors were transformed into ones that were shared by the general public, and as such readers were positioned to belong to the same imagined feeling community (Berezin, 2002; Kitch, 2003; Martin, 2004; Stenvall, 2008).

In the context of food safety, journalists in both societies steer clear of an otherwise possible social disorder through presenting and representing negative emotions ('insecurity' and 'dissatisfaction') of ordinary citizens and elites towards risk food. Hence, the possibility of inflicting a social conflict between the dominant and dominated is kept at arm's length. In short, despite the distorting effects of these negative emotions, 'the social order cannot be sustained without moral emotional arousal' (J. H. Turner & Stets, 2006, p. 5).

That said, we have witnessed different centres of social values being construed in Chinese and Australian hard news reporting on risk events. In the Australian context, the centre of social values holding the nation together is construed through ordinary citizens, whereas in the Chinese context the centre is construed through power elites. The rituals of emotionality have been mobilized in service of distinctive purposes. In the Australian context, and perhaps more broadly in Anglo-American societies, we have witnessed the rise of 'therapeutic culture' (Pantti, 2010, p. 168), in which 'individual emotions and experience have acquired an unprecedented significance' (Furedi, 2004, p. 44). The concept of therapeutic culture stems from psychotherapy analysis in Western societies but it is translated to culture studies to signify means of imposing a new conformity through manipulating people's emotions. Social orders are intimately connected with private inner emotional orders of individuals. In such therapy news reports as those examined in the present article, the public display of emotions is not as much considered a threat to political or social stability as it was. Privileging the voices of victims provides counsel and comfort to victims and the bereaved families. However, in the Chinese context journalists still subscribe to the Elite culture (官本位) in which the behaviour of power elites constitutes the centre of social order. On this view, Chinese journalists are cautious about attending to the voices of the powerless (e.g. citizens and individual risk makers).

Taken together, the corpus findings suggest that the presentation and representation of emotions in news discourse functions to 'bind the nation and nurture a collective climate of rational opinion formation' (Hendy, 2013, p. 38). This corroborates interview findings with journalism practitioners by Pantti (2010, p. 179),

> Emotion did not present a challenge to the rationales of factuality and objectivity. On the one hand, presenting and interpreting 'relevant' individual and collective emotions were seen as a part of journalism's aim to reveal reality, as 'fact', without which the whole truth is not told; on the other hand, the main objective of emotional storytelling was to enhance the political and social knowledge of audience, to facilitate the understanding of news.

6.6 Summary

To conclude, the analysis of strategic rituals of emotionality in Australian and Chinese print media hard news reporting on risk events has indicated that emotions are vital means of journalistic stance taking and also central to bond journalistic pursuit of objectivity with the formation of social togetherness. The corpus findings have pointed to the distinction in the ways Australian and Chinese journalists construct different centres of social values in the face of risk events through mediating emotions of news actors with different social standings. However, this chapter did not examine how emotions and social orders are mapped onto lexico-grammatical patterns (but see Huan, 2015 for attempts in this regard), and that is a topic worth further exploration.

References

Abu-Lughod, L., & Lutz, C. A. (1990). Introduction: Emotion, discourse, and the politics of everyday life. In C. A. Lutz & L. Abu-Lughod (Eds.), *Language and the politics of emotion* (pp. 1–23). Cambridge: Cambridge University Press.

Bednarek, M. (2006). *Evaluation in media discourse: Analysis of a newspaper corpus*. London/New York: Continuum.

Bednarek, M. (2008). *Emotion talk across corpora*. Basingstoke/New York: Palgrave Macmillan.

Bednarek, M., & Caple, H. (2014). Why do news values matter? Towards a new methodological framework for analysing news discourse in Critical Discourse Analysis and beyond. *Discourse & Society, 25*(2), 135–158. https://doi.org/10.1177/0957926513516041.

Bell, A. (1991). *The language of news media*. Oxford/Cambridge MA: Blackwell.

Berezin, M. (2001). Emotions and political identity: Mobilizing affection for the polity. In J. Goodwin, J. Jasper, & F. Polletta (Eds.), *Passionate politics: Emotions and social movements* (pp. 83–98). Chicago: University of Chicago Press.

Berezin, M. (2002). Secure states: Towards a political sociology of emotion. In J. Barbalet (Ed.), *Emotions and Sociology* (pp. 33–52). Oxford: Blackwell.
Blommaert, J. (2005). *Discourse: A critical introduction*. Cambridge: Cambridge University Press.
Chalaby, J. K. (1998). *The invention of journalism*. Houndmills: Macmillan Press.
Clark, C. (1997). *Misery and company: Sympathy in everyday life*. Chicago: The University of Chicago Press.
Fairclough, N. (2010). *Critical discourse analysis: The critical study of language*. Harlow: Pearson Education Limited.
Franklin, B. (1997). *Newszak and news media*. London: Arnold.
Franklin, B. (2005). Broadloid. In B. Franklin, M. Hamer, & M. Hanna (Eds.), *Key concepts in journalism studies* (pp. 28–29). Thousand Oaks, CA: Sage.
Furedi, F. (2004). *Therapy culture: Cultivating vulnerability in an uncertain age*. London: Routledge.
Gee, J. P. (2014). *An introduction to discourse analysis: Theory and method* (4th ed.). New York: Routledge.
Harrington, S. (2008). Popular news in the 21st century Time for a new critical approach? *Journalism, 9*(3), 266–284.
Hartley, J. (1996). *Popular reality: Journalism, modernity, popular culture*. Arnold.
Hendy, C. (2013). *Public service broadcasting*. Basingstoke: Palgrave Macmillan.
Huan, C. (2015). *Journalistic stance in Chinese and Australian hard news* (Doctoral thesis). Macquarie University, Sydney.
Huang, C. (2016). Towards a broadloid press approach: The transformation of China's newspaper industry since the 2000s. *Journalism, 17*(5), 652–667.
Hunston, S. (2011). *Corpus approaches to evaluation: Phraseology and evaluative language*. New York: Routledge.
Kitch, C. (2000). A news of feeling as well as fact: Mourning and memorial in American newsmagazines. *Journalism, 1*(2), 171–195.
Kitch, C. (2003). Mourning in America: Ritual, redemption, and recovery in news narrative after September 11. *Journalism Studies, 4*(2), 213–224.
Martin, J. R. (2004). Mourning: How we get aligned. *Discourse & Society, 15*(2), 321–344.
McNair, B. (1999). *Journalism and democracy*. London: Routledge.
McNair, B. (2011). *An introduction to political communication*. New York: Routledge.
Mindich, D. (1998). *Just the facts: How objectivity came to define American journalism*. New York: New York University Press.
Molek-Kozakowska, K. (2013). Towards a pragma-linguistic framework for the study of sensationalism in news headlines. *Discourse & Communication, 7*(2), 173–197.
Pantti, M. (2010). The value of emotion: An examination of television journalists' notions on emotionality. *European Journal of Communication, 25*(2), 168–181.
Pantti, M., & Husslage, K. (2009). Ordinary people and emotional expression in Dutch public service news. *Javnost-The Public, 16*(2), 77–94.
Pantti, M., & Sumiala, J. (2009). Till death do us join: Media, mourning rituals and the sacred centre of the society. *Media, Culture and Society, 31*(1), 119–135.
Pantti, M., & Van Zoonen, L. (2006). Do crying citizens make good citizens? *Social Semiotics, 16* (2), 205–224.
Pantti, M., & Wieten, J. (2005). Mourning becomes the nation: Television coverage of the murder of Pim Fortuyn. *Journalism Studies, 6*(3), 301–313.
Peters, C. (2011). Emotion aside or emotional side? Crafting an 'Experience of Involvement' in the News. *Journalism, 12*(3), 297–316.
Schudson, M. (1978). *Discovering the news: A social history of American newspapers*. New York: Basic Books.
Schudson, M. (2001). The objectivity norm in American journalism. *Journalism, 2*(2), 149–170.
Schudson, M., & Anderson, C. (2009). Objectivity, professionalism, and truth seeking in journalism. In K. Wahl-Jorgensen & T. Hanitzsch (Eds.), *The handbook of journalism studies* (pp. 88–101). New York & London: Routledge.

Scollon, R. (1998). *Mediated discourse as social interaction: A study of news discourse*. New York: Routledge.

Sparks, C. (1998). Tabloidisation and the media. *Javnost-The Public, 2*(2), 5–10.

Stenglin, M. K. (2004). *Packaging curiosities: Towards a grammar of three-dimensional space* (Doctoral thesis). University of Sydney, Sydney.

Stenvall, M. (2008). On emotions and the journalistic ideals of factuality and objectivity: Tools for analysis. *Journal of Pragmatics, 40,* 1569–1586.

Stenvall, M. (2014). Presenting and representing emotions in news agency reports. *Critical Discourse Studies, 11*(4), 461–481. https://doi.org/10.1080/17405904.2013.866588.

Stets, J. E., & Turner, J. (2006). *Handbook of sociology of emotions*. New York: Springer.

Telle, N.-T., & Pfister, H.-R. (2016). Positive empathy and prosocial behavior: A neglected link. *Emotion Review, 8*(2), 154–163.

Thomson, E., White, P. R. R., & Kitley, P. (2008). "Objectivity" and "hard news" reporting across cultures: Comparing the news report in English, French, Japanese and Indonesian journalism. *Journalism Studies, 9*(2), 212–228.

Tiffen, R. (2006a). Political economy and news. In S. Cunningham & G. Turner (Eds.), *The media and communications in Australia* (2nd ed., pp. 28–42).

Tiffen, R. (2006b). The press. In S. Cunningham & G. Turner (Eds.), *The media and communications in Australia* (2nd ed., pp. 97–112). Sydney: Allen & Unwin.

Tuchman, G. (1972). Objectivity as strategic ritual: An examination of newsmen's notions of objectivity. *American Journal of Sociology, 77,* 660–679.

Tudor, A. (2003). A (macro) sociology of fear? *The Sociological Review, 51*(2), 238–256.

Turner, J. H., & Stets, J. E. (2006). Introduction. In J. E. Stets & J. H. Turner (Eds.), *Handbook of the sociology of emotions* (pp. 1–10). New York: Springer.

Van Dijk, T. A. (1988). *News as discourse*. Hillsdale, NJ: L. Erlbaum Associates.

Wahl-Jorgensen, K. (2013a). The strategic ritual of emotionality: A case study of Pulitzer prize-winning articles. *Journalism, 14*(1), 129–145.

Wahl-Jorgensen, K. (2013b). Subjectivity and story-telling in journalism: Examining expressions of affect, judgement and appreciation in Pulitzer prize-winning stories. *Journalism Studies, 14* (3), 305–320.

White, P. R. R. (1998). *Telling media tales: The news story as rhetoric* (Unpublished Ph.D. thesis). University of Sydney, Sydney.

Wodak, R., & Meyer, M. (2009). Critical discourse analysis: History, agenda, theory and methodology. In R. Wodak & M. Meyer (Eds.), *Methods for critical discourse analysis* (2nd ed., pp. 1–33). London: Sage.

Yell, S. (2012). Natural disaster news and communities of feeling: The affective interpellation of local and global publics. *Social Semiotics, 22*(4), 409–428.

Zhao, Y. (2008). *Communication in China: Political economy, power, and conflict*. Lanham, MD: Rowman & Littlefield Publishers.

Chapter 7
Judgement Patterns

7.1 Introduction

This chapter intends to interrogate the ways behaviours of news actors (i.e. individuals or institutions written about in a news report) are judged in relation to social values in Chinese and Australian hard news reporting on risk events. Features of judgement are significant semantic sources for journalists to undertake divergent stances in (re)constructing social values in the face of risk events. A number of recent important studies have shifted our understanding of JUDGEMENT from a traditional view that considers JUDGEMENT as linguistic markers in texts to a practice-focused view that studies JUDGEMENT as discursive acts of stance taking by writers/speakers vis-à-vis people, objects or propositions concerned (e.g. Du Bois, 2007; Jaffe, 2009; Martin & White, 2005; Perrin, 2012; Vertommen et al., 2012; Wahl-Jorgensen, 2013b).

This chapter builds on this view by considering expression of JUDGEMENT (a subsystem of ATTITUDE) in news discourse as journalists' discursive practices in enacting and concealing certain social and professional values. An important means of practising journalism is realized by lexico-grammatical resources. Hence, this chapter takes language resources of JUDGEMENT as the analytical point of entry to understand how language patterns of JUDGEMENT (re)produce social values and how social values regulate the actual expression of JUDGEMENT in a specific discourse context, namely Chinese newspaper reports on risk events.

7.2 A Brief Review of JUDGEMENT Studies

As indicated in Chap. 6, in the field of journalism practices, journalistic ATTITUDE, (including journalists' expression of emotions and judgement of people's behaviours), is often dismissed as a marker of unprincipled and flawed journalism

C. Huan, *Journalistic Stance in Chinese and Australian Hard News*,
https://doi.org/10.1007/978-981-13-0791-1_7

(Chalaby, 1998; Mindich, 1998; Peters, 2011; Schudson & Anderson, 2009). Journalistic ATTITUDE—authorial (i.e. journalists' own attitude) or observed (i.e. reporting third parties' attitudinal responses) (Stenvall, 2014; Thomson, White, & Kitley, 2008, p. 225)—has largely been discussed in relation to journalists' professional norms of objectivity or neutrality. Research has demonstrated that journalistic authorial ATTITUDE, especially authorial judgement, is hardly present in quality journalism in the Anglo-American tradition of news reporting, but that the reporting of observed ATTITUDE has become increasingly explicit (e.g. Bednarek, 2006, 2008; Martin & White, 2005; Peters, 2011; Pounds, 2010; Stenvall, 2008, 2014; Wahl-Jorgensen, 2013a; White, 1997). A growing number of studies have argued that the inclusion of observed ATTITUDE in news discourse is considered as a strategic ritual of objectivity in journalism practices (e.g. Tuchman, 1972; Wahl-Jorgensen, 2013a, 2013b; White, 1998). However, as Peters (2011, p. 298) observes, "in recent years the dominance of objectivity as a fundamental paradigm in Anglo-American journalism has increasingly been called into question, not only by academics but within the industry itself (Frank, 2003; Rosen, 1999)".

Additionally, research into ATTITUDE in news discourse in line with the APPRAISAL framework has tended to focus on the analysis of 'affect' or emotions (e.g. emotional responses) (see Chap. 6). The ways news actors are judged in news (e.g. how behaviours or characters of news actors are ethically evaluated in accord with social norms) have as yet tended to be neglected (see Feez, Iedema, & White, 2008 for an exception). This is particularly the case in Chinese news discourse, although studies of APPRAISAL have sparked increasing scholarly interest in China since 2001 (Wang, 2001).

Research interest in attitudinal language among Chinese linguists is of recent origin (Iwasaki & Yap, 2015, p. 2). Most studies on attitude in general (not following the APPRAISAL framework) in Chinese have largely laid emphasis on the exposition of syntactic and semantic idiosyncrasies or taken a grammaticalisation perspective (e.g. Endo, 2013; Lim, 2011; Su, 2004; Tao, 2003, 2007; F. Wu, 2011; H. Wu, 2015; R.-J. R. Wu, 2004; Yang & Yap, 2015; but see Liu & Stevenson, 2013 for a small-scaled constractive analysis of appraisal in Chinese and Australian disaster news). The study of Liu and Stevenson (2013) is one of few studies available in the literature examining JUDGEMENT features in the context of Chinese news reporting. They examined JUDGEMENT features in fifteen news stories concerning the 2008 Sichuan Earthquake in China (five from *People's Daily*, five from *Australian Chinese Daily*, and five from *Sydney Morning Herald*). They found that the prominent JUDGEMENT features in *Peoples' Daily* and *Australian Chinese Daily* were related to the 'tenacity' of rescue workers and that of the Chinese leadership, followed by evaluation of their 'capacity' and 'propriety'. However, in *Sydney Morning Herald* the primary JUDGEMENT feature related to participants' 'capacity' to carry out rescue work. However, they did not study valences of JUDGEMENT features or the lexico-grammatical patterns of JUDGEMENT.

Hence, we have so far obtained insufficient understanding of how journalistic voices (e.g. reporter voice) are more or less compatible with journalists' expression of JUDGEMENT. The social factors that give rise to the realization of JUDGEMENT in Chinese news discourse are underexplored as well. On this view, this chapter focuses on patterns of JUDGEMENT in Chinese and Australian hard news. Patterns of JUDGEMENT are defined as phraseological patterns in which judgement markers are embedded, patterned distribution of semantic features of judgement, and patterned relations between semantic features of judgement, their valences, and social statuses of news actors. This chapter focuses on the link between specific lexico-grammatical expressions of JUDGEMENT, semantic features of JUDGEMENT, and the underpinning social values in Chinese and Australian hard news reporting.

7.3 Overview of Corpus Analytic Findings

This section outlines corpus analytic findings in relation to semantic features of JUDGEMENT, their valences, and social statuses of news actors. Table 7.1 shows the normalized percentage of the distribution of JUDGEMENT features in the corpus.

We can observe from Table 7.1 that overall the number of positive 'social esteem' (comprising 'normality', 'capacity' and 'tenacity') markers (46%) overtakes that of negative markers (10%) but the reverse is true in the realization of 'social sanction'. Neutral JUDGEMENT markers are minimally relevant in the realization of JUDGEMENT. If we continue examining the valences of 'social esteem' and 'social sanction', we will find that all 'social esteem' features (i.e. 'normality', 'capacity' and 'tenacity') prefer positivity over negativity. This is also the case in realizing 'veracity', a feature of 'social sanction'. However, in realizing 'propriety', negative markers (34%) by far outnumber positive ones (4%).

This finding largely corroborates that presented in the study of Liu and Stevenson (2013). They have found that Chinese news coverage of risk events (i.e. the 2008 Sichuan Earthquake) tended to foreground 'tenacity', 'capacity' and 'propriety' of Chinese power elites, and also presented cross-cultural differences in the distribution of JUDGEMENT features. These findings point to the cultural

Table 7.1 Distribution of JUDGEMENT in relation to polarity in the Chinese corpus

		Positive		Negative		Neutral		Total	
		No.	%	No.	%	No.	%	No.	%
Social esteem	Normality	12	**1**	5	**1**	3	**0**	20	**2**
	Capacity	137	**17**	47	**6**	0	**0**	184	**22**
	Tenacity	232	**28**	24	**3**	18	**2**	274	**33**
Social sanction	Veracity	19	**2**	8	**1**	1	**0**	28	**3**
	Propriety	36	**4**	283	**34**	0	**0**	319	**39**
	Total	436	**53**	367	**44**	22	**3**	825	**100**

The percentage was calculated by dividing the number of the occurrence of each JUDGEMENT feature by the total occurrence (i.e. 825). This rule also applies to the following tables and figures in this chapter

Table 7.2 Distribution of JUDGEMENT in relation to polarity in the Australian corpus

		Positive		Negative		Neutral		Total	
		No.	%	No.	%	No.	%	No.	%
Social esteem	Normality	5	**7**	8	**11**	0	**0**	13	**18**
	Capacity	11	**15**	15	**21**	11	**15**	37	**52**
	Tenacity	7	**10**	0	**0**	0	**0**	7	**10**
Social sanction	Veracity	2	**3**	1	**1**	0	**0**	3	**4**
	Propriety	3	**4**	8	**11**	0	**0**	11	**15**
	Total	28	**39**	31	**44**	11	**15**	71	**100**

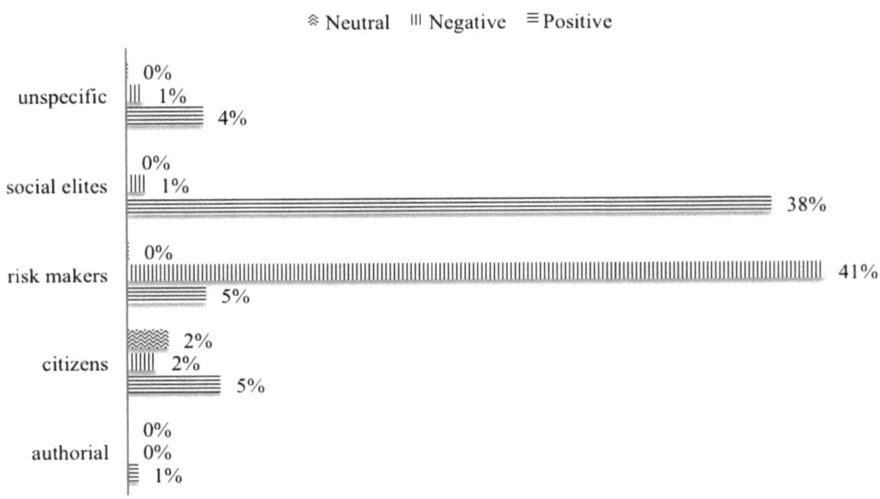

Fig. 7.1 Distribution of JUDGEMENT valences in relation to news actors in the Chinese corpus

distinction of JUDGEMENT in news discourse, suggesting that it is necessary to probe more fully into the underpinning socio-cultural values to understand the expression of JUDGEMENT in news discourse (see Sect. 7.6).

Table 7.2 shows that overall negative JUDGEMENT markers (44%) slightly outnumber positive ones (39%) in the Australian corpus. This is also the case in the realization of 'social sanction'. The number of positive markers of 'social esteem' resembles that of negative ones. Due to the limited number of JUDGEMENT markers in the Australian corpus, their distributions across corpora are not directly comparable. Despite that, we can find that the Australian corpus tends to foreground 'capacity', 'normality' and 'propriety', whereas the occurrences of 'tenacity' and 'veracity' are less frequent.

Figure 7.1 displays corpus distribution of news actors in relation to the valences of JUDGEMENT features in the Chinese corpus.

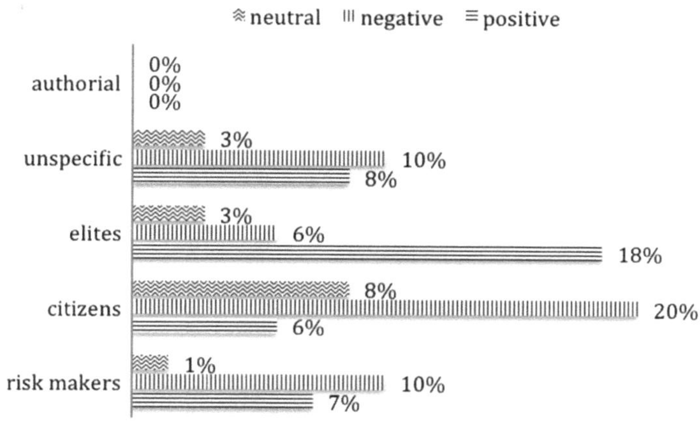

Fig. 7.2 Distribution of JUDGEMENT valences in relation to news actors in the Australian corpus

The most obvious difference lies in the fact that risk makers are predominantly judged negatively, but social elites are overwhelmingly judged in a positive manner. Such a contrast may not be particularly striking, but the details are of interest (see Sect. 7.4 below). Neutral JUDGEMENT makers chiefly relate to JUDGEMENT of citizens and they are hardly enacted in judging other news actors. Hence, my discussion on JUDGEMENT markers will focus on positive and negative markers. Additionally, the analysis will foreground three groups of news actors, namely risk makers, social elites and citizens, in that JUDGEMENT of other news actors is minimally relevant in the corpus. More specifically, the number of authorial JUDGEMENT is negligible with five occurrences, and four of them are realized by the marker 仔细 (*careful*) to show journalists' careful reading of the information of a risky product (e.g. food with potential health risk). Unspecific news actors will be ignored because we are unable to know who are judged in news reporting.

Figure 7.2 exhibits corpus distribution of JUDGEMENT valences in relation to news actors in the Australian context. Authorial markers of JUDGEMENT are absent in the Australian corpus. In comparison with findings presented in Fig. 7.1, the Australian corpus also records more positive JUDGEMENT upon elites, yet negative markers are noticeable as well. The Australian corpus documents more negative markers of JUDGEMENT upon risk makers, but positive markers are noticeable. In regard to citizens, Australian corpus shows a preference towards negativity, which is in sharp contract with that in the Chinese corpus.

Let us now turn to examine the relationship between JUDGEMENT features and news actors. Table 7.3 shows the distribution of JUDGEMENT features vis-à-vis their polarity orientations and the social statuses of selected news actors.

Table 7.3 shows that negative 'propriety' markers are predominantly adopted to judge risk makers (279 occ.) rather than to judge social elites (1 occ.) or citizens (0 occ.). Positive markers of 'capacity' and 'tenacity' are mainly deployed to judge social elites. The predominant negative markers in relation to JUDGEMENT of social

Table 7.3 Distribution of JUDGEMENT features in relation to news actors and valences in the Chinese corpus

	Risk makers				Social elites				Citizens			
	Positive		Negative		Positive		Negative		Positive		Negative	
	No.	%	No.	%	No.	%	No.	%	No.	%	No.	%
Normality	1	**0**	2	**0**	5	**1**	0	**0**	6	**1**	3	**0**
Capacity	6	**1**	25	**3**	117	**14**	8	**1**	4	**0**	9	**1**
Tenacity	23	**3**	22	**3**	163	**20**	0	**0**	28	**3**	2	**0**
Veracity	6	**1**	8	**1**	8	**1**	0	**0**	2	**0**	0	**0**
Propriety	2	**0**	279	**34**	18	**2**	1	**0**	5	**1**	0	**0**

Table 7.4 Distribution of JUDGEMENT features in relation to news actors and valences in the Australian corpus

	Risk makers				Social elites				Citizens			
	Positive		Negative		Positive		Negative		Positive		Negative	
	No.	%	No.	%	No.	%	No.	%	No.	%	No.	%
Normality	0	**0**	1	**1**	3	**4**	1	**1**	1	**1**	5	**7**
Capacity	1	**1**	4	**6**	5	**7**	2	**3**	3	**4**	9	**13**
Tenacity	1	**1**	0	**0**	4	**6**	0	**0**	0	**0**	0	**0**
Veracity	0	**0**	0	**0**	1	**1**	1	**1**	0	**0**	0	**0**
Propriety	2	**3**	3	**4**	0	**0**	0	**0**	0	**0**	0	**0**

elites relate to their negative 'capacity' (8 occ.). Citizens are hardly judged negatively by reference to 'social sanction' (i.e. 'veracity' and 'propriety'). Positive JUDGEMENT of citizens mostly relates to their 'tenacity', whereas negative JUDGEMENT mostly has to do with their 'capacity'.

As Table 7.4 shows, risk makers are mainly judged in relation to their negative 'capacity' and 'propriety', whereas social elites are chiefly judged in relation to their positive 'capacity' and 'tenacity'. By contrast, citizens are predominantly judged in relation to their negative 'normality' and 'capacity', but not in relation to 'social sanction'. This table also indicates that we can hardly conduct local grammatical analysis of JUDGEMENT patterns in relation to news actors. This is mainly because overall JUDGEMENT markers are rather infrequent in the Australian corpus (71 occ. in total). As such, most JUDGEMENT features are realized by less than five markers in the corpus, failing to meet our threshold for pattern analysis. In recognition of this, we have decided to foreground local patterns of JUDGEMENT in the Australian corpus in relation to their part-of-speech instead of semantic features. Co-selection of JUDGEMENT features and news actors will also be discussed.

Bringing together the corpus analytic findings in this section, it appears that 'social esteem' is oriented towards positivity whilst 'social sanction' is oriented towards negativity in the Chinese corpus. In comparison, 'social esteem' in the Australian corpus does not display polarity preferences, but 'social sanction' is oriented towards negativity. Among all news actors concerned in the Chinese corpus, risk makers are predominantly judged negatively, but social elites are overwhelmingly judged positively. This is also the case in the Australian corpus, but positive judgement upon risk makers and negative judgement upon social elites are more noticeable in the Australian corpus. In both corpora, negative JUDGEMENT of risk makers primarily relates to 'propriety', and positive JUDGEMENT of social elites chiefly concerns their 'capacity' and 'tenacity'. In the next section I examine the local patterns of JUDGEMENT markers in each corpus.

7.4 Patterns of JUDGEMENT in Chinese Corpus

This section presents patterns of JUDGEMENT in the Chinese corpus. For reasons of scope and due to their infrequent occurrences (see Sect. 7.3 above), markers of 'normality' and 'veracity' will be excluded from pattern analysis. In other words, I will focus on the local patterns of 'capacity', 'tenacity' and 'veracity' in relation to risk makers, citizens and social elites (see Table 7.5). Those markers with less than five occurrences will be excluded from analysis in that they are infrequent to establish a solid ground for pattern analysis.

In order to avoid generating a pattern analysis that is too dense to be comprehensible, I decided to further confine pattern analysis to verbal and adjectival patterns of 'capacity', 'tenacity' and 'propriety' in relation to citizens, risk makers and social elites. Nominal and adverbial patterns will be briefly discussed here due to their infrequent occurrences. Specifically, Table 7.5 shows that nouns mainly realize positive 'capacity' and positive 'propriety', and that adverbs chiefly realize positive 'capacity' and negative 'propriety'.

All the six nominal markers of 'capacity' serve to positively judge social elites (困难–5 occ.; 艰难险阻–1 occ.; both meaning difficulties) in the pattern of *Shubin* (see example (26)).

(1) 救援车队正在**克服各种困难**加快速度赶到灾区。(Shubin)
The rescue traffic is **overcoming various difficulties** to arrive at the disastrous areas faster.

Table 7.5 Distribution of 'capacity', 'tenacity' and 'propriety', and their valences across POS

	Capacity				Tenacity				Propriety			
	Positive		Negative		Positive		Negative		Positive		Negative	
	No.	%	No.	%	No.	%	No.	%	No.	%	No.	%
Noun	6	**1**	0	**0**	1	**0**	0	**0**	6	**1**	3	**0**
Adverb	11	**1**	0	**0**	3	**0**	1	**0**	0	**0**	58	**7**
Verb	23	**3**	6	**1**	6	**1**	4	**0**	6	**1**	9	**1**
Adjective	87	**11**	36	**4**	204	**25**	19	**2**	10	**1**	210	**25**

The stance noun itself (困难, *difficulty*) bears a negative meaning. However, when it is adopted in the pattern of *Shubin* and especially when collocating with the verb *overcome* (克服), it enacts positive evaluation of the 'capacity' of the rescue team.

Likewise, all nominal markers of 'propriety' (i.e. 爱心—*love*, 6 occ.) construe positive judgement of social elites. The APPRAISAL item 爱心 (love) often collocates with the verb 献 (donate) in the pattern of *Shubin* (see example (27) below). The beneficiaries are typically earthquake victims or those persons influenced by the disaster. As such, news actors (social elites in this case) who perform the donating actions are positively judged.

(2) 中央和国家机关各部门各单位干部职工踊跃捐款,向灾区人民献上一片**爱心**。(Shubin)

Staffs from all sectors of the CPC and national bureaus donate money enthusiastically to show their **love** to those in the disaster areas.

In addition to the *Shubin* pattern, the corpus has documented the pattern of *Dingzhong* (attributive + head noun) (see example (28) below), in which the head explicates the persons under evaluation while the attributive assigns a positive JUDGEMENT value.

(3) X已接收社会各界及**爱心**人士捐赠款2.4171亿多元。(Dingzhong)

X has received the donation of 241.71 million CNY from **caring** people from all walks of life and those.

Bringing together nominal patterns of positive 'capacity' and positive 'propriety', it was found that they both prefer the pattern *Shubin*, and that they both serve to positively judge social elites.

As to adverbial markers, although no single adverbial marker of positive 'capacity' occurs more than five times in the corpus to be eligible for pattern analysis, it is interesting to notice that all adverbial markers of positive 'capacity' occur in the same pattern (i.e. *Zhuangzhong*) to positively judge social elites (see example (29)).

(4) 胡锦涛总书记,温家宝总理…要求**千方百计**救援受灾群众。(Zhuangzhong)

General Secretary Hu Jintao, and Premier Wen Jiabao requested (government officials) to **spare no efforts to** rescue those people in the disaster areas.

In like manner, the primary pattern of adverbial markers in realizing negative 'propriety' is also that of Zhuangzhong (see example (30)). However, all these markers serve to negatively judge risk makers, who illegally produce risky food.

(5) 经查,犯罪嫌疑人高某、宋某某等…**非法**牟取暴利。(Zhuangzhong)

The investigation shows that the criminals Gao and Song **illegally** obtained profits.

Collating adverbial patterns of positive 'capacity' and negative 'propriety' in the corpus, it was found that they both favoured the pattern *Zhuangzhong*. However, the target of JUDGEMENT in adverbial patterns of positive 'capacity' was social elites, whereas the target in adverbial patterns of 'propriety' was risk makers.

7.4.1 Patterns of 'Capacity'

Table 7.6 shows that verbal markers of 'capacity' mainly serve to negatively judge risk makers (6 occ.) but to positively judge social elites (22 occ.). This is also the case for adjectival markers of 'capacity'.

As to verbal markers, both negative 'capacity' of risk makers (see example (32)) and positive 'capacity' of social elites (see example (31)) tend to occur in the pattern *Zhuwei*.

(6) 习近平...详细了解工程建设情况 (Zhuwei)
Xi Jinping...**discerned** in detail the construction situation.

(7) 王老板称，他非常了解一些地下加工厂制作猪红的制作过程。(Zhuwei)
Mr. Wang said, he **was quite familiar with** the processes of lards production in illegal workshops.

It is worth noting that the same JUDGEMENT item in the same pattern may realize rather different valences of JUDGEMENT. For instance, the JUDGEMENT marker *discern* (了解 in the examples (31) and (32)) is employed to inscribe positive JUDGEMENT when news actors under evaluation are the powerful voice. By contrast, when news actors under evaluation are powerless, it realizes negative JUDGEMENT. The finding thus points to an important fact that valences of JUDGEMENT are closely linked to social status of news actors under evaluation.

Adjectival markers of 'capacity' of risk makers, citizens and social elites all primarily take the pattern Zhuangzhong (adverbial+head verb), in which the adjectives modify a verbal group (see example (33)). In this pattern nominal group, preceding adjectival markers realize the target of JUDGEMENT, and the verbal group explicates their behaviours.

(8) 几名妇女麻利地将它们捡到塑料袋里。(Zhuangzhong)
Several women **swiftly** picked them up and throw to the plastic bags.

Despite the similarity, local adjectival patterns in realizing 'capacity' of risk makers, citizens and social elites also exhibit disparity. For instance, another salient adjectival patterns in realizing 'capacity' of risk makers is that of Zhongbu (head + complement), with the head realized by a verbal group (example (34)).

(9) 厂家称是商家储存不当 (Zhongbu)
The factory said this was because dealers **improperly** store (the goods).

Table 7.6 Distribution of 'capacity' of selected news actors across POS and valences

	Risk makers				Social elites				Citizens			
	Positive		Negative		Positive		Negative		Positive		Negative	
	No.	%	No.	%	No.	%	No.	%	No.	%	No.	%
Verb	0	**0**	6	**1**	22	**3**	0	**0**	0	**0**	0	**0**
Adjective	6	**1**	19	**2**	77	**9**	8	**1**	4	**0**	9	**1**

By contrast, other prominent adjectival patterns in realizing ‘capacity’ of social elites are Dingzhong (attributive + head) and Zhuwei (subject + predicate). In the former pattern, social elites (political figures in most cases) are grammatically realized as the head and are directly modified by the evaluative adjectives (e.g. ***高效、务实的***党委、政府—***Efficient and pragmatic*** *Party Committee and government.*). In the latter pattern, adjectival markers of ‘capacity’ function as the predicate of the clause (e.g. 他认为中国政府很了不起。 *He thinks the Chinese government is* ***doing a good job***.).

Due to the infrequent occurrences, it is difficult to observe the preferred local adjectival patterns in realizing ‘capacity’ of citizens other than Zhuangzhong. However, bringing together the pattern differences in realizing ‘capacity’ of risk makers, citizens and social elites, we find that the pattern Zhongbu (head + complement) (see example (35)) appears to be associated with a negative value of JUDGEMENT of ‘capacity’ of risk makers.

(10) 元宵有霉变的味道可能是消费者储存不当造成。(Zhongbu)
The mouldy smell of lantern festival dumplings may be caused by consumers **improperly** storing (them).

In addition, the pattern Zhongbu is hardly adopted to evaluate ‘capacity’ of social elites. This finding suggests that social statuses of news actors may select certain local patterns and largely determine valences of JUDGEMENT.

7.4.2 Patterns of ‘Tenacity’

Table 7.7 shows that the ‘tenacity’ of risk makers, social elites and citizens is primarily realized in adjectival forms and that verbal markers of ‘tenacity’ of these three news actors only sporadically occur. Thus, this section will focus on adjectival markers of ‘tenacity’.

Adjectival markers of both positive and negative JUDGEMENT of ‘tenacity’ of risk makers are primarily embedded in the pattern Zhuangzhong (adverbial + head verb), in which the JUDGEMENT adjectives serve to modify the following verb. It counters our expectation to find more adjectival markers of positive ‘tenacity’ than those negative ones in relation to risk makers. However, a close examination of the targets of JUDGEMENT reveals that positive ‘tenacity’ of risk makers relates to institutions (e.g. large food factories) (see example (36)), whereas negative

Table 7.7 Distribution of ‘tenacity’ of selected news actors across POS and valences

	Risk makers				Social elites				Citizens			
	Positive		Negative		Positive		Negative		Positive		Negative	
	No.	%	No.	%	No.	%	No.	%	No.	%	No.	%
Verb	0	**0**	3	**0**	4	**0**	0	**0**	2	**0**	1	**0**
Adjective	23	**3**	18	**2**	156	**19**	0	**0**	25	**3**	1	**0**

'tenacity' relates to individual food producers (see example (37)). In the event of food safety, institutions are represented as news actors who actively seek cooperation with government in dealing with the risk or in initiating food recall. By contrast, individuals are represented as those who recklessly place or produce food.

(11) 北京X食品有限公司负责市场的廖姓工作人员表示,将**积极**配合政府有关部门解决此事。(Zhuangzhong)
Mr. Liao, a staff responsible for marketing in the Beijing X Food Corporation, said that (they) will **actively** collaborate with relevant government departments to solve the issue.

(12) 食监人员到生产现场调查看到…部分食品盛器**随意**放在地上 (Zhuangzhong)
Officials of Food and Medicine Administration saw on the production site that some food was **recklessly** placed on ground.
All adjectival markers of 'tenacity' in relation to social elites are positive in terms of valence. The primary local pattern is that of Zhuangzhong as well (see example (38)), expressing JUDGEMENT of political figures' resolute, careful and serious dealing with risk situations. In addition, the pattern Dingzhong (attributive + head) is noticeable (see example (39)). This pattern often positively judges the resolute leadership of the central government. The adjectival marker (i.e. attributive) directly modifies and thus evaluates political figures and Chinese government (i.e. head).

(13) 习近平来…**认真**查看工程规划展板。(Zhuangzhong)
Xi Jinping…**earnestly** watched the reconstruction plan.

(14) 有党中央、国务院的**坚强领导**…我们一定能打赢抗震救灾这场硬仗。(Dingzhong)
With the **resolute leadership** of the Central Party Committee and State Council, we will eventually win the battle against earthquake after-effects.
Adjectival markers of 'tenacity' in relation to citizens are typically collocated to their left with a modal verb, expressing obligation (see example (40)) primarily in the pattern Zhuangzhong.

(15) 工商部门提醒,市民在购买乳饮料时要**仔细**查看产品包装上的标签标识是否齐全。(Zhuangzhong)
The Administration for Industry and Commerce reminds that citizens should **carefully** check product labels before purchasing any dairy drink.
In short, positive JUDGEMENT of 'tenacity' upon citizens is often associated with kind reminder offered by elites.

Table 7.8 Distribution of 'propriety' of selected news actors across POS and valences

	Risk makers				Social elites				Citizens			
	Positive		Negative		Positive		Negative		Positive		Negative	
	No.	%	No.	%	No.	%	No.	%	No.	%	No.	%
Verb	1	**0**	9	**1**	5	**1**	0	**0**	0	**0**	0	**0**
Adjective	1	**0**	209	**25**	7	**1**	1	**0**	2	**0**	0	**0**

7.4.3 Patterns of 'Propriety'

Table 7.8 shows that both verbal and adjectival markers mainly realize negative JUDGEMENT of risk makers and positive JUDGEMENT of social elites, and that adjectival markers far outnumber verbal ones.

Verbal markers of positive 'propriety' in relation to social elites mainly express their adherence to the common interest of the mass in the event of earthquake, but no single marker occurs frequent enough to be eligible for pattern analysis. Hence, I turn to examine verbal markers of negative 'propriety' in relation to risk makers, as in example (41).

(16) 还有些经营者**伪造**食品生产日期。(Zhuwei)
Some dealers **fake** the production date of food.
Negative 'propriety' mainly concern the process of faking food (假冒, 伪造). The verbal markers are mainly realized in the pattern of Zhuwei as above where the first nominal group refers to individuals or institutions under evaluation.
As to adjectival markers of 'propriety', markers of positive 'propriety' are primarily adopted to evaluate social elites in the local pattern of *Zhuangzhong* (adverbial + head verb). These markers mainly refer to how selfless social elites are in donating money to those persons influenced by the disaster at issue. The only negative JUDGEMENT of 'propriety' of social elites refers to an anonymous disgraced government official as in the local phrase of ***腐败***官员 (a *corrupted* official). I will not present those patterns here due to their infrequent occurrence (less than five occurrences). Instead I now turn to adjectival markers of negative 'propriety' in relation to JUDGEMENT of risk makers.
While positive JUDGEMENT of 'propriety' of social elites favours the pattern *Zhuangzhong*, negative JUDGEMENT of 'propriety' of risk makers prefers the pattern *Dingzhong*. In the former pattern, the JUDGEMENT item is adopted to evaluate the action conducted by social elites, whilst in the latter pattern the JUDGEMENT item directly judges the character of risk makers against morality and law-abidingness (e.g. ***黑心***商户—***black-hearted*** *businessmen*; ***地下***窝点—***illegal*** *food workshop*).
There are also cases where markers that are usually adopted to evaluate entities (i.e. APPRECIATION) may realize JUDGEMENT of 'propriety'. For instance, the

APPRAISAL marker 假冒 (*counterfeited*) in example (42) realizes APPRECIATION of the soy source at issue in its immediate local pattern (i.e. *Dingzhong*).

(17) 该犯罪团伙自2009年初大肆生产、销售**假冒**酱油...(Shubin)
This criminal group has been producing and selling **counterfeited** soybean source since early 2009.
However, it is also embedded in a larger pattern of *Shubin* (verb + object) in which the entire local pattern of *Dingzhong* functions as the object. It is in the pattern of *Shubin* that the APPRAISAL item (i.e. 假冒—*counterfeited*) realizes and triggers the negative JUDGEMENT of 'propriety'. Examples of this kind are typical cases of what Thompson (2014: 47) called "Russian dolls". ATTITUDINAL markers of this kind have posed substantial challenges for their annotation and subsequent analysis. On the other hand, these markers are significant for understanding the interwoven relation between evaluative language and local patterns (e.g. Hunston, 2011).

7.5 Patterns of JUDGEMENT in the Australian Corpus

Since the Australian corpus has merely documented one nominal social sanction marker and two nominal social esteem markers, I will not present them here and instead focus on the adjectival, verbal and adverbials forms of social sanction and social esteem.

7.5.1 Verbal Patterns

Resembling the marginal occurrences of nominal judgement markers (3 occ.) in the Australian corpus, verbal judgement markers (8 occ.) occur rather infrequently as well. Among these eight occurrences, two realizes positive social sanction in relation to social elites (examples (43) and (44)) and six realize negative social esteem (examples (45)–(48)). Verbal social esteem markers may be realized in both passive and active voices. It should be noted that in the passive pattern of 'n V-ed by n' (examples (43)–(45)), the mapping of stance categories on these passive patterns relies heavily on the stance verbs. For instance, in example (45), stance categories are projected onto the passive pattern of 'n V-ed by n' in the order of 'JUDGEMENT target, JUDGEMENT item and JUDGEMENT trigger', whereas in example (44) the positions of JUDGEMENT target and JUDGEMENT trigger are swapped. The JUDGEMENT target in example (44) is social elite, whereas that in the example (45) is civil citizen. This finding may point to the hypothesis that social actors with different social statuses may be mapped onto different local patterns in Australian news report. However, the limited occurrences of verbal patterns of 'social esteem' do not allow us to make more grounded generalizations than this hypothesis.

(18) But many volunteers … say Mr Shepherd's efforts should be **honoured** in full. **[n be V-ed]**

(19) "With 400 fires having burnt across NSW since July 1 and winter rainfall at record lows, Koperberg's ranks are likely to be needed—and **trusted** by the public—more so than ever this summer. We are shaping up particularly badly." Koperberg says. **[n V-ed by n]**

(20) Country Fire Authority (CFA) volunteers have been **traumatised** by many of their gruesome discoveries and…**[n V-ed by n]**

The active voice pattern of 'n V n' (examples (47) and (48)) occurs the most frequently, although my corpus records one occurrence of 'n V *wh*-clause' (example (46)). In the active pattern of 'n V n', JUDGEMENT categories are always mapped in the order of 'JUDGEMENT target, JUDGEMENT verb and JUDGEMENT trigger'. Such a way of the mapping of JUDGEMENT categories resembles that in realizing AFFECT. However, the targets in judgement pattern are not those who express the affective emotions, but are those who are judged by the speaker or writer. For instance, 'crews' in 'crews now **fear** the worst as the humidity drops' signals that they are the emotion experiencer of 'fear'; however in example (47) 'too many people' who are negatively judged by the writer. Examples (46) and (48) realize negative judgement of 'capacity' upon government officials in the Australian corpus whereas example (47) judges citizens' negative capacity in preventing their losses from bush fire.

(21) "Perhaps of greater concern is the widespread perception that the ACT government does not really understand or **appreciate** what motivates and drives entrepreneurs," the council said. **[n V wh-clause]**

(22) Too many people **ignore** the most critical part of a fire plan to prevent the loss of their home—house construction. **[n V n]**

(23) WA went solo last year and **ignored** the roll-out of a national system, claiming State Alert was better. **[n V n]**

Broadly, analysis of verbal patterns of JUDGEMENT has shown that social elites in the Australian corpus are judged positively as much as they are negatively. Although more grounded generalization of the interconnected relation between social statuses of news actors and local verbal patterns is confined by limited occurrences of verbal markers of judgement in my Australian corpus, this points to further studies in this regard.

7.5.2 Adverbial Patterns

As mentioned previously, among the 26 adverbial judgement markers, 25 of them realize judgement of 'social esteem'. The only one adverbial marker of 'social sanction' (example (49)) is found in the pre-verbal position in relation to an unspecific actor. That said, I will focus on the adverbial patterns of 'social esteem' in this Section.

(24) There had never been a reported case of a person being harmed by someone **maliciously** altering their implantable medical device, he said. [**Pre-verbal**] Adverbial markers of social esteem have been recorded in the Australian corpus to frequently occur before the main event verb (17 occ.) (examples (52) and (53)). In comparison, the 'post-verbal' patterns appear less frequently (8 occ.) (examples (50) and (51)) and there is only one case where adverbial social esteem occurs in the final position (example (54)) and no initial position is found to be occupied by adverbial judgement markers. The final position is less frequently adopted in the adverbial realization of all ATTITUDE in the Australian corpus. This may be due to the fact that "these [positions] are less efficient for listeners, since the proposition has been processed before hearing [or reading] the speaker's stance" (Conrad & Biber, 2000, p. 72).

(25) Ewan Waller from the Department of Sustainability and the Environment (DSE) said people should think **carefully** about travel plans on Saturday. [**Post-verbal**]

(26) A Newspoll survey for the Food Safety Information Council found nearly one in five Australians were taking risks by not handling foods containing raw eggs **correctly**. [**Post-verbal**]

(27) "...the implications of Australia's highly concentrated grocery market should be **carefully** examined as part of this inquiry." [**Pre-verbal**]

(28) The owner of a popular Deakin yum cha restaurant has been fined nearly $50,000 after a 2010 health inspection found the kitchen was filthy, food was **improperly** stored and there were insects stuck to the custard tarts. [**Pre-verbal**]

(29) "We've got through today, all things considered, very **well** indeed." [**Final**]

Concerning news actors in adverbial patterns of 'social esteem', citizens (11 occ.) are more frequently represented than social elites (6 occ.) and risk makers (4 occ.). Social elites are mainly represented in a positive way (5 occ.) in relation to their 'capacity' (e.g. *FESA was generally **well** prepared with effective community engagement and public information.*) or their 'tenacity' (e.g. *More than 100 fire-fighters are **desperately** working to contain the fire in Bunyip State Park as it nears a number of small townships.*). By contrast, citizens are negatively represented (6 occ.) in relation to their internationality in causing bushfires (e.g. *Detectives charged the man late last night with **intentionally** causing a fire and being reckless as to its spread.*). Likewise, risk makers receive negative judgement in relation to their improper storage of food (e.g. *The owner of a popular Deakin yum cha restaurant has been fined nearly $50,000 after a 2010 health inspection found the kitchen was filthy, food was **improperly** stored and there were insects stuck to the custard tarts.*).

To sum up, adverbials of JUDGEMENT (social esteem) incline towards an earlier position in a clause but prefer the pre-verbal position, although the occurrence of post-verbal position is noticeable. My corpus records no initial position of judgement (social esteem) adverbials. While social elites are predominantly judged positively in relation to their 'capacity' and 'tenacity', citizens and risk makers are mainly judged negatively in relation to their 'normality' and 'capacity' respectively.

7.5.3 Adjectival Patterns

In adjectival patterns of judgement (34 occ.) in the Australian corpus, 'social esteem' markers (23 occ.) far outnumber 'social sanction' markers (11 occ.). It is noticeable that citizens and social elites are exclusively evaluated in relation to 'social esteem', whereas risk makers are more likely to be represented in relation to 'social sanction' (5 occ.) than they are in relation to 'social esteem' (3 occ.). On this view, and also considering the fact that 'social esteem' and 'social sanction' incline towards different polarity orientations, I examine their patterns separately in the following.

7.5.3.1 Social Esteem

In the realization of 'social esteem' the most frequent pattern is the 'predicative pattern' of 'n be ADJ' (example (55)-(60)) in which the JUDGEMENT triggers may be realized by '*when*-clause, *to*-infinitive clause, *because*-clause', and 'prepositional group', etc. JUDGEMENT triggers can remain implicit and as such undirected adjectival social esteem patterns are produced in which JUDGEMENT targets are often explicated in the context and are realized by a nominal group preceding the social esteem adjective. JUDGEMENT of 'social esteem' in the predicative pattern often concern 'capacity' of citizens (examples (55)-(57)), risk makers and elites (example (59)). Social elites (e.g. Mr Garland, a divisional commander and firefighter, in example (61)) are also judged in relation to their 'tenacity' and 'normality'.

(30) "People need to be **careful** when they are driving on the road." [**n be ADJ when-clause**]

(31) "We are asking everyone to be especially vigilant, monitor your surroundings, stay up to date and be **careful** not to undertake any activity that may start a fire," he said. [**be ADJ to-inf**]

(32) "People aren't **careful** enough with these things." [**n be ADJ with n**]

(33) Raw egg poisoning risk higher at Christmas December 15, 2012 Eggnog could have nasty side effects this Christmas if consumers are not **careful**, experts warn. [**n be ADJ**]

(34) FESA urged motorists to be **careful**. [**n to be ADJ**]

(35) "I am **determined** to see this thing implemented across the nation in a nationally consistent way as rapidly as possible in the year ahead." [**n be ADJ to-inf**]

(36) Mr Garland was fit, **well-known** and much loved by his friends, family and colleagues and would be "extremely missed", Ms Barnes said. [**n be ADJ**]

The attributive pattern of 'ADJ n' (examples (62)-(64)) occurs less frequently than the predicative pattern. In the attributive pattern, the nominal group is more often than not an animate human being or an inanimate human behaviour, and it triggers the judgement of social esteem.

(37) He was trapped by the tree and despite **frantic** efforts from those around him was caught under the tree and passed away, NPWS head Sally Barnes said. [**ADJ n from n**]

(38) We are **passionate** supporters of the JDRF and this is a step towards the cure that everyone is after. [**ADJ n**]

(39) She said George Jackson, a **well-known** St Andrews delivery driver, had been found dead in his burnt-out kitchen. [**ADJ n**]

7.5.3.2 Social Sanction

In contrast to social esteem in which an explicit attributive or predicative pattern may be discerned, adjectival social sanction has somehow posed challenges to follow this clear two-fold adjectival stance pattern. This is because in cases such as examples (67) and (68) the adjectival social esteem is adopted to directly modify things rather than human beings or human behaviors but such a local pattern of 'ADJ n' is embedded in the larger structure of 'human do ADJ things'. For this reason, it is human behavior realized by 'do things' that is evaluated by the speaker. In the examples of (65) and (66), the JUDGEMENT triggers are realized by the last nominal group which refers to human intention or human acts. The difference between the predicative patterns in realizing social sanction (examples (69) and (70)) and in realizing social esteem lies in the choice of the JUDGEMENT items. It is noteworthy that social sanction is predominantly concerned with risk makers in relation to judgement of their positive 'propriety' (examples (67) and (68)).

(40) The experts say it is because many devices are not properly secured and are therefore susceptible to being hacked by someone with **malicious** intent. [**n with ADJ n**]

(41) …to do more to make sure they are secure from **malicious** acts. [**ADJ n**]

(42) "The vast majority of kebab shop owners do the **right** thing," Mr Macdonald said in a statement. [**n v ADJ n**]

(43) "We know the overwhelming majority of food businesses in the ACT are doing the **right** thing, but…[**n v ADJ n**]

(44) "It's signed, sealed and delivered that we're **guilty**." [**n be ADJ**]

(45) Under Queensland's Food Act, a person found **guilty** of purposely contaminating food faces up to 10 years in jail. [**n v ADJ of-ing**]

To briefly summarize adjectival JUDGEMENT patterns in the Australian corpus, I have found social elites and citizens are exclusively judged in relation to social esteem in predicative and attributive patterns, whereas risk makers are mainly judged positively in relation to their 'propriety', a finding that stands in sharp contrast with that presented in the Chinese corpus.

7.6 Discussion

Collating the corpus analytic findings in this chapter, it is the case that positive markers of 'normality', 'capacity', 'tenacity' and 'veracity' in the Chinese corpus outnumber the negative ones but that the reverse is true in the case of 'propriety'. Negative JUDGEMENT is chiefly concerned with risk makers, whereas positive JUDGEMENT is mainly linked to social elites. In other words, social elites are more likely to be positively judged, but risk makers are less likely to be so. Among negative JUDGEMENT of risk makers, it is their 'propriety' that is often foregrounded, whereas positive JUDGEMENT of social elites highlights 'tenacity' and 'capacity'. By contrast, in the Australian corpus 'social esteem' does not exhibit polarity preferences, but 'social sanction' is oriented towards negativity. Resembling findings in the Chinese corpus, social elites are also overwhelmingly judged positively, yet negative judgement upon them is noticeable as well. While risk makers and citizens are predominantly judged negatively in the Australian corpus, there are considerable amount of positive markers. In both corpora, negative JUDGEMENT of risk makers primarily relates to that of 'propriety', and positive JUDGEMENT of social elites chiefly concerns their 'capacity' and 'tenacity'.

The choice of JUDGEMENT markers in hard news appears to be incompatible with journalistic professional norms of objectivity or neutrality of news reporting. Instead, it signals Chinese and Australian journalists' ATTITUDINAL stance vis-à-vis news actors and events in news discourse. By positively judging behaviours of social elites, Chinese journalists position themselves in alignment with the powerful. This is immediately relevant to the social values (see Chap. 10 for more detailed discussion) that are currently operational in news production in the Chinese context where journalists and their affiliated newspapers need to toe the government line (Lee, He, & Huang, 2007; Zhao, 1998, 2008). The primary and guiding working principle of all Chinese news agencies is that of *dang guan meiti* (The government should supervise the work of Chinese news agencies), as prescribed in media policies (http://www.gapp.gov.cn). Under this principle, what is considered to be of social import by the government will and should be augmented accordingly by Chinese news agencies in news production processes and in news products (e.g. news stories) as well. In this sense, newspapers are supposed to disseminate the social-political values desired by the government. To do so, it is necessary that power elites be discursively construed in a positive way in news reporting, for instance how resolute and capable they are in dealing with risk situations. This explains in part our corpus analytic findings concerning the predominant positive JUDGEMENT of 'capacity' and 'tenacity' of social elites in the Chinese corpus.

In the Australian context of news production, Australian journalism practitioners also share the social-political values of the government. However, Australian journalists are less likely to defer to news values criteria and professional values in news production in harmony with the dominant social values. This is largely because on one hand Australian journalists need to rely on elite news sources to fill in daily press space, and on the other hand Australian news production is driven by economic profits (Tiffen, 2006a, 2006b) rather than political requirements (see Chap 8 for more discussions around news sources and journalistic stance). Thus, Australian journalists are accorded with more press power to criticize power elites, as an effort to win readership in the pursuit of maximizing economic profits for stakeholders and media proprietors.

In the context of increasing media competition and decreasing government subsidies, Chinese press tends to augment the news values of Eliteness (i.e. the high status of individuals, institutions or nations involved in an event) and Positivity (i.e. the positive aspects of an event) to cater to the political power of the government, and at the same time to foreground the news values of Personalisation (i.e. the personal or 'human' face of an event) and Negativity (i.e. the negative aspect of an event) to accrue economic profits. Such a distinctive way of enacting news values in the Chinese press is relevant to my corpus analytic finding that the powerful (i.e. social elites) are predominantly evaluated in a positive manner whereas the powerless (risk makers) are negatively evaluated. This trend is also observed in the Australian corpus, but the pairing of Negativity and Eliteness, and that of Positivity and Personalisation are noticeable as well. In both corpora, the media pursuit of economic profits may partly explain why institutional risk makers are more likely to be represented positively, in marked contrast with the way individual risk maker are represented. Another sharp contrast between Chinese and Australian corpus analytic findings is that Australian journalists are more likely to positively judge risk makers in relation to their 'capacity' in dealing with food risk, but negatively judge risk makers in relation to their 'capacity' in intentionally causing bushfires.

Additionally, the involvement of JUDGEMENT markers in Chinese and Australian hard news requires revisiting the often-assumed natural relationship between 'reporter voice' and the genre of hard news, especially in the Western context of hard news reporting. According to Feez et al. (2008, p. 201), 'reporter voice' is a feature of 'authorial voice' which is defined as "certain language features in texts that contribute to a sense of the presence or personality of a writer". The system of 'authorial voice' is divided into those language resources that are reserved for expressing objectivity (i.e. 'reporter voice') and those that are adopted to be subjective (i.e. 'writer voice'). 'Writer voice' is further divided into 'correspondent voice' (where JUDGEMENT is confined to values of 'social esteem') and 'commentator voice' (which has access to the full array of JUDGEMENT values of 'social esteem' and 'social sanction', with a tendency to give prominence to 'social sanction') (Feez et al., 2008, p. 211). As Feez et al. (2008, p. 198) point out, the objective of hard news reporting is to construct a 'reporter voice' featuring an impersonal, anonymous or even absent authorial voice. In other words, as White (1997, p. 107) observes, "the meanings typically avoided [in journalistic reporter voice] include explicit value judgements by the reporter about the morality, competence, normality, etc. of participants". According to Thomson et al. (2008, p. 212), "within English-language journalism, authorial 'neutrality' and use of the 'inverted pyramid' structure are frequently seen to be distinctive features of the modern hard news report and one of the grounds by which journalists assert the 'objectivity' of their writing". However, my corpus analytic finding has shown the involvement of JUDGEMENT of esteem and sanction in Chinese and Australian hard news. The finding indicates that, on the one hand, there is no natural relation between reporter voice and hard news; at least this is not necessarily true in Chinese and Australian hard news reporting on risk events. On the other hand, the shift from a 'reporter voice' to a 'commentator voice' in hard news points to an important pragmatic function of hard news, that is to (re) produce the dominant power relations in news discourse. This is because adopting a 'commentator voice' can substantially facilitate undertaking certain stances by journalists in news discourse.

The present study has also demonstrated the interlocked relationship between local patterns of JUDGEMENT markers and their corresponding JUDGEMENT features. For instance, the JUDGEMENT marker of *kunnan* can only express JUDGEMENT of 'capacity' in the pattern *Shubin*. By examining language patterns of JUDGEMENT, I found that the same JUDGEMENT marker (e.g. *liaojie*) in the same grammatical pattern may realize different valences of JUDGEMENT in relation to news actors of different social statuses. In addition, certain grammatical patterns (e.g. Zhongbu) are less likely to be adopted to judge the 'capacity' of social elites. Furthermore, there seems to be a close link between JUDGEMENT meanings and word classes. For instance, in the Chinese corpus 'tenacity' is chiefly realized in adjectival forms, but seldom in other forms. The limited amount of JUDGEMENT markers in the Australian corpus has not allowed us to make similar observations but several hypotheses.

7.7 Summary

To conclude, the study of the ways Chinese and Australian journalists judge behaviours or characters of different news actors in newspaper hard news reporting has documented an interwoven relation between semantic features of JUDGEMENT, their valences, social statuses of news actors and local grammatical patterns of JUDGEMENT markers. Such an intimate relation is mediated by journalistic stance taking strategies. Their judgement upon elites and non-elites not only concern the articulation of news values, (re)production of symbolic power, but also journalistic manoeuvre of dialogic space of divergent news voices, which constitutes the prime focus of the next chapter.

References

Bednarek, M. (2006). *Evaluation in media discourse: Analysis of a newspaper corpus*. London/New York: Continuum.

Bednarek, M. (2008). *Emotion talk across corpora*. Basingstoke/New York: Palgrave Macmillan.

Chalaby, J. K. (1998). *The invention of journalism*. Houndmills: Macmillan Press.

Conrad, S., & Biber, D. (2000). Adverbial marking of stance in speech and writing. In S. Hunston & G. Thompson (Eds.), *Evaluation in text: Authorial stance and the construction of discourse* (pp. 56–73). Oxford: Oxford University Press.

Du Bois, J. W. (2007). The stance triangle. In R. Englebretson (Ed.), *Stancetaking in discourse: Subjectivity, evaluation, interaction* (pp. 130–182). Amsterdam: Benjamins.

Endo, T. (2013). Epistemic stance in Mandarin conversation: The positions and functions of wo juede "I think". In Y. Pan & D. Kádár (Eds.), *Chinese discourse and interaction: Theory and practice* (pp. 12–34). London: Equinox.

Feez, S., Iedema, R., & White, P. R. R. (2008). *Media literacy*. Surry Hills, N.S.W.: NSW Adult Migrant Education Service.

Frank, R. (2003). These 'crowded circumstances': When pack journalists bash pack journalism. *Journalism, 4*(4), 441–458.

Hunston, S. (2011). *Corpus approaches to evaluation: Phraseology and evaluative language*. New York: Routledge.

Iwasaki, S., & Yap, F. H. (2015). Editorial: Stance-marking and stance-taking in Asian languages. *Journal of Pragmatics, 83,* 1–9.

Jaffe, A. (2009). *Stance: Sociolinguistic perspectives*. Oxford: Oxford University Press.

Lee, C. C., He, Z., & Huang, Y. (2007). Party-market corporatism, clientelism, and media in Shanghai. *The Harvard International Journal of Press/Politics, 12*(3), 21–42.

Lim, N. E. (2011). From subjectivity to intersubjectivity: Epistemic marker wo juede in Chinese. In Y. Xiao, L. Tao, & H. L. Soh (Eds.), *Studies in Chinese linguistics in the new era* (pp. 265–300). Cambridge: Cambridge University Press.

Liu, L., & Stevenson, M. (2013). A cross-cultural analysis of stance in disaster news reports. *Australian Review of Applied Linguistics, 36*(2), 197–220.

Martin, J. R., & White, P. R. R. (2005). *The language of evaluation*. Basingstoke: Palgrave Macmillan.

Mindich, D. (1998). *Just the facts: How objectivity came to define American journalism*. New York: New York University Press.

Perrin, D. (2012). Stancing: Strategies of entextualizing stance in newswriting. *Discourse, Context & Media, 1*(2–3), 135–147.

Peters, C. (2011). Emotion aside or emotional side? Crafting an 'experience of involvement' in the news. *Journalism, 12*(3), 297–316.

Pounds, G. (2010). Attitude and subjectivity in Italian and British hard-news reporting: The construction of a culture-specific 'reporter' voice. *Discourse Studies, 12*(1), 106–137.

Rosen, J. (1999). *What are journalists for?* New Haven, CT: Yale University Press.

Schudson, M., & Anderson, C. (2009). Objectivity, professionalism, and truth seeking in journalism. In K. Wahl-Jorgensen & T. Hanitzsch (Eds.), *The handbook of journalism studies* (pp. 88–101). New York & London: Routledge.

Stenvall, M. (2008). On emotions and the journalistic ideals of factuality and objectivity: Tools for analysis. *Journal of Pragmatics, 40,* 1569–1586.

Stenvall, M. (2014). Presenting and representing emotions in news agency reports. *Critical Discourse Studies, 11*(4), 461–481. https://doi.org/10.1080/17405904.2013.866588.

Su, L. I.-W. (2004). Subjectification and the use of the complementizer SHUO. *Concentric: Studies in Linguistics, 30,* 19–40.

Tao, H. (2003). Phonological, grammatical, and discourse evidence for the emergence of zhidao constructions in mandarin conversation. *Zhongguo Yuwen [中国语文], 4*(295), 291–302.

Tao, H. (2007). Subjectification and the development of special-verb existential/presentative constructions. *Language and Linguistics, 2*(2), 575–602.

Thompson, G. (2014). Affect and emotion, target-value mismatches, and Russian dolls. In G. Thompson & L. Alba-Juez (Eds.), *Evaluation in context* (pp. 47–66). Amsterdam: John Benjamins.

Thomson, E., White, P. R. R., & Kitley, P. (2008). "Objectivity" and "hard news" reporting across cultures: Comparing the news report in English, French. *Japanese and Indonesian Journalism. Journalism Studies, 9*(2), 212–228.

Tiffen, R. (2006a). Political economy and news. In S. Cunningham & G. Turner (Eds.), *The media and communications in Australia* (2nd ed., pp. 28–42).

Tiffen, R. (2006b). The press. In S. Cunningham & G. Turner (Eds.), *The media and communications in Australia* (2nd ed., pp. 97–112). Sydney: Allen & Unwin.

Tuchman, G. (1972). Objectivity as strategic ritual: An examination of newsmen's notions of objectivity. *American Journal of Sociology, 77,* 660–679.

Vertommen, B., Vandendaele, A., & Van Praet, E. (2012). Towards a multidimensional approach to journalistic stance. Analyzing foreign media coverage of Belgium. *Discourse, Context & Media, 1*(2), 123–134.

Wahl-Jorgensen, K. (2013a). Subjectivity and story-telling in journalism: Examining expressions of affect, judgement and appreciation in Pulitzer prize-winning stories. *Journalism Studies, 14* (3), 305–320.

Wahl-Jorgensen, K. (2013b). The strategic ritual of emotionality: A case study of Pulitzer prize-winning articles. *Journalism, 14*(1), 129–145.

Wang, Z. (2001). 评价系统及其运作 [Appraisal systems and their operations: A new development in the systemic functional linguistics]. *Journal of Foreign Languages, 6,* 13–20.

White, P. R. R. (1997). Death, disruption and the moral order: The narrative impulse in mass-media hard news reporting. In F. Christie & J. R. Martin (Eds.), *Genres and institutions: Social processes in the workplace and school* (pp. 101–133). London: Cassell.

White, P. R. R. (1998). *Telling media tales: The news story as rhetoric* (Unpublished Ph. D. thesis). University of Sydney, Sydney.

Wu, R.-J. R. (2004). *Stance in talk: A conversation analysis of Mandarin final particles.* Amsterdam/Philadelphia: John Benjamins.

Wu, F. (Ed.). (2011). *Hanyu Zhuguanxing yu Zhuguanhua Yanjiu (studies in subjectivity and subjectification in Chinese).* Beijing: Commercial Press.

Wu, H. (2015). Encoding subjectivity with totality: A corpus-based study of [zhengge yi (CL) + X] in Mandarin. *Journal of Pragmatics, 83,* 27–40.

Yang, Y., & Yap, F. H. (2015). "I am sure but I hedge": Fear expression kǒngpà as an interactive rhetorical strategy in Mandarin broadcast talk. *Journal of Pragmatics, 83,* 41–56.

Zhao, Y. (1998). *Media, market, and democracy in China: Between the party line and the bottom line.* Urbana: University of Illinois Press.

Zhao, Y. (2008). *Communication in China: Political economy, power, and conflict.* Lanham, Maryland: Rowman & Littlefield Publishers.

Chapter 8
Engagement Patterns

8.1 Introduction

In this chapter, I explore the ways Chinese and Australian journalists engage with different news sources in print media hard news reporting on risk events. It is widely acknowledged that 'journalists rely primarily on other people's accounts of events in their authoring of stories' (Bell, 1991, p. 56; see also Cotter, 2010; Fishman, 1980; Gans, 2004/1979; Tiffen et al., 2014; Van Dijk, 1988). Sigal (1986) even considers that sources make the news. According to Van Dijk (2013), understanding sources of knowledge and how they are presented in news discourse is relevant to 'epistemic discourse analysis, [...] the systematic and explicit study of the ways knowledge is interactively "managed" (activated, expressed, presupposed, implied, conveyed, construed, etc.) in the structures and strategies of text and talk' (Van Dijk, 2013, p. 497).

The epistemic analysis of news discourse is pivotal for understanding '[how] news mediates the wider socio-political environment to its audience' (Tiffen, 1989, p. 32). In mediating such knowledge, quoting news sources does not simply mark sources of knowledge, but more importantly it manages knowledge through appraising news sources. As such, the choice of news sources and the way to present them are discursive resources or mediational means (Jones & Norris, 2005; Scollon, 1998, 2001) by which journalists undertake stances towards the knowledge being advanced in news discourse (Bednarek, 2006; Calsamiglia & Ferrero, 2003; Hanks, 2012; Jullian, 2011; Martin & White, 2005; Mushin, 2001, 2013; White, 2003, 2012). Journalists are believed to be skilful in putting their words in the mouth of the sources quoted (Bell, 1991; Sleurs, Jacobs, & Van Waes, 2003). Hence, the epistemic analysis of news discourse is intimately interconnected with the analysis of how journalists position themselves with respect to the knowledge in news. As Caldas-Coulthard (2002, p. 304) puts it, 'the choice of who is given voice depends on the importance given to some people instead of others [...] The selection of the speakers reflects cultural belief systems and power structures'

C. Huan, *Journalistic Stance in Chinese and Australian Hard News*,
https://doi.org/10.1007/978-981-13-0791-1_8

(p. 304). That is to say, sources are not selected and mediated equally in news discourse. As Caldas-Coulthard (1994, p. 304) points out, 'a lot of what is reported is associated with power structures'. This corroborates the argument of Tiffen et al. (2014, p. 375) that 'the power relationship is pivotal – and the news that results highly pertinent to the larger exercise of political power'.

Previous studies of journalists engaging with news sources (e.g. quoting practices) in news discourse have mostly centred on objectivity/subjectivity, authority and reliability of news reporting (e.g. Fowler, 1991; Gans, 2004/1979; Hsieh, 2008; Sigal, 1986; Tuchman, 1978; Van Dijk, 1988; Zelizer, 1989, 1990). This line of scholarly inquiry has focused on truth functionality and certainty of knowledge, but has largely ignored the negotiation of dialogic positioning vis-a-vis propositions in news (White, 2012).

Scholars have only recently attempted to fill this gap by investigating the relationship between journalistic stance (e.g. dialogic positions vis-a-vis a proposition) and the way news voices are engaged in news discourses (e.g. Bednarek, 2006; Biber, Johansson, Leech, Conrad, & Finegan, 1999; Hanks, 2012; Jullian, 2011; Martin & White, 2005; Mushin, 2013; White, 2003, 2012). Engaging with different news sources is considered in this book as an important means for journalism practitioners to reorganize the structure of socio-cultural knowledge in the acquisition, perpetuation and change of ideology and power relations. The pragmatic and ideological significance of journalists engaging with news sources has as yet been underexplored in Chinese news discourse, and as such cultural differences in this regard have been poorly understood. This is particularly true in the changing face of the Chinese press since the 2000s (Z. Hu, 2003; Winfield & Peng, 2005; Zhao, 2000) (see Chap. 10).

8.2 Overview of Journalistic Engagement Markers

This section presents an overview of the distribution of 'engagement' markers in each corpus. The normalized percentage of the distribution of 'engagement' markers (see Table 8.1) shows that the percentage of 'acknowledge' markers in the Australian corpus (90%) overtakes that in the Chinese corpus (70%), suggesting that in general the quoted voices are more negotiable in the Australian corpus. Despite the predominant amount of 'acknowledge' markers in both corpora, Chinese journalists favour direct witness (i.e. 'attest', 17%) in reporting the risk event at issue, while the Australian journalists show their reluctance to do so (4%). This is also the case in endorsing other voices (12% in the Chinese corpus vs. 5% in the Australian corpus). Both Chinese and Australian journalists disfavour frequent adoption of 'distance' and 'pronounce' markers since such explicit journalistic intervention into a text may jeopardize journalists' professional norms.

The summary of 'contract' and 'expand' features in Table 8.1 indicates that both Chinese and Australian journalists open up the dialogic space for alternative positions more than they close it down. However, Chinese journalists are more

Table 8.1 Key engagement features in each sub-corpus

N.	Engagement	Chinese corpus		Australian corpus	
		Frequency	Per cent	Frequency	Per cent
1	Acknowledge	3735	70	2516	90
2	Attest	916	17	116	4
3	Endorse	653	12	151	5
4	Pronounce	25	0	7	0
5	Distance	26	0	10	0
	Contract	1594	30	274	10
	Expand	3761	70	2526	90
Total		5355	100	2800	100

likely to contract the dialogic space (30%) than their Australian peers in this respect (10%). In other words, Australian journalists are more likely to open up the dialogic space than Chinese journalists.

In the following examination of 'engagement' patterns, I will exclusively focus on 'attest', 'endorse' and 'acknowledge' which are involved in the engagement with other news voices and meanwhile appear frequently in each corpus. This is not to deny the importance of other 'engagement' features, but my focus on journalists engaging with various voices in news reports lies more in *who* is/are positioned and *how* they are dialogically positioned, rather than in how 'engagement' features are realized and distributed in news.

8.3 Attest Patterns in the Australian and Chinese Corpora

As previously defined, 'attest' relates to direct witness through human sensory senses, the primary one of which is through visual sense (e.g. see). Unlike other 'engagement' features that involve explicit quotation of other sources, 'attest' is related to journalists' engaging with authorial or non-authorial sources by means of introducing attested fact in reporting an event. Figure 8.1 shows that the major source of 'attest' in each corpus differs from the others.

In general, Australian journalists are more likely to mediate the attested knowledge from news sources of government officials, experts and those unspecified (officials and experts) than their Chinese peers are. However, the opposite is the case when it comes to mediating the attested knowledge from news sources of journalists themselves (i.e. authorial), ordinary citizens and risk makers.

To be specific, the Australian corpus (Fig. 8.2) shows that government officials are the chief source of witness of the reported events (44 occ., 38%). There are considerable cases where sources of eye-witnessed events are unspecified by Australian journalists (37 occ., 32%). By unspecified sources, I mean those sources that are not immediately known in the context. The sources of ordinary citizens (25 occ., 21%) are

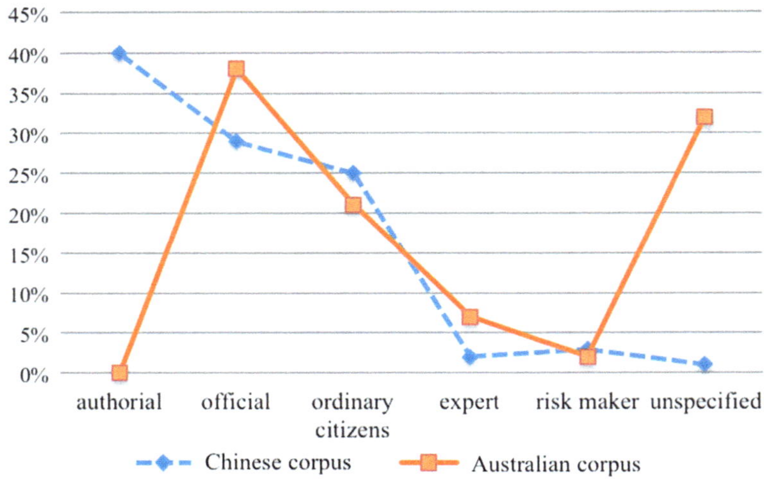

Fig. 8.1 Comparing attest sources in Chinese and Australian corpora

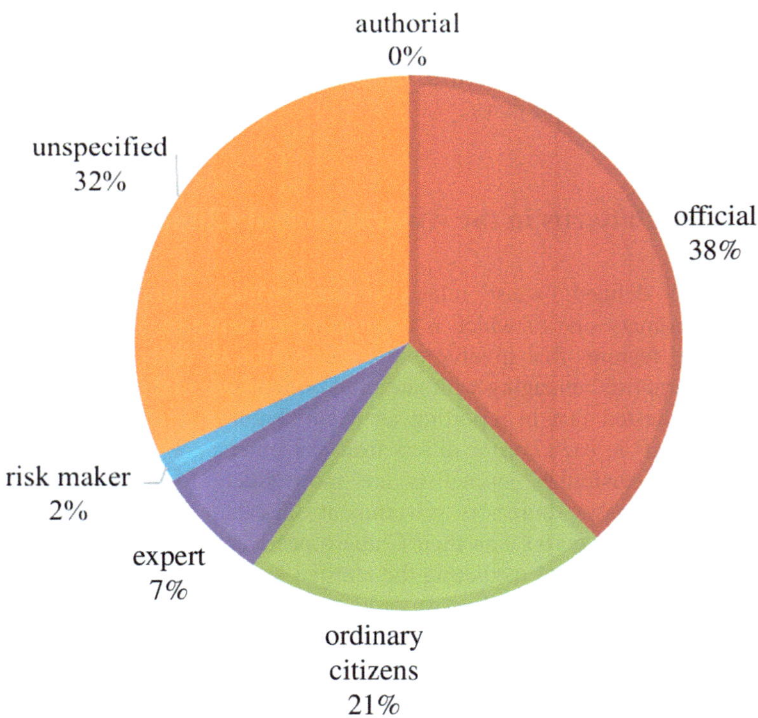

Fig. 8.2 Distribution of attest sources in the Australian corpus

noticeable, but the expert sources (8 occ., 7%) and those of risk makers (2 occ., 2%) are rather marginal. Risk makers are those individuals or institutions who have done things that put others at risk despite degrees of risk they produce and degrees of their intention. The Australian corpus has not displayed any instance of journalistic authorial 'attest'. The 'attested' sources in the Australian corpus are illustrated in examples (71)–(74):

(71) … health authorities discovered a cockroach infestation and shoddy cleaning practices at the store. (Officials)
(72) Solvents are found in many common products, including… (Unspecified)
(73) Doctors Kacey O'Rourke, Stuart McMaster and Karin Lust said similar cases of hepatitis after methoxyflurane had been found in women who had received the drug during labour. (Experts)
(74) … Mr. Gissara and Mr. Crosby saw a fireball emerge from the landscape. (Ordinary citizens)

The rare occurrences of risk makers' voice and no presence of journalistic authorial voice in attesting the risk event at issue suggest that Australian journalists are rarely on site to be able to directly access knowledge pertaining to risk events. Another potential explanation is that they are on site, but in writing up the news item they background their own sensory experience in line with the Anglo journalistic convention of backgrounding journalistic subjectivity. Among 'attest' sources in reporting risk events, Australian journalists rely heavily on the official voice (38%) and unspecified voice (e.g. officials and experts, 32%), but the voice of risk makers is hardly heard therein. This finding indicates that in 'resemioticizing' (Iedema, 2003) risk events into news stories, Australian journalists tend to marginalize the knowledge about risk from risk makers, but to prioritize the knowledge from official sources.

Let us turn to the 'attest' patterns in the Chinese corpus. Chinese journalists primarily rely on journalistic authorial voice (363 occ., 40%) in witnessing risk events (Fig. 8.3). Official sources (265 occ., 29%) are less frequently mediated than journalistic authorial sources, but the former still occurs more frequently than the sources of ordinary citizens (230 occ., 25%). The heavy reliance on authorial voice in the Chinese corpus stands in sharp contrast to that in the Australian corpus in which there is no occurrence of authorial source. There are more sources of risk makers in the Chinese corpus (33 occ.) than those in the Australian corpus (2 occ.) in attesting risk events or issues. Resembling their Australian peers in mediating sources of experts (8 occ.), Chinese journalists tend to marginalize the voice of experts (16 occ., 2%). However, unspecified sources (9 occ., 1%) are negligible in the Chinese corpus.

Attest sources in the Chinese corpus are illustrated in examples (75)–(79):

(75) 记者见到了小佳脖子右侧有一个大肿块
(Authorial) Reporter saw a lump on the right of Xiaojia's neck.
(76) 记者看到两侧山上都出现滑坡…
(Authorial) Reporter saw slides on both sides of the mountain.

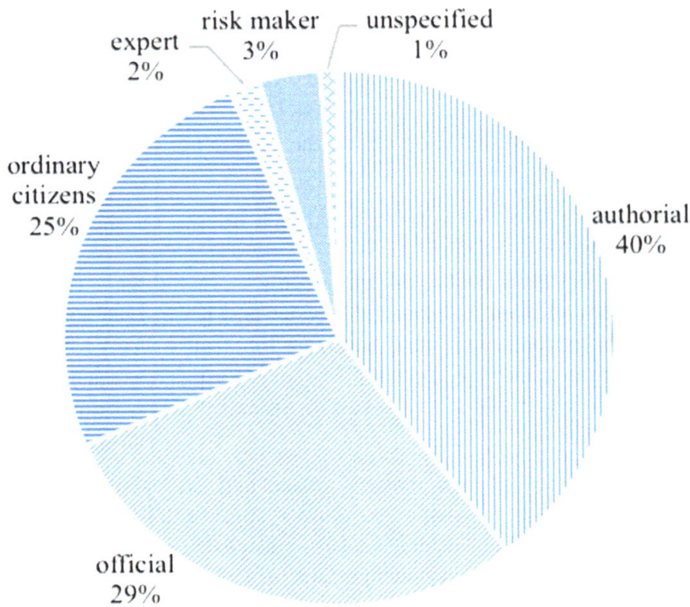

Fig. 8.3 Distribution of attest sources in the Chinese corpus

(77) 执法人员发现了一个糕点黑作坊...
(Officials) Law enforcers found an illegal workshop producing dim sum.

(78) 何春凯说:‘在这次地震中, 我们发现一些用轻钢板做屋盖的木屋架的学校房屋表 现不错。
(Experts) He Chunkai said ‘in this earthquake, we found some wooden school buildings with light steel as the roof performed well’.

(79) 江女士给本报热线打来电话称,... 她发现饮料内居然漂着一只死蟑螂。
(Ordinary citizens) Ms. Jiang called the hotline of our newspaper and said she had found a dead cockroach floating on her soft drink.

To summarize, the significant difference of engaging ‘attest’ sources in Chinese and Australian corpora is that Chinese journalists tend to foreground their own voice in reporting risk events, whereas Australian journalists are more likely to background journalistic authorial voice. This point is relevant to the high frequency of journalistic authorial voice in the Chinese corpus and the low frequency of authorial voice in the Australian corpus.

8.4 Endorse Patterns in the Australian and Chinese Corpora

While 'attest' voices take human beings as news sources, endorsed voices may have both inanimate entities and human beings as news sources. The Australian corpus has shown that objective reports, surveys, scientific analysis, official investigation or photos constitute the primary and the most frequently quoted source (84 occ., 56%) that are endorsed in the Australian corpus such as those in (80) and (81). These sources are equivalent to the base of knowledge—Proof—in Bednarek's (2006, p. 640) discussion of epistemological position, with proof being 'a marking of the proposition as being based on some sort of "hard proof"'(p. 640). Hence, these sources will be referred to hard proof sources from this point onwards. It is noteworthy that hard proof sources in the Australian corpus mainly come from official sources and various professional organizations:

(80) Food regulators have called on wholesalers and retailers across Australia to remove White Rabbit Creamy Candies after New Zealand testing found 'sufficiently high levels' of melamine. (Hard proof sources)
(81) But the director-general Kieran McNamara has expressed full confidence in Mr. Commins, and said an independent inquiry found he was not careless. (Hard proof sources)
(82) Canned tuna was also found to have elevated BPA levels though… (Unspecified)

As shown in Fig. 8.4, the next frequently endorsed sources after hard proof sources are official sources (35 occ., 23%), followed by unspecified sources (17 occ., 11%) such as that in example (12). Voices of experts (8 occ., 5%), risk makers (4 occ., 3%) and ordinary citizens (3 occ., 2%) are rather marginal in the Australian corpus.

In the Chinese corpus, hard proof sources (535 occ., 82%) are the primary source endorsed by Chinese journalists in reporting risk events as well, as illustrated in examples (13) and (14). In the Australian corpus, government officials and unspecified voices are the two most frequently endorsed sources, following hard proof sources. By contrast, the Chinese journalists are more likely to endorse sources of news/risk makers (97 occ., 15%) than their Australian peers are (3%). However, the sources of risk makers are exclusively introduced by two reporting verbs in the Chinese corpus—交待-jiāodài and 承认-*chéngrèn* (to confess or to admit something reluctantly). The two reporting verbs indicate that risk makers in the Chinese corpus remain in a powerless situation. Their speeches are only endorsed by journalists to establish the truth of their risk-producing actions and thus discourage challenges by alternative voices. The amount of official sources (14 occ., 2%) and unspecified sources (1 occ., 0%) are minimally relevant in the Chinese corpus (Fig. 8.5):

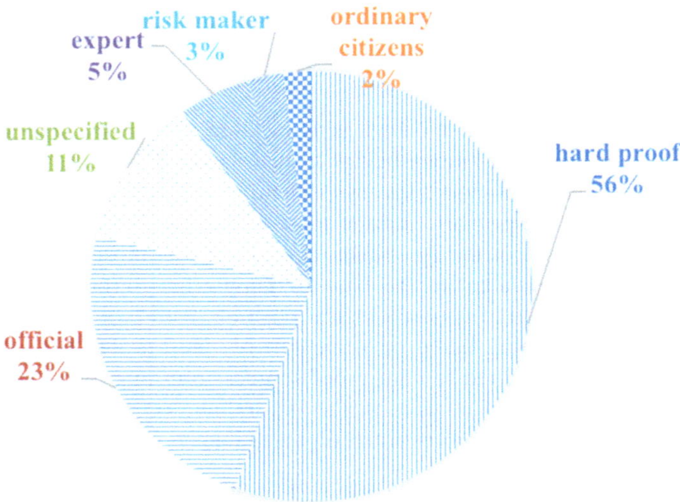

Fig. 8.4 Distribution of endorse sources in the Australian corpus

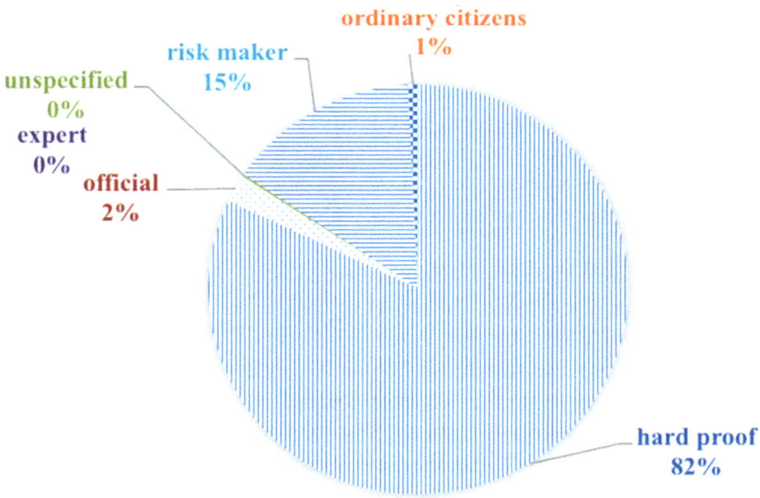

Fig. 8.5 Distribution of endorse sources in the Chinese corpus

(83) 审计结果表明, 灾后恢复重建整体进展顺利… (Hard proof sources)
Audit results show the restoring works are progressing well.

(84) 质量监测结果显示 3 个批次质量不合格。(Hard proof sources)

Quality testing results show 3 batches of goods are below the quality standard.

It may sound as if Chinese journalists decline to endorse official voices, but a scrutiny of those hard proof sources reveals that they are predominantly released by the Chinese government such as those in examples (83) and (84). Simply put, Chinese journalists have managed to endorse official sources in disguise by replacing official human sources with inanimate government investigation results and reports (hard proof sources). In so doing, journalists have adopted a stance in alignment with the government sources.

Comparing 'endorse' patterns in Chinese and Australian corpora, Chinese journalists are more likely to endorse hard proof sources results (82%) than their Australian peers do (56%), but Chinese journalists are less likely to explicitly endorse government officials. However, this does not necessarily mean that Chinese journalists are detaching themselves from official sources. On the contrary, Chinese journalists have replaced explicit endorsing of official human sources with implicit hard proof sources released by the government. Another point is that the voice of risk makers is more salient in the Chinese corpus than it is in the Australian corpus. However, the involvement of knowledge about risk events from risk makers mainly serves to negatively judge their actions in producing risks.

8.5 Acknowledge Patterns in the Australian and Chinese Corpora

Rather than exhausting all 'acknowledge' patterns in the Australian and Chinese corpora, for reasons of scope I have decided to focus on the most frequent 'acknowledge' marker (i.e. 'said', 528 occ., and '说': 'shuō, say', 448 occ.) only in the food- safety sub-corpus.

The corpus software WordSmith (V6.0; http://www.lexically.net/wordsmith/) has been adopted to investigate the way knowledge about food safety is reorganized in the Australian corpus through acknowledging other news sources. In the collocation analysis, the mutual information (MI) score was adopted to measure the strength of collocations, and a default 5:5 window (five words to the left and five words to the right of the node word) was used. The MI score has been used widely in corpus linguistics as a measure of collocational strength (McEnery, Xiao, & Tono, 2006). Concordances of 'said' in the Australian food-safety corpus are illustrated in Fig. 8.6. This figure is sorted by the frequency of collocation of the searched word 'said', with the word immediately to its left (L1). It shows that 'said' is most frequently collocated with 'he' to its left, followed by 'she' and others in the 'L1' column. If continuing reading the collocates of 'said' with those in the 'L1' column in Fig. 8.6, we may find that the most frequently mediated voice in communicating food risk in Australian press is the official voice, as evidenced by frequent collocation of 'said' with 'spokeswoman, FSANZ, spokesman, council, Macdonald (NSW Primary Industries Minister), Buchtmann (spokeswoman Ms. Lydia Buchtmann of FSA),

N	L5	L4	L3	L2	L1	Centre	R1	R2	R3	R4	R5
1	THE	THE	SAID	MR	HE	SAID	THE	WAS	HAD	THE	THE
2	TO	AND	THE	DR	SHE		IT	THE	THE	TO	OF
3	OF	FOOD	OF	THE	SPOKESWOMAN		THERE	HAD	STATEMI	OF	TO
4	AND	OF	MINISTE:	MS	FSANZ		IN	WOULD	OF	NOT	FOR
5	IN	FOR	FOOD	HEALTH	SPOKESMAN		HE	HEALTH	TO	WERE	HAD
6	HEALTH	TO	SPOKESI	STEVE	COUNCIL		DR	ARE	WAS	WAS	IN
7	FOR	BE	DR	PROFESS	MACDONALD		THAT	OF	SAID	NO	THAT
8	PRIMARY	HEALTH	AUSTRAI	IN	BUCHTMANN		WE	FOOD	NOT	FOOD	WAS
9	BE	IN	SAFETY	LYDIA	WHAN		THEY	AND	NO	BE	WERE
10	FOOD	HE	AND	IAN	AMES		WHILE	HAS	WERE	HAD	SAFETY
11	AT	AUSTRAI	DIRECTC	SAID	GALLAGHER		YESTERI	THIS	BEEN	FOR	NOT
12	WITH	INDUSTR	BUT	IT	PHILLIPS		IT'S	DRUG	IS	ON	IS
13	HAVE	CHIEF	FOR	AUSTRAI	KINGMA		FOOD	COMPAN	ALSO	THAT	AND
14	IS	THERAPE	IT	ADMINIS	GUEST		THIS	WERE	WOULD	NEED	THERAPE
15	OR	IS	HEALTH	JUDGE	ALSO		THESE	SAID	HAVE	ALL	SAID
16	SAID	OFFICER	OFFICER	THIS	WOOLLARD		SHE	WHO	AND	ABOUT	FOOD
17	STILL	OR	AUSTRAI	TGA	HOUSE		AUSTRAI	COULD	SHOULD	IS	AT

Fig. 8.6 Selected concordances of "said" in the Australian food-safety corpus

N	Concordance
1	altering their implantable medical device, he said. Mr Miller said that despite this,
2	to date with the latest attack techniques," he said. "This will ensure that all realistic risks
3	the artificial pancreas. "It's bittersweet," he said. "It's quite emotional to see this coming
4	Minister Steve Whan said in a statement. He said some of the offences included
5	have moved to establish tolerable levels," he said. "The Choice report notes BPA has
6	infection and stop it spreading further. He said members of the public were not at risk
7	Zealanders had gone one step further, he said, launching a campaign against the
8	25th or Saturday 26th November," he said. "Food safety inspections of the
9	life. "But it's a good proof of principle," he said. Another diabetes expert, Professor
10	of keeping blood sugar steady overnight, he said. Over 100,000 people in Australia are

Fig. 8.7 Examples of collocation of "said" with "he" in the Australian corpus

Whan (Mr. Steve Whan, Primary Industry minister), Phillips (Professor Paddy Phillips, state's chief medical officer)'.

To understand the persons whom 'he' and 'she' refer to in the corpus, I went through all collocates of 'he' with 'said' in the co-text (Fig. 8.7) and also collocates of 'she' with 'said'. The manual analysis shows that among the 85 collocates of 'he' with 'said', official sources (31 occ.) account for 36%, sources from different associations (24 occ.) amount to 28%, expert sources (22 occ.) occupy 26% and risk makers' sources (8 occ.) account for 9.4%. These news sources are illustrated in examples (85)–(88). Among the 34 collocates of 'she' with 'said', official sources account for 62% (21 occ.), ordinary citizens' sources take 21% (7 occ.), while expert sources and risk makers' sources, each with three occurrences, occupy less than 1%. For space limitations, these news sources will not be illustrated here:

(85) 'We assessed them [two cafes were unclean, failing to maintain temperature control for critical food items, etc.] as being a clear risk to the public health', he said. (Paul Dugdale, chief health officer on duty for ACT) (Officials)

(86) The plastic had been declared safe by Food Safety Australia New Zealand, he said. (Plastics and Chemicals Industries Association (PACIA) chief executive Michael Catchpole) (Associations)

(87) He said that although some of the chemicals had been banned in Australia, they persisted in the environment, including in people's homes and in food. (Dr. David Carpenter, the director of the Institute of Health and the Environment at the University of Albany in New York) (Experts)

(88) Sales manager Cheng Zhou said they sold the products to about 50 shops in small orders. 'Some (shops) only take 10 packs, 20 packs. Normally 10 packs', Mr. Zhou said. He said the company had not imported White Rabbit lollies for some months. (Risk makers)

To produce 'acknowledge' patterns in the Chinese corpus, I have relied on the corpus concordance tool SysConc. The most frequent 'acknowledge' marker, '说' (say), was adopted to illustrate how different news sources were mediated to channel knowledge about risk events in Chinese news discourse.

Due to the unique nature of Chinese language, there is no corpus linguistic software that can produce collocation of Chinese words of the kind produced for the English data. To examine the patterns of Chinese journalists acknowledging different news sources, I manually checked all concordances of the searched word 'shuo'. The analysis shows that among the 448 concordances, Chinese journalists prioritize the voice of risk makers (41%, 183 occ.), followed by that of consumers (24%, 106 occ.), government officials (19%, 86 occ.), experts (13%, 60 occ.), associations (1.6%, 7 occ.) and journalists themselves (1.3%, 6 occ.). In comparison with the voices presented in the Australian corpus, the Chinese corpus highlights those of risk makers and consumers. Examples (89)–(93) illustrate the voice of risk makers, consumers, government officials, experts and associations in tandem:

(89) 昨日，生产厂家说:瓜子里有虫子，证明是无公害的绿色天然食品。(Risk makers)
Yesterday, the manufacturer said worms were found in sunflower seeds, and it proved that these sunflower seeds were organic green food.

(90) 张先生说, 厂家不认同蛆虫是火腿肠自身产生的, 他便当着大家的面剥开了火腿肠 剩余的部分, 同样发现了蛆虫。(Consumers)
Mr. Zhang said the manufacturer did not agree that the maggots were formed in the sausage, so he pealed the rest of sausage in face of all involved parties and also found maggots.

(91) X工商所长高峰说， 柠檬黄不能用作花椒的添加剂， 这是违法添加。(Government officials)
Gao-Feng, the director of the X Administration of Industry and Commerce, said lemon citron could not be used as an additive of pepper and it was an illegal additive.

(92) X大学食品学院副院长熊善柏说，植物生长调节剂等添加剂均属激素类，使用不能 过量。(Experts)
Xiong Shanbo, the deputy dean of the Faculty of Food Science at the X University, said additives such as plant growth regulator belonged to steroids and could not be overused.

(93) 近日，山西省醋产业协会副会长王建忠在接受媒体采访时说，市面上的山西陈醋 95%为勾兑醋，且大多添加防腐剂… (Associations)
Recently, Wang Jianzhong, the deputy president of Shanxi Vinegar Industry, said in an interview with the press 95% of Shanxi Vinegar sold in the market were vinegar blend and most of them contained preservatives…

In short, Chinese journalists prioritize the voices of consumers and risk makers, whereas in the Australian corpus the official voice is far more frequently acknowledged than other voices.

8.6 Discussion

To briefly summarize 'attest', 'endorse' and 'acknowledge' patterns in the Chinese and Australian corpus as presented in this chapter, when aligning with a position by adopting markers of 'attest' and 'endorse', Australian journalists prioritize official sources and unspecific sources; however, Chinese journalists foreground their presence in attesting risk events. In endorsing a proposition, Chinese journalists endorse official sources in disguise through endorsing hard proof sources (e.g. official test or investigation results). In acknowledging other sources, Australian journalists rely heavily on official sources that are presented as one of the many alternative voices. However, Chinese journalists primarily engage with risk makers and ordinary citizens and thus hesitate to align with the propositions being advanced by these sources. To attest or endorse a position narrows down the dialogic space for alternative voices, whereas to acknowledge a position opens up the dialogic space for the position being advanced. On this view, Chinese journalists are less likely to open up the dialogic space for alternative voices in mediating the official sources, whereas the dialogic space of the official source is opened up (i.e. acknowledged) as much as it is closed down (i.e. attested and endorsed) by Australian journalists. The findings are significant for understanding the ways journalistic stances are undertaken across cultures.

The choice of reporting verbs is not simply about the indication of knowledge status towards the reported events, but more importantly it signals journalists' dialogistic positioning in relation to the news sources being advanced in news texts. Generally speaking, corpus findings suggest that Chinese journalists take a stance in alignment with official sources, whereas Australian journalists do not position themselves to align with official sources. The different journalistic stances undertaken by Australian and Chinese journalists are, however, inevitably conditioned by socio-cultural, institutional and professional values and beliefs about news reporting in each context.

In the Australian context of news production, Australian newspapers are privately owned rather than State-owned so as to allow people to access a diversity of media voices (Cunningham & Turner, 2006; Finkelstein, 2012; Papandrea, 2013). The Australian press are detached from any State capital given by the government. In this sense, the Australian press are dissociated from any specific political party and government, and consequently, they are not obliged to fulfil any propaganda objectives. It is the media proprietors rather than any specific political party that exercise editorial control over news production. Accordingly, the symbolic power (Bourdieu, 1989, 1991) of the Australian government is minimally relevant in enacting journalistic stance. Instead, the Australian news institutions possess significant power to decide what makes news in their newspapers during editorial meetings. In so doing, Australian journalism practitioners reproduce the institutional values preferred by media proprietors in news production.

In the Chinese context, the primary aim of news production, especially that of Party papers (e.g. organs of the Communist Party of China at different levels), is to disseminate the socio-political values of the government (Z. Hu, 2003; Lee, He, & Huang, 2007; Tong, 2009; Zhao, 2000, 2005). Chinese journalists need to prioritize what the government considers as newsworthy. Australian journalism practitioners also share (and only sometimes challenge) socio-political values of the power elites, as has been shown in work on racist ideology (e.g. Van Dijk, 1998; Wodak & Van Dijk, 2000). However, Chinese and Australian journalism practitioners defer to different news values criteria and professional values in news production. Simply put, the Australian press are dominated by commercial values (Tiffen, 2006a, 2006b), whereas the Chinese press foreground socio-political values (Zhao, 1998, 2005, 2008). In the Australian press, the ultimate goal of news production is to maximize the economic profits for stakeholders and media proprietors, while to praise or criticize the government is only a means to achieve this end. The reverse is the case in the Chinese press in the sense that to promote the political propaganda is the end of all Chinese press, while to pursue economic profits is only an efficient means to achieve this end.

The different relationship between news institutions and government in each context has greatly influenced journalistic stance towards official sources. In the Chinese context, the interpersonal relationship between journalists and official sources depends on the nature and status of the newspapers where journalists work. Chinese journalists in Party papers have privilege in accessing official sources and official events. In the transaction between Chinese journalists and official sources, the news institutions accrue economic profits while official sources promote the political ideology. Negotiating relationships between the power elites and the press is key to the enactment of journalistic stances. In this negotiation process, Chinese journalists have taken a stance in alignment with the power elites. This in part explains why Chinese journalists consider official sources as less negotiable than other sources.

With the tightening budget in the Australian press, Australian journalists tend to rely heavily on prefabricated news from regular sources (Papandrea, 2013; Tiffen, 2006a, 2006b; G. Turner, 2006). News sources from officials, experts and organizations are the primary sources adopted by Australian journalists in mediating knowledge about risk. Regular and frequent access to news sources from ordinary citizens is less likely to be affordable with the tightening budget in the Australian context. This is relevant to the corpus finding that sources of ordinary citizens are less frequently adopted than official sources or other sources (e.g. sources from experts and organizations) in reporting risk events. The changing economic situation in Australian newspapers also explains why Australian journalists rely on elite sources in Australian news discourse. However, reliance on elite sources itself does not necessarily mean a compromised Fourth Estate as suggested by Lewis, Williams, and Franklin (2008), although it consciously or subconsciously sustains the status quo. What also matters is the way that elite sources are mediated in news discourses. The corpus findings have shown that in the Australian corpus, although elite sources (e.g. official sources) are the primary source in mediating risk communication, they are adopted to attest risk events at issue (38%) as much as they are acknowledged (36%). This suggests that the dialogic space of elite voice is likely to be opened up as much as it is closed down in the Australian news discourse. As such, Australian journalists do not take a stance to please the power elites as their Chinese peers do. However, this is not to suggest that media proprietors of Australian press cannot exchange media responsibility with non-media interests. The point is that my corpus findings on discursive stances in the Australian news discourse have not showed strong evidence supporting a compromised Fourth Estate in the Australian press in general.

8.7 Summary

To conclude, the epistemic analysis of Australian and Chinese print media hard news reporting on risk events has recorded different patterns of journalists engaging with news sources. The textual patterns have pointed to distinction in the ways social, institutional and professional values are reproduced in news production and to different (power) relations between journalists and news sources, issues that will be discussed more fully in the next two chapters.

The linguistic analysis of stance markers in this book has been conducted by primarily drawing on the ATTITUDE (Chaps. 5–7) and ENGAGEMENT system (this chapter) of the APPRAISAL framework at the expense of the GRADUATION system. GRADUATION system concerns the intensification and mitigation of ATTITUDE or ENGAGEMENT sources, and GRADUATION resources may also express a writer's or a speaker's stance (Hood, 2010; Martin & Hood, 2005; Martin & White, 2005). The investigation of journalists engaging different voices in news reports in this chapter has been exclusively focused on the categories of 'attest', 'endorse' and 'acknowledge', while ignoring other less frequent categories such as 'affirm', 'entertain', 'distance', 'deny', 'counter', and 'pronounce', etc. Such a decision was, however, made for practical reasons (e.g. limited time, limited resources). This is not to deny or to downplay the significance of other resources in expression of stance in news. Instead of exploring the repertoire of APPRAISAL features which may have ended up with overloaded description of evaluative language in news text (in particular the GRADUATION resources), the restriction of selected APPRAISAL features has provided a detailed insight into the patterns of discursive stances undertaken by Chinese and Australian journalists.

References

Bednarek, M. (2006). Epistemological positioning and evidentiality in English news discourse: A text-driven approach. *Text & Talk, 26*(6), 635–660. https://doi.org/10.1515/text.2006.027.
Bell, A. (1991). *The language of news media*. Oxford/Cambridge, MA: Blackwell.
Biber, D., Johansson, S., Leech, G., Conrad, S., & Finegan, E. (1999). *Longman grammar of spoken and written English*. London: Longman.
Bourdieu, P. (1989). Social space and symbolic power. *Sociological Theory, 7*(1), 14–25.
Bourdieu, P. (1991). *Language and symbolic power*. Cambridge, MA: Harvard University Press.
Caldas-Coulthard, C. R. (1994). On reporting: The representation of speech in factual and factional narratives. In M. Coulthard (Ed.), *Advances in written text analysis* (pp. 295–308). London/New York: Routledge.
Caldas-Coulthard, C. R. (2002). On reporting reporting: The representation of speech in factual and factional narratives. In M. Coulthard (Ed.), *Advances in written text analysis* (pp. 295–308). London/New York: Routledge.
Calsamiglia, H., & Ferrero, C. L. (2003). Role and position of scientific voices: Reported speech in the media. *Discourse Studies, 5*(2), 147–173. https://doi.org/10.1177/14614456030050023O8.
Cotter, C. (2010). *News talk: Investigating the language of journalism*. Cambridge: Cambridge University Press.
Cunningham, S., & Turner, G. (Eds.). (2006). *The media and communications in Australia*. Sydney: Allen & Unwin.
Finkelstein, R. (2012). *Report of the Independent Inquiry into aspects of the media and media regulation (The Finkelstein Report)*. Canberra: Department of Broadband, Communications and the Digital Economy.
Fishman, M. (1980). *Manufacturing the news*. Austin: University of Texas Press.
Fowler, R. (1991). *Language in the news: Discourse and ideology in the press*. London/New York: Routledge.
Gans, H. J. (2004/1979). *Deciding what's news: A study of CBS evening news, NBC nightly news, newsweek, and time*. Illinois: Northwestern University Press.
Hanks, W. F. (2012). Evidentiality in social interaction. *Pragmatics and Society, 3*(2), 169–180.
Hood, S. (2010). *Appraising research: Evaluation in academic writing*. Basingstoke: Palgrave Macmillan.
Hsieh, C.-L. (2008). Evidentiality in Chinese newspaper reports: Subjectivity/objectivity as a factor. *Discourse Studies, 10*(2), 205–229.
Hu, Z. (2003). The Post-WTO restructuring of the Chinese media industries and the consequences of capitalisation. *Javnost-The Public, 10*(4), 19–36.
Iedema, R. (2003). Multimodality, resemiotization: Extending the analysis of discourse as multi-semiotic practice. *Visual Communication, 2*(1), 29–57.
Jones, R. H., & Norris, S. (Eds.). (2005). *Discourse in action: Introducing mediated discourse analysis*. New York: Routledge.

Jullian, P. M. (2011). Appraising through someone else's words: The evaluative power of quotations in news reports. *Discourse & Society, 22*(6), 766–780. https://doi.org/10.1177/0957926511411697.

Lee, C. C., He, Z., & Huang, Y. (2007). Party-market corporatism, clientelism, and media in Shanghai. *The Harvard International Journal of Press/Politics, 12*(3), 21–42.

Lewis, J., Williams, A., & Franklin, B. (2008). A compromised fourth estate? *Journalism Studies, 9*(1), 1–20.

Martin, J. R., & Hood, S. (2005). Invoking attitude: The play of graduation in appraising discourse. *Revista Signos, 38*(58), 195–220.

Martin, J. R., & White, P. R. R. (2005). *The language of evaluation*. Basingstoke: Palgrave Macmillan.

McEnery, T., Xiao, R., & Tono, Y. (2006). *Corpus-based language studies*. London: Routledge.

Mushin, I. (2001). *Evidentiality and epistemological stance: Narrative retelling*. Amsterdam: John Benjamins.

Mushin, I. (2013). Making knowledge visible in discourse: Implications for the study of linguistic evidentiality. *Discourse Studies, 15*(5), 1–19. https://doi.org/10.1177/1461445613501447.

Papandrea, F. (2013). *State of the newspaper industry in Australia*. Canberra: University of Canberra.

Scollon, R. (1998). *Mediated discourse as social interaction: A study of news discourse*. New York: Routledge.

Scollon, R. (2001). *Mediated discourse: The nexus of practice*. London: Routledge.

Sigal, L. V. (1986). Sources make the news. In R. K. Manoff & M. Schudson (Eds.), *Reading the news* (pp. 9–37). New York: Pantheon.

Sleurs, K., Jacobs, G., & Van Waes, L. (2003). Constructing press releases, constructing quotations: A case study. *Journal of Sociolinguistics, 7*(2), 192–212.

Tiffen, R. (1989). *News and power*. Sydney: Allen & Unwin.

Tiffen, R. (2006a). Political economy and news. In S. Cunningham & G. Turner (Eds.), *The media and communications in Australia* (2nd ed., pp. 28–42).

Tiffen, R. (2006b). The press. In S. Cunningham & G. Turner (Eds.), *The media and communications in Australia* (2nd ed., pp. 97–112). Sydney: Allen & Unwin.

Tiffen, R., Jones, P. K., Rowe, D., Aalberg, T., Coen, S., Curran, J., et al. (2014). Sources in the news: A comparative study. *Journalism Studies, 15*(4), 374–391.

Tong, J. (2009). Press self-censorship in China: A case study in the transformation of discourse. *Discourse & Society, 20*(5), 593–612.

Tuchman, G. (1978). *Making news*. New York: Free Press.

Turner, G. (2006). Public relations. In S. Cunningham & G. Turner (Eds.), *The media and communications in Australia* (pp. 227–237). Sydney: Allen and Unwin.

Van Dijk, T. A. (1988). *News as discourse*. Hillsdale, NJ: L. Erlbaum Associates.

Van Dijk, T. A. (1998). *Ideology: A multidisciplinary study*. London: Sage.

Van Dijk, T. A. (2013). The field of epistemic discourse analysis. *Discourse Studies, 15*(5), 497–499.

White, P. R. R. (2003). Beyond modality and hedging: A dialogic view of the language of intersubjective stance. *Text & Talk, 23*(2), 259–284.

White, P. R. R. (2012). Exploring the axiological workings of 'reporter voice' news stories—Attribution and attitudinal positioning. *Discourse, Context & Media, 1*(2), 57–67.

Winfield, B. H., & Peng, Z. (2005). Market or party controls?: Chinese media in transition. *International Communication Gazette, 67*(3), 255–270.

Wodak, R., & Van Dijk, T. A. (Eds.). (2000). *Racism at the top. Parliamentary discourses on ethnic issues in Six European states*. Klagenfurt: Drava.

Zelizer, B. (1989). 'Saying'as collective practice: Quoting and differential address in the news. *Text & Talk, 9*(4), 369–388.

Zelizer, B. (1990). Where is the author in American TV news? On the construction and presentation of proximity, authorship, and journalistic authority. *Semiotica, 80*(1–2), 37–48.

Zhao, Y. (1998). *Media, market, and democracy in China: Between the party line and the bottom line*. Urbana: University of Illinois Press.
Zhao, Y. (2000). From commercialization to conglomeration: The transformation of the Chinese press within the orbit of the party state. *Journal of Communication, 50*(2), 3–26.
Zhao, Y. (2005). The state, the market, and media control in China. In P. Thomas & Z. Nain (Eds.), *Who owns the media: Global trends and local resistance* (pp. 179–212). Penang, Malaysia: Southbound.
Zhao, Y. (2008). *Communication in China: Political economy, power, and conflict*. Lanham, Maryland: Rowman & Littlefield Publishers.

Chapter 9
News Values and Journalistic Stance

9.1 Introduction

The aim of this chapter is to identify and examine the news values that are articulated and prioritized in Chinese and Australian news discourses. To foreground or prioritize different news values can considerably influence journalistic social practices (e.g. stance taking in news writing) since the prioritized news values are transformed to mediational means or cultural tools by which journalism practitioners reconstruct events into newsworthy stories. It is based on this view that the articulation of news values affords means of enabling certain journalistic stances but disabling others in news discourse. The relationship between journalistic stance and news values is that journalistic stances construct the articulated and prioritized news values and at the same time news values constitute cultural tools or mediational means to afford and/or constraint certain stances in news discourse.

Previous studies have suggested that news values exist in the minds of journalists as guidelines for journalists to judge or measure the newsworthiness of events (e.g. Cotter, 2010; Donsbach, 2004; Harrison, 2006; Kepplinger & Ehmig, 2006; J. Palmer, 2000; Richardson, 2007; Schultz, 2007; Strömbäck, Karlsson, & Hopmann, 2012). This depiction of news values has largely focused on journalists' cognitive perception at the expense of the equally important social and discursive aspects of news values. Socially, news values reflect ideologies and priorities that are currently operational in society and news institutions (Bell, 1991). For this reason, news values are hardly neutral, but they reproduce ideologies in news institutional practices and in journalistic social practices. Discursively, news values are not only reflected in but more importantly constituted by discursive resources in the final news texts (Bednarek & Caple, 2012a).

The discursive aspect of news values should not be considered to replace the social or cognitive aspects. Rather, what is present in news texts establishes and sustains news values as much as what is absent. Van Dijk (1991) considers what is "unsaid" may sometimes prove to be more illuminating than what is "said". Hence,

C. Huan, *Journalistic Stance in Chinese and Australian Hard News*,
https://doi.org/10.1007/978-981-13-0791-1_9

the investigation of the discursive facets of news values should be examined in conjunction with their cognitive and social-institutional aspects. The social-institutional aspects stabilize and anchor news values so as to sustain the daily routine of news conceptualization and construction in the newsroom, whereas the cognitive and discursive aspects afford journalists flexibility to accommodate surprisingly unscheduled events and to construct reality through diverse discursive resources.

That said, this research will examine the discursive, cognitive and social-institutional aspects of news values in the Chinese context of print media hard news reporting while in the Australian context only the discursive aspect of news values will be examined, the reason for which is twofold. On one hand, it is because news values and more generally news production have been substantially examined in the Australian context (e.g. Bednarek & Caple, 2012a) and other similar English-speaking contexts such as the U.K. (e.g. Bednarek, 2006; Brighton & Foy, 2007; Harcup & O'Neill, 2001), the U.S. (e.g. Cotter, 2010; Fuller, 1996; Gans, 2004/1979; Herman & Chomsky, 1988) and New Zealand (e.g. Bell, 1991). However, research on news values in the Chinese news discourse has received scant scholarly attention perhaps largely due to restricted access to Chinese news institutions. On the other hand, it is due to the different datasets collected and different methodologies adopted in the investigation of news values in each context. I have conducted ethnographic research in the Chinese news institutions to understand the Chinese press, but relied on secondary sources (e.g. previous studies) to understand the Australian press for practical reasons (e.g. limited time, limited resources).

For these reasons, I will draw on my ethnographic studies in the examination of news values (see Sect. 3.5 in Chap. 3 for methodology) in the Chinese context, but I will examine news values in the Australian context by drawing on previous studies on news values in the Western English speaking context of news production.

9.2 Towards a Taxonomy of News Values

This section presents four prevalent approaches to news values in the research literature (see Caple & Bednarek, 2013 for a detailed review), the chief purpose being to formulate a classification of news values to enable subsequent data coding and analysis and to explore the epistemological underpinnings of news values in each approach.

The first approach primarily conceptualizes news values as properties of news events and as adopted by journalists to determine newsworthiness (Bell, 1991; Cotter, 2010; Galtung & Ruge, 1965; Harcup & O'Neill, 2001; Schultz, 2007). News values are accordingly perceived as existing independently of journalists and embedded in news events (e.g. Conley & Lamble, 2006). Content analysis of news values (e.g. Harrison, 2006) is the prevailing research method in this regard. However, if news values simply reside in news events, then we would have unanimous news values across cultures and media outlets. As mentioned previously, this is not the case according to research findings in the literature. This notwithstanding, the analytical method of content analysis "would not necessarily explain why that story was selected above other potential stories containing similar elements" (Harcup & O'Neill, 2001, p. 268) and it largely ignores the influence of political and economic factors (McQuail, 1994).

To overcome such a caveat, the second approach problematizes "the rationale of news selection in the first place" (Hartley, 1982, p. 79). News values are thus investigated in relation to the social-political and economic conditions, which give rise to news reports (e.g. Allern, 2002; Brighton & Foy, 2007; Donsbach, 2004; Gans, 2004/1979; Herman & Chomsky, 1988; Machin & Niblock, 2006). Cultural and semiotic studies of news (e.g. Hall, 1980; Hall, Critcher, Jefferson, Clarke, & Roberts, 2000; Hartley, 1982) are among those research traditions highlighting the ideological imprint in the process of news selection. What has been manifested in this approach is that news values are diverse, distinctive and dynamic in different cultures and societies. At its extremes, this approach does not dispute that news values (or more broadly the production and distribution of media content) are ideological, but rather takes them for granted as obvious, unproblematic and transparent (Sinclair, 2006, p. 18). Social-cultural conditions are considered in this approach to be deterministic of the meanings of news values. Hence, the dynamism of news values within a certain society or institution is dismissed. This viewpoint has unnecessarily ignored the role played by the major social agents—journalism practitioners—in a society and/or news institution in negotiating meanings of news values. In short, "judgement of news texts might be superficial without a more profound cultural understanding of practice and its 'insider' entailments" (Cotter, 2010, p. 86).

In recognition of such a point, the third approach conducts participant observation of journalistic social practices and/or interviewing of journalists to elicit a list of news values perceived by professional journalism practitioners and those required by news institutions (e.g. Fowler, 1991; Gans, 2004/1979; Van Dijk, 1988). News values in the production processes of news discourse indicate that a range of daily occurring events are tailored by editorial decision-makers to satisfy requirements of newspaper agenda and their current framing in news agencies. In comparison with the first approach, one that perceives news as reflecting or mirroring reality, this approach assumes that journalists reconstruct reality in news items in rapport with news values currently operational in their institution. News values therefore do not presuppose that news is out there, which reporters will endorse or exclude (e.g. Harcup & O'Neill, 2001; McQuail, 1994), but indicate that journalists manufacture news and in so doing reconstruct reality (Cotter, 2010). However, to avoid taking this interpretive stance to its extremes, it is necessary to acknowledge the structural affordances and constraints for journalists to reconstruct the news values of an event, as foregrounded in the second approach.

Resembling the third approach, a fourth approach, which is termed as the discursive approach (Bednarek & Caple, 2012a, 2012b, 2014; Caple & Bednarek, 2013, 2015), sets out to problematize the ways journalists reconstruct events as newsworthy stories. The focal point of analysis of the discursive approach however is on its close examination of discursive construction of news values through semiotic resources such as language and images (Bednarek & Caple, 2014; Caple & Bednarek, 2015). Bednarek and Caple (2014) consider the discursive approach to complement rather than to replace the above three approaches, the reason for which will be explained below.

Since the seminal work by Galtung and Ruge (1965) on news values in Scandinavian news discourse, various taxonomies of news values have been provided by researchers (e.g. Bell, 1991; Brighton & Foy, 2007; Cotter, 2010; Gans, 2004/1979; Harcup & O'Neill, 2001; Harrison, 2006; Machin & Niblock, 2006; Montgomery, 2007; Richardson, 2007; Schulz, 1982; Van Dijk, 1988). As Bednarek and Caple (2012a, p. 40) rightly point out, researchers have not yet reached consensus about the number and the kinds of news values to be covered under the overriding rubric of news values, and news values have been grouped in different ways by researchers. Hence, "it is questionable whether or not they should all be covered by the same term" (Bednarek & Caple, 2012a, p. 40).

Despite different labels of different values, news values are generally categorized into three groups (Bednarek & Caple, 2012a, p. 41; Bell, 1991): values in news actors and events (see Table 9.1), values in the news process (see Table 9.2) and values in the news text. In Table 9.1, I have added one news value—**positivity**—to the list based on my study of news values in the Chinese news discourse. This news value may be not a significant value in the Western context of news discourse, but, as will be shown in Sect. 9.3.1 below, it is fairly salient in the Chinese context.

This study will adopt the list of news values proposed by Bednarek and Caple (2012a) in the examination of the discursive aspect of news values (Table 9.1) mainly because their updated and clearly delimited taxonomy is derived from the

Table 9.1 News values in news actors and events (after Bednarek & Caple, 2012a, p. 41; Caple & Bednarek, 2015)

Negativity	The negative aspects of an event or issue
Positivity	The positive aspects of an event or issue
Timeliness	The relevance of an event or issue in terms of time: recent, ongoing, about to happen or seasonal
Proximity	The geographical and/or cultural nearness of an event or issue
Eliteness	The high status of the individuals, organizations or nations involved in an event or issue
Consonance	The stereotypical aspects of an event or issue; adherence to expectations
Impact	The high significance of an event or issue in terms of its effects or consequences
Novelty	The new and/or unexpected aspects of an event or issue
Superlativeness	The large scope or scale of an event or issue
Personalization	The personal or human interest aspects of an event or issue, including eyewitness reports

Table 9.2 News values in the news process (after Bell, 1991, p. 159)

Continuity	Once a story appears as news it continues as news
Competition	The competition among news institutions for scoops and the competition among stories for coverage
Co-option	Associating one story with a more newsworthy one
Composition	The balance of different sorts of news stories reported in the newspaper.
Predictability	The scheduling of news, such as press conferences to fit the news cycle
Prefabrication	The existence of prefabricated input sources

discursive approach that can afford means to bridge analysis of different aspects of news values.

However, the discursive approach focuses exclusively on values in news actors and events and studies in this area seldom conducts ethnographic studies in newsrooms to investigate news values in the news selection process. It is perhaps in this sense that Bednarek and Caple (2014) argued that the discursive approach was not meant to replace other approaches to news values. For this reason, I will rely on Bell's (1991) list of news values in the news process to examine the news values as highlighted in the news selection process (see Table 9.2). To make it clear, I will rely on Bednarek and Caple's list to study news values in news actors and events, and will rely on Bell's list to study news values in the news selection process.

News values in the news text incorporate three aspects—**clarity**, **brevity** and **colour** (Bednarek & Caple, 2012a, p. 40; Bell, 1991, p. 160)—concerning those news stories that are interpreted by journalists in a clear, accurate and unambiguous fashion and written in a reader-friendly manner. These values in the news text "are more like general characteristics demanded of news story in order to be included" (Bednarek & Caple, 2012a, p. 40). Hence, subsequent analysis will focus on news values in actors and events and those in the news process and will only mention values in the news text in passing when necessary. The above frameworks will be applied not only in relation to my analysis of corpus data but also in relation to other data.

This research adopts a much broader conceptualization of news values, one where news values can relate to the process, the story and events (i.e. on the level of the published news story) whereas Bednarek and Caple (Bednarek & Caple, 2012b, 2014; Caple & Bednarek, 2015) focus on news values on the level of events per se. For instance, I define the news value of personalization in relation to news stories that are discussed as attracting readers, while Bednarek and Caple (Bednarek & Caple, 2012b, 2014; Caple & Bednarek, 2015) define that in relation to news events that are constructed as involving ordinary people. Impact on the level of news event is considered as news events that are constructed as having significant effects, whereas on the level of news story it refers to news stories that are discussed as creating reader/leader feedback and reactions.

The conflation of news values from different approaches should not be considered as problematic. Rather, the resemioticizing of events into newsworthy stories is the result of the mapping of the cognitive, social-institutional and discursive aspects of news values.

9.3 News Values in Chinese and Australian Hard News Reporting

In the following, I will apply the list of news values presented above to investigate news values in Chinese and Australian news discourse. However, due to the different datasets collected in each context, news values in Australian news discourse will be investigated by following the discursive approach (e.g. Bednarek & Caple, 2014) focusing on news values in actors and events in the Australian news corpus. However, the lack of fine-grained corpus tagging sets to reliably code the Chinese data has made it impossible to follow the discursive analysis of news values in Chinese news texts of the kind carried out by Bednarek and Caple (2014). Instead, this research will explore the prioritized news values as discursively constructed in journalistic stance patterns in news texts. For this reason, news values in Chinese and Australian hard news discourse are not meant to be directly comparable across cultures. Additionally, journalistic stance is a key device in enacting news values, though not the only one (Bednarek & Caple, 2012a). In other words, I am unable to examine those news values that are not typically construed in journalistic stances, such as proximity or timeliness.

Values in the news process to be briefly discussed in Australian news discourse are not based on direct observation of newsroom practices, but premised on deduction in light of stance patterns. I will take the Australian bushfire sub-corpus as an example to examine how news values are (re)articulated in stance patterns surrounding part-of-speech tags, lexical semantics, polarity orientations and stance patterns. This is because on one hand the corpus tool—W-Matrix—can only process a limited amount of texts each time and on the other my study has not found significant difference in terms of news values exhibited in each sub-corpus. In contrast, news values in the news selection process in Chinese news discourse are based on my participant observation in one typical Chinese news institution.

Bednarek and Caple, taking a discursive approach to news values (e.g. Bednarek & Caple, 2012a, 2014), "assume that it is difficult to determine an event's fixed or inherent newsworthiness and that, rather, events are given newsworthiness by the media, via the construction of particular news values" (Bednarek & Caple, 2014, p. 5). Taking this point further, I argue that the newsworthiness of an event, albeit difficult to be pinned down, is governed by journalists' professional experience in relation to their awareness of the social-institutional affordances and constraints, and that news values are eventually constructed by semiotic resources in news reporting. The articulation of news values constitutes mediational means by which journalism practitioners undertake stances.

9.3.1 News Values in Chinese Hard News Reporting

This section firstly investigates the prominent news values as inscribed in media policy documents in a Chinese news institution (Sect. 9.3.1.1). Secondly, it examines news values in Chinese print media hard news as spelt out in daily editorial meetings (Sect. 9.3.1.2). Thirdly, it probes into the ways news values are prioritized by journalists (Sect. 9.3.1.3). Lastly, it briefly explores the ways salient news values are projected on stance patterns (Sect. 9.3.1.4).

9.3.1.1 News Values as Inscribed in News Policy Documents

This section elaborates on news values as rubrics adopted by the news institution under investigation to evaluate daily news stories. In addition to other criteria necessary for the operation of news institution, policy makers prescribe a range of news values as yardsticks for the news review panel to evaluate news reports published every day. The news institution under investigation lists several criteria to select the so-called "best" news stories. The policy documents under investigation exclusively refer to two documents. One is the *Regulation of Performance Assessment* (hence Regulation 1), and the other is the *Regulation of Rewards and Penalties* (hence Regulation 2).

The prioritized news values in news events and actors in the 'Regulation 1' are translated and quoted as such: "Top news stories must 1) report on a significant event or issue (in most cases, it refers to a political event); 2) reflect key and hot social issues concerned by readers; 3) result in great public impact among readers; 4) arouse attentions of high rank officials; 5) be widely cited by other news agencies; 6) create positive social benefits; 7) be reported timely, or 8) be novel."

The more criteria a news story satisfies, the more newsworthy it is. Significant news events refer to the reporting of those activities concerning power elites or superlative events with significant consequences. Hence, they realize the news values of **eliteness** and **superlativeness** depending on the nature of reported events. Key and hot social issues refer to those events that are close and relevant to the life of ordinary readers and as such can easily arouse readers' attention or emotional reactions. The news values of **consonance** and **personalization** are thus emphasized. The **impact** of a news story is judged by reference to three standards. Tentatively, I name the first standard as market standard as it highlights the impact among readers. The second standard is political standard since it emphasizes the praise or criticism from authorities. The third standard is professional standard because it brings into view the influence among other Chinese media. As prescribed in the official documents, the selection of top news reports needs to consider all these professional, political and market factors. Other news values in news events as prioritized in the official document incorporate **positivity**, **timeliness** and **novelty**. It is noteworthy that the news value of **negativity**, as frequently provoked in Australian hard news reporting, is neither brought into focus in news editorial meetings nor is it highlighted in institutional documents. Rather, **positivity** receives special attention in evaluating top news as prescribed in official documents. Corpus findings in Chaps. 6–8 have revealed that those are often positively portrayed in news stories are the powerful (e.g. government officials), the reasons for which will be discussed in Sect. 9.3.1.4 below and also in Sect. 9.4.

The salient news values in news selection process in the 'Regulation 1' are mainly demonstrated by the following two criteria: "1) the best news stories are scoops or present exclusive content, exclusive opinions or exclusive interpretation in comparison with those reported by other local news institutions; and 2) the best continuous news report must incorporate dynamic news and the predictable superlative news". Exclusive news stories are judged by reference to the news value of **competition** in news selection process whereas continuous news stories are judged by reference to the **predictability** and **co-option** of news. Predictable news stories often concern significant official events such as national congress or official activities of local/national leaders. Dynamic news stories mostly refer to those related to the life of ordinary people. For instance, food safety issues are significant news events for journalists. They are dynamic because they happen unpredictably but frequently in China. Hence, news stories about food safety can be considered as continuous, albeit irregularly.

According to the 'Regulation 2', the author of the top news selected in tune with the above listed criteria will be rewarded a bonus of 300 CNY (approx. 50 USD). Adding to such a daily incentive, top news will be selected on a monthly and yearly basis with increased amount of bonus, and national-award winning news may be rewarded up to 100,000 CNY (20,000 USD). To strive for such economic benefits and the so-called "professional award", Chinese journalists have no choice but to conform to the news values as preferred by the authority.

9.3.1.2 News Values as Highlighted in Daily Editorial Meetings

The Chinese news institution under investigation held two editorial meetings every day. The morning session started from 11.00 a.m. and normally lasted for 30 min. The afternoon session started from 4.00 p.m. and lasted for one to one and half hours. The time was said to be "*unshakeable by thunder*" (*léi dă bù dòng*), meaning these two editorial sessions start on time every day and are not to be altered under any circumstances. Only the head of each department could attend the editorial meetings, while journalists and editors were not encouraged to do so. In fact, the limited space of the meeting room could only accommodate the head of each department. The morning session served to present and determine the everyday budget/list of news that each head had received so far from journalists in their respective editorial department. The afternoon session mainly focused on reviewing the newspaper published on that day, and arranging news stories on each page to be published in the next day. After the review of their own newspaper, the review panel would devote substantial efforts to compare the quality of news stories against that in other local competing newspapers. The main points of the daily afternoon

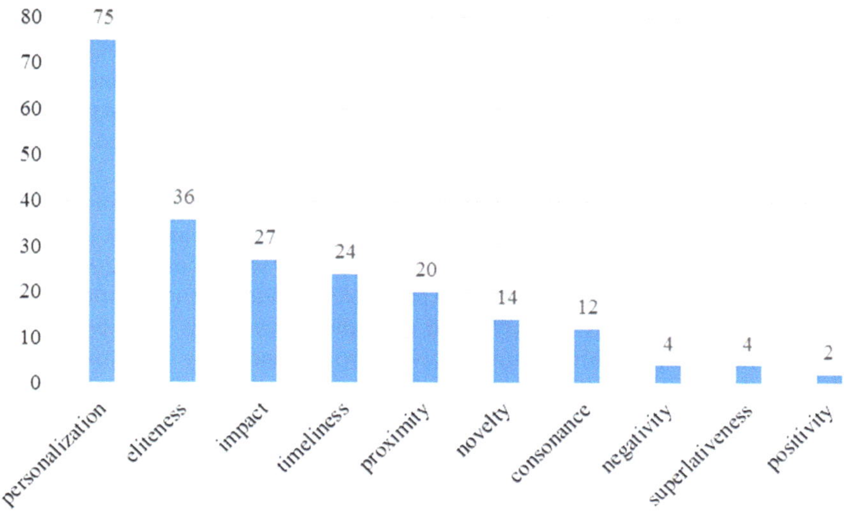

Fig. 9.1 News values in news events and actors highlighted in editorial meeting

editorial session would be summarized within 70 Chinese characters by an administrative staff and sent via mobile phone to all staff in the news institution. The set of data analyzed in this part is constituted by such short messages.

Overall, the results of analysis (see Fig. 9.1) show that daily editorial meeting prioritized news values in news events and actors ($N = 218$) over news values in news selection process ($N = 46$). Among news values in news events and actors, the value of **personalization** ($N = 75$) occurs more frequently than do others. The number here means the number of time each news value is mentioned in the editorial meeting.

The value of personalization concerns the attraction of reader's attention and interest of reading. For instance, the editor-in-chief (EIC) commented on one news story about an exposition and said "the news report on [X] expo needs to focus on what readers are concerned with most". In his another comment on a report about an official field trip of the CPC (Communist Party of China) leaders Xi Jinping and Li Keqiang, he said "news reports concerning field trips of Xi Jinping [the General Secretary of the CPC] and Li Keqiang [the Premier] should appeal to readers". Even the reports authored by local official leaders will need to accommodate an appealing style, as the EIC commented, "the original report by local municipal leaders on the first page is tediously long. Our journalists need to take actions to appeal to our readers".

The desk editor whom I interviewed told me that they used to adopt a stereotyped style (八股—bāgǔ) of news reporting of official events, but their newspaper shifted away to emphasizing the attraction of readers' attention. The stereotyped style (八股—bāgǔ) means that the news stories are written in a bureaucratic tone or a clichéd style with boring news content. This shift of focus has thus prioritized the news value of **personalization** in news events and actors, as the desk editor explained, one reason for this shift being that "if ordinary citizens are not interested in reading our news stories, then we are unable to disseminate the official ideology to them". That is to say, to disseminate the official ideology to ordinary citizens, especially to the young generation of readers, the Chinese press, at least the Party paper under investigation, is reconfiguring the priority of news values.

The second most frequently emphasized news value concerns the parameter of **eliteness** ($N = 36$). It involves significant national events such as the 18th CPC's national congress, national figures such as Mo Yan (the winner of the 2012 Nobel Prize in Literature), local Mayors and experts, etc. In selecting news sources and major news makers, the EIC emphasized that "the interviewees must be authoritative and have a high social status". News reports concerning local or national leaders were supposed to appear on the most prominent cover page of the newspaper, regardless of the newsworthiness of their activities. Failing to do so would be criticized or sometimes censored by the managing editors. For instance, a report on a regular field trip of local leaders did not appear on the cover page of the newspaper, and in the editorial meeting the EIC criticized such an arrangement by saying that "the report on the field trip of the provincial secretary of the CPC should appear on the cover page of the newspaper", though he later admitted that this report was not newsworthy by professional standard. In so doing, he prioritized the news value of **eliteness** over other news values and also relinquished professional perception of news values to the social-institutional priorities of news values.

The parameters of **impact** ($N = 27$) and **timeliness** ($N = 24$) were also significant. In contrast with **impact** as defined in the Anglo-American context, one that refers to the influence of news stories among readers, it also means the positive or negative feedback provided by official leaders in the Chinese context. A news story that has been praised by authorities is considered as a good story with high impact, at least this is what the EIC indicated. For instance, when commenting on two news stories, he said "[names], Ministers of the provincial Publicity Department and the review panel of provincial Publicity Department, have positively appraised our report on the 18th Party congress". In contrast, a news story that as criticized by authorities would be considered as poorly written with undesirable impact, as suggested by the EIC's comment on a news story "leaders of the municipal CPC have criticized the poor quality of report on the visit of foreign officials."

The news value of **timeliness** incorporates two aspects. On one hand, it concerns daily deadline in newsroom, as emphasized by the EIC, "all reporters and editors should strictly follow the daily deadline for distributing the press proof of their respective page". On the other hand, it relates to the timely report of recent news events since delayed news reports are considered to be detrimental to the reputation of newspaper. For instance, the EIC said in his comment on a news story, "the delayed news reports on PM2.5 and migratory birds are detrimental to the authoritativeness/reputation of our newspaper".

The value of **proximity** ($N = 20$) was found important as well. My interviews with journalists and senior editors of the news institution reveal that journalists has internalized this concept and that senior editors consider proximity as a chief determinative factor for the selection of news events occurring in a remote place. They have developed a jargon for such a concept, "luòdì", translated literally as "to land", meaning to establish relevance of the event to the local city. Only those news events happened elsewhere that can establish a relevance to local readership will be reported.

As for the news values in the news selection process, the four most prominent ones are **competition** ($N = 20$), **continuity** ($N = 13$), **predictability** ($N = 7$) and **co-option** ($N = 5$) whereas other news values were less frequently mentioned. An exclusive news report by journalists will be rewarded by their affiliated newspapers while an ignorance of news in comparison with other local newspapers will be fined by the news institutions in which they are working. News stories that are a continuation of previous reports (i.e. continuity) more easily attract reader attention. Predictable or prescheduled events relate primarily to prominent activities involving high rank officials at national or local levels. The priority of such events is consonant with the current press system in China where Chinese newspapers are prohibited from criticizing the Party committee with which they are affiliated to direct editorial censorship (Zhao, 2000). Hence, Chinese press are required by the CPC to promote official policies and to construct an image of a harmonious and consensual society in order to serve the interests of the Party and the local/national council. The prescheduled events are mutually beneficial for both official news makers and journalists, since the authorities publicize the official ideology while journalists obtain stories to fill the space in their newspaper. Such events also foreshadow potential **continuous** news, which may occasion scoops or afford journalists the means to delve new angles by framing them in relation to the prominent theme in consonance with reader expectation. The priority of **competition** reflects news institutional pursuit of economic profits.

9.3.1.3 News Values as Perceived by Chinese Journalists

While the above investigation of news values in official documents and those highlighted in news editorial meetings may reveal the kind of news values promoted at the social-institutional level, it tells us little about how journalists perceive them in the process of news reporting. In this research, I have exclusively drawn on semi-structured interviews with the Chinese journalists to elicit their perception of news values. I am certainly aware of alternative means to do so, for instance, through large scale surveys of the kind conducted by Strömbäck et al. (2012). This strand of research would nevertheless require the participation of a substantial number of Chinese journalists, to which I have no access.

"Working journalists tend to become uncharacteristically inarticulate when asked for their own philosophy of news values. Answers tend to be like 'It's obvious' or 'You just know'" (Brighton & Foy, 2007, p. 14). This is the case in my interviews with Chinese journalists as well. For instance, a junior journalist (Q) told me, "for me, the news value of an event is sometimes just an instinct/intuition", and a senior journalist (T) said, "it's all about your professional experience". Another senior journalist (P), elaborating on her professional experience, told me:

> For predictable news, you will know where news values may situate after you check its background information, and then what you need to do is go and find these news values on site. For unpredictable news, such as a car accident, you will already have had a general picture in mind about what questions to ask.

Depending on the genre of news journalists frequently report (e.g. political, economic, infotainment), their professional perception of news values may differ. For instance, a senior journalist (S), who has been working for eleven years on reporting political/official events in relation to the municipal leaders, said "to decide the newsworthiness of events is an important and basic skill for journalists and if you have been working on reporting political news for a long time, you will have accumulated some experience", and she added, "if you are not sure about the news values in an event, then you can ask the responsible government department about what the significance and key points are of the policies or conference at issue". In this sense, news values are not purely cognitive, but negotiable between journalists and authorities.

The Chinese journalists whom I interviewed overall prioritized news values in news events and actors ($N = 20$) over values in the news selection process ($N = 3$). The low frequency of values in the news selection process is hardly unexpected since journalists were not encouraged to participate into the daily editorial meetings where news stories were selected. Among news values in news events and actors, my interviewees, akin to editorial meetings, prioritized the two values of **personalization** ($N = 5$) and **eliteness** ($N = 5$), whereas other news values in this regard were less salient. The journalist Q whom I have mentioned earlier said the increasing emphasis on the news value of personalization was caused by increasingly fierce competition from local newspapers. "With the increasing competition in newspapers, reporting on political news now needs to appeal to readers and find out what readers are concerned with most, rather than report in the previous 'bāgǔ' style (stereotyped writing)", she said, adding that "some political news tend to highlight the presence of leaders rather than focusing on events. Some procedural official conferences having no news values are now covered within 200–300 words, but previously we needed to make the procedures more complicated." Reporting on news without any news values, as she said, was due to the institutional influences upon them and their news reports. That is to say, these news stories should not have been published had journalists not been constrained by external influences. On one hand, this finding suggests that 'external influences' are a news value as well. On the other hand, it indicates that Chinese journalists have surrendered their professional judgement of newsworthiness of events to the social-institutional priorities of news values. Involving professionals and/or official authorities in news reports was considered by a junior journalist (L) as a means of increasing the news values in news events and actors, and also of enhancing the credibility of news events.

9.3.1.4 News Values as Reproduced in Discursive Stances

To maintain public trust in Chinese media, Chinese journalism practitioners need to sustain their professional identity by exercising oversight on the actions of the Party and government officials on behalf of ordinary citizens. Failure to do so will result in the media losing public credibility, while any inappropriate discursive actions to deal with the political issues in the news reports may bring in political risks to the institution or journalists themselves (Tong, 2009). News institutions and journalists alike therefore need to develop practical strategies to navigate a way through such a conflicting situation. Maneuvering discursive resources is one such key strategy.

The corpus findings in Chap. 6 have shown that Chinese journalists are more likely to provoke people's emotions in mediating risk communication than their Australian peers are. However, Chinese journalists mediate the emotions of ordinary citizens and those of authorities in distinctive ways. In mediating the positive affect in reporting risk events, Chinese journalists often show how caring and considerate the prominent figures (e.g. government/CPC leaders) are towards those victims in risk situations, but the positive emotions of ordinary citizens are often illustrated by how satisfied they are with the efforts of government in battling risks, or by how fond they are of certain entities (e.g. food). In mediating the negative affect, officials show their grief, but the ordinary citizens often express their worries and fears.

When judging human behaviours in risk communication, Chinese journalists tend to positively judge the authorities by reference to their capacity in dealing with risks, but negatively judge the risk makers by reference to their unethicalness and unlawfulness.

While Australian journalists tend to downplay their presence on site in reporting risk events, Chinese journalists prefer to augment their presence by frequently deploying authorial 'attest' sources (e.g. reporters saw…). In so doing, Chinese journalists increase the credibility of their reports and they are more likely to produce an exclusive news report. In contrast, ordinary news makers, although frequently acknowledged by Chinese journalists, are considered less reliable than official sources. However, framing risk makers in negative ways construct news values of **negativity** and **personalization** and framing power elites in positive ways construct news values of **positivity** and **eliteness**.

In short, Chinese journalists undertake different stances to please those powerful elites by means of constructing news values of **eliteness** and **positivity**, among others, to please their readership through construing news values of **personalization** and **proximity**, inter alia, to sustain their professional identity and to maintain the institutional pursuit of public mandate via casting a negative light onto those lower-level state officials, corporations and ordinary citizens who break the law or infringe social morality.

9.3.2 News Values in Australian Hard News Reporting

Due to the different datasets collected and different methodologies adopted in the investigation of news values in each context, the results are not directly comparable. However, the cognitive, discursive and social-institutional aspects of news values in Chinese news discourse have shown a clear and consistent pattern of prioritizing the news values of **personalization**, **eliteness** and **positivity** in news actors and events. Although the cognitive and social-institutional aspects of news values in the Australian context are not examined in this research, the discursive aspect of news values is expected to suggest the prioritized news values in the news selection process in Australian news discourse.

The frequency of particular POS tags (Table 9.3), semantics (Table 9.4) and APPRAISAL features will be interpreted as revealing associated news values. However, to avoid oversimplifying the investigation of such a nuanced and complex phenomenon as news values, the quantitative frequency will be complemented by qualitative analysis of stretches of text that shows how particular expressions operate in context. This is because an interpretive conclusion about news values can hardly be read off the mere occurrence of a lexical item.

In order to produce valid findings I will provide snapshot of some frequent POS tags and semantic tags in the Australian corpus and intend to find the coupling between lexical, semantic patterns and their corresponding news values. Figures 9.2, 9.3, 9.4, 9.5 and 9.6 present some most salient words surrounding singular weekday noun, adverbs after nominal head, singular month noun, singular temporal noun and the *-ing* form of lexical verbs respectively. The reason to group them together is that they all refer to recent or ongoing actions and as such they are more likely to realize the news value of **timeliness**, indicating that the reported bushfire events are relevant to the readership in terms of time.

Figures 9.7 and 9.8 illustrate the ten most salient POS tags surrounding singular noun of direction and singular locative noun. These POS tags refer to a location in Australia where bushfires were spotted or ongoing, and as such they realize the news value of **proximity**, indicating that the news stories are relevant to the readers in terms of geographical location.

'NNU2' (plural unit of measurement), 'DAR' (comparative after-determiner) and 'MC' (cardinal number) have been presented in Figs. 9.9, 9.10 and 9.11 respectively. They are presented together because they concern the extent or magnitude of the reported bushfires through emphasizing the size of land in hectares impacted by bushfire in question (Fig. 9.9) or the number of firefighters was required to contain the bushfire (Figs. 9.10 and 9.11). The news stories were therefore intensified and the news values of **superlativeness** and **impact** were realized therein. In an indirect way, the considerable impact of magnitude bushfires at issue expressed how negative and terrifying these events were and as such construed the news value of **negativity**.

However, this is not to suggest that there is a one-to-one correspondence between lexical choices and their associated news values. Instead, the relationship

Table 9.3 Top 20 key POS tags in the bushfire corpus against the BNC written sampler

N.	Item	Glosses	O1	%1	O2	%2	LL
1	NPD1	singular weekday noun	364	0.61	408	0.04+	1057.72
2	ND1	singular noun of direction	376	0.63	700	0.07+	836.03
3	NNU2	plural unit of measurement	147	0.25	251	0.03+	344.34
4	RA	adverb, after nominal head	97	0.16	167	0.02+	226.12
5	NPM1	singular month noun	234	0.39	1231	0.13+	194.53
6	VBN	been	354	0.60	2552	0.26+	169.57
7	NNL1	singular locative noun	103	0.17	339	0.04+	148.05
8	VBDR	were	406	0.69	3319	0.34+	145.10
9	VVG	-ing participle of lexical verb	1202	2.03	13,564	1.40+	136.57
10	NN2	plural common noun	4087	6.90	55,665	5.75+	119.74
11	DAR	comparative after-determiner	150	0.25	875	0.09+	106.41
12	VH0	have, base form (finite)	341	0.58	2971	0.31+	102.60
13	VVD	past tense of lexical verb	1788	3.02	22,749	2.35+	96.65
14	VVN	past participle of lexical verb	1902	3.21	24,675	2.55+	88.02
15	MC	cardinal number, neutral for number	1085	1.83	13,154	1.36+	82.11
16	CSN	than (as conjunction)	141	0.24	981	0.10+	72.70
17	NN	common noun, neutral for number	320	0.54	3059	0.32+	72.14
18	VHZ	has	307	0.52	2901	0.30+	71.95
19	II	general preposition	4537	7.66	65,675	6.78+	60.09
20	NNT1	temporal noun, singular	387	0.65	4177	0.43+	54.36

Note Column O1 represents observed frequency in this sub-corpus; O2 is observed frequency in normalized data in BNC written sampler; %1 and %2 values show relative frequencies in the texts. '+' indicates overuse in O1 relative to O2, while '−' indicates underuse in O1 relative to O2. 'LL' shows the log-likelihood (LL) value, according to which the figure is sorted. The LL value expresses how many times more likely the POS tags are in the Bushfire corpus than those in the BNC written sampler. The higher the LL value is, the more likely a corresponding POS tag is in the Bushfire corpus

may be that of one-to-many in some cases. For instance, the common nouns in Fig. 9.12 involve powerful individuals (e.g. firefighters and authorities) and thus realize the news value of **eliteness**. Commons nouns in Fig. 9.13 involve the presentation of human faces in news reporting on bushfire events and accordingly the news value of **personalization** is realized. When these common nouns collocate with cardinal numbers (e.g. 300 firefighters, hundreds of people), they may express the news values of **impact** and **superlativeness**.

Such an analysis should not be considered as exhaustive, because more in-depth analysis of text may reveal other news values as inscribed in the news texts. For instance, a scrutiny of the time span of the reported events shows that all news stories have been reported on hotter and drier seasons of the year in Australia. Hence, it was likely that the reported event was to some extent 'predictable' to the journalists and that there might have been already other stories that were reported previously. In this sense, the possible news values that were realize include

Table 9.4 Top 20 most frequent semantic tags in the bushfire corpus against the BNC written sampler

N.	Item	O1	%1	O2	%2	LL	Glosses
1	O4.6+	2282	3.85	988	0.10+	9131.45	Temperature: hot/on fire
2	A1.1.2	538	0.91	815	0.08+	1348.07	Damaging and destroying
3	W4	352	0.59	770	0.08+	704.09	Weather
4	Q2.1	1106	1.87	7024	0.73+	678.51	Speech: communicative
5	H4	469	0.79	1592	0.16+	654.54	Residence
6	T1.3	1173	1.98	8327	0.86+	580.35	Time: period
7	A15-	223	0.38	370	0.04+	531.13	Danger
8	G1.1	652	1.10	3542	0.37+	516.92	Government
9	N5.1+++	76	0.13	1	0.00+	423.09	Entire; maximum
10	N3.6	124	0.21	93	0.01+	422.20	Measurement: area
11	O4.6	126	0.21	110	0.01+	405.93	Temperature
12	A5.1—	104	0.18	54	0.01+	396.89	Evaluation: bad
13	M4	258	0.44	843	0.09+	373.38	Sailing, swimming, etc.
14	W2	58	0.10	0	0.00+	330.94	Light
15	M7	744	1.26	5888	0.61+	288.33	Places
16	M6	1078	1.82	9859	1.02+	280.67	Location and direction
17	M3	347	0.59	2171	0.22+	218.63	Vehicles/transport on land
18	E3-	283	0.48	1647	0.17+	201.52	Violent/angry
19	W5	88	0.15	225	0.02+	156.99	Green issues
20	A13	26	0.04	0	0.00+	148.35	Degree

364 occurrences.				Extend context
but guests were evacuated on	Friday		. </p> <p> " Every now and ag	1 More | Full
in the valley . </p> <p> On	Friday		, Ms Keneally told Warringah	2 More | Full
ions of NSW (LGSA) said on	Monday		the decision should wait unti	3 More | Full
The trip flare was found on	Saturday		by two women riding their hor	4 More | Full
larney Vale , was charged on	Sunday night		over a fire at Kangoo Road ,	5 More | Full
Kangoo Road , Somersby , on	Saturday		. </p> <p> On that day staff	6 More | Full
already been refused bail on	Sunday		during a brief hearing in whi	7 More | Full
would not have saved them on	Sunday		, given half the properties l	8 More | Full
the delays in the system on	Sunday		but says only one-way warning	9 More | Full
Forest at 8.30pm (AEST) on	Friday		, with fire crews backburning	10 More | Full

Fig. 9.2 Snapshot of the ten most prominent NPD1 (singular weekday noun)

timeliness and **consonance** in news events and actors and **predictability** and **continuity** in news selection process. However, from the text alone, this is difficult to infer, and without investigating the news production processes in the Australian newsroom or actually looking at whether or not similar stories had previously been published, it can only remain a hypothesis.

Adding to the realization of news values in the frequent POS tags, semantic patterns can reveal the prioritized news values in reporting bushfire events as well.

97 occurrences.			Extend context	
<p> The blaze started just before	2pm	, NSW Rural Fire Service spokeswoma	1 More	Full
year-old near his Katoomba home at	8.30am	yesterday over a blaze that spread	2 More	Full
ire broke out in Frenchs Forest at	8.30pm	(AEST) on Friday , with fire crew	3 More	Full
> <p> The blaze was reported about	11.30pm	on Tuesday night . </p> <p> Mr Irvi	4 More	Full
ition following the incident about	5pm	(WST) yesterday.They will be flow	5 More	Full
and rushed to leave the area about	10.30pm	yesterday . </p> <p> Others , howev	6 More	Full
an Morgan was still on his roof at	1am	on Friday morning hosing down as th	7 More	Full
ire continued to burn . </p> <p> "	1am	and I 'm on my roof hosing it down	8 More	Full
ets been full of fire trucks since	9pm	, on my way back out to keep watch	9 More	Full
southerly breeze took hold around	9.15pm	. </p> <p> Residents were initially	10 More	Full

Fig. 9.3 Snapshot of the ten most prominent RA (adverb, after nominal head)

234 occurrences.			Extend context	
	December 9	, 2007 <p> More than 300 firefig	1 More	Full
within containment lines . </p>	February 16	, 2009 <p> THOUSANDS of elderly	2 More	Full
ice over expansion plans . </p>	February 16	, 2009 <p> Any decision on allow	3 More	Full
eing built in such areas . </p>	October 16	, 2008 <p> A discarded army flar	4 More	Full
e defence spokesman said . </p>	February 10	, 2009 <p> A 31-YEAR-OLD man cha	5 More	Full
Farrell will apply for bail on	February 16	. </p> <p> The NSW Premier , Nat	6 More	Full
n fuelled flames in the west 12	February 2011	The Australian Weather alone did	7 More	Full
engagement , Suellen Shea . In	May last	year , a revised edition of WA '	8 More	Full
ntrolled burning policy'' since	February 2000	, because frequent burning ` ` f	9 More	Full
t not being done , '' he says .	October 25	, 2011 <p> MORE than 100 firefig	10 More	Full

Fig. 9.4 Snapshot of the ten most prominent NPM1 (singular month noun)

387 occurrences.			Extend context	
on their property through the	day	but CFS crews were trying to k	1 More	Full
said the family had spent the	day	making sure they were " prepar	2 More	Full
a escarpment . </p> <p> And a	week	after Victoria 's bushfire dis	3 More	Full
dreadful lessons of the past	fortnight	. " </p> <p> Only one road run	4 More	Full
lodged in 2005 , prior to her	time	as planning minister , but she	5 More	Full
n Saturday . </p> <p> On that	day	staff at a nearby car dealersh	6 More	Full
avaged outer Perth early this	week	AUTHORITIES have blamed powerf	7 More	Full
estroying 72 homes early this	week	. But apart from extreme weath	8 More	Full
e fire started shortly before	midday	in the hillside suburbs of Kel	9 More	Full
alian revealed throughout the	week	, a ` ` no burn'' policy imple	10 More	Full

Fig. 9.5 Snapshot of the ten most prominent NNT1 (temporal noun, singular)

1202 occurrences.			Extend context	
han 300 firefighters are	battling	three blazes still burnin	1 More	Full
tling three blazes still	burning	out of control on South A	2 More	Full
y roads closed and smoke	drifting	across the island and ove	3 More	Full
d the wind was gradually	blowing	the blaze from Flinders C	4 More	Full
eir 18-month-old son are	staying	at the property , but gue	5 More	Full
said . </p> <p> " We 're	expecting	it to (hit) at some sta	6 More	Full
said spot fires had been	flaring	on their property through	7 More	Full
e day but CFS crews were	trying	to keep them under contro	8 More	Full
family had spent the day	making sure	they were " prepared " wh	9 More	Full
ers had been involved in	fighting	the blaze over the past f	10 More	Full

Fig. 9.6 Snapshot of the ten most prominent VVG (-ing participle of lexical verb)

376 occurrences.			Extend context
urning out of control on	South Australia	's Kangaroo Island , with	1 More | Full
ha . </p> <p> A fire on	South Australia	's Yorke Peninsula at War	2 More | Full
and blocks . </p> <p> At	North Turramurra	- a peninsula surrounded	3 More | Full
xford Falls in Sydney 's	north	. </p> <p> The developmen	4 More | Full
ed a bushfire on the NSW	south	coast but the Defence Dep	5 More | Full
on fuelled flames in the	west	12 February 2011 The Aust	6 More | Full
ue Mountains community ,	west of Sydney	. </p> <p> Police arreste	7 More | Full
a bushfire in Sydney 's	north	, but say properties in t	8 More | Full
oad , Fitzpatrick Avenue	West	, Grace Avenue and Sorlie	9 More | Full
imum temperatures in the	southwest	hovering around the mid-	10 More | Full

Fig. 9.7 Snapshot of the ten most prominent ND1 (singular noun of direction)

103 occurrences.			Extend context
ontinuing to burn at Western	River	Conservation Park , D'Estrees	1 More | Full
the area , while the Western	River	fire had burned 2140 ha . </p	2 More | Full
ar where a fire broke out at	Mount	Penang Parkland shortly after	3 More | Full
ide Cliff Drive and Birdwood	Avenue	in Katoomba . </p> <p> Do you	4 More | Full
y Wellman Road , Fitzpatrick	Avenue	West , Grace Avenue and Sorli	5 More | Full
zpatrick Avenue West , Grace	Avenue	and Sorlie Road , the NSW Rur	6 More | Full
hris Irvine said the fire at	Mt Roland	was estimated to have scorche	7 More | Full
ble country on the slopes of	Mt Roland	, about 10 kilometres west of	8 More | Full
orth of the Nicholls Rivulet	Road	. </p> <p> Senior ranger Mike	9 More | Full
between Kununurra , the Gibb	River	Road and El Questro Wildernes	10 More | Full

Fig. 9.8 Snapshot of the ten most prominent NNL1 (singular locative noun)

147 occurrences.			Extend context
fires had burnt more than 21,000	hectares	of the island , with the small co	1 More | Full
D'Estrees fire had burned 9,400	hectares	of bush in an area where access w	2 More | Full
ders Chase fire had burned 4,100	hectares	and crews were planning further b	3 More | Full
bushfire burnt out 4,000 square	metres	of bush and took two hours to ext	4 More | Full
ing winds today of around 30- 40	kilometres	[an hour] . These are	5 More | Full
chool . </p> <p> It destroyed 19	hectares	of bush and took firefighters abo	6 More | Full
st , has ravaged more than 2,400	hectares	in the South East Forest National	7 More | Full
imated to have scorched about 50	hectares	so far . </p> <p> " It is burning	8 More | Full
e slopes of Mt Roland , about 10	kilometres	west of Sheffield , " he said . <	9 More | Full
ire that has blackened about 200	hectares	of buttongrass plains and bush ,	10 More | Full

Fig. 9.9 Snapshot of the ten most prominent NNU2 (plural unit of measurement)

150 occurrences.			Extend context
December 9 , 2007 <p>	More	than 300 firefighters are battli	1 More | Full
CFS) said the fires had burnt	more	than 21,000 hectares of the isla	2 More | Full
nd they come in and throw a bit	more	water on it , " he said . </p> <	3 More | Full
ate statement from the CFS said	more	than 300 firefighters , five wat	4 More | Full
<p> It is understood there are	less	than 30 permanent residents of t	5 More | Full
f those already there need much	more	scrutiny to ensure our communiti	6 More | Full
t couple of years . And that 's	more	houses than we 've lost since th	7 More | Full
eas has risen sharply . ` ` The	more	activities humans conduct in bus	8 More | Full
es humans conduct in bush , the	more	fires there will be , ' ' says FE	9 More | Full
he says . October 25 , 2011 <p>	MORE	than 100 firefighters and a wate	10 More | Full

Fig. 9.10 Snapshot of the ten most prominent DAR (comparative after-determiner)

1085 occurrences.			Extend context		
December 9 ,	2007	<p> More than 300 firefighters	1	More	Full
cember 9 , 2007 <p> More than	300	firefighters are battling thre	2	More	Full
300 firefighters are battling	three	blazes still burning out of co	3	More	Full
the fires had burnt more than	21,000	hectares of the island , with	4	More	Full
e authorities to get an extra	300	firefighters to help fight the	5	More	Full
necessary numbers , so around	300	extra firefighters are needed	6	More	Full
t from the CFS said more than	300	firefighters , five water bomb	7	More	Full
more than 300 firefighters ,	five	water bombing aircraft and six	8	More	Full
ve water bombing aircraft and	six	surveillance aircraft were cur	9	More	Full
rking on the fires . </p> <p>	Three	fires are continuing to burn a	10	More	Full

Fig. 9.11 Snapshot of the ten most prominent MC (cardinal number)

4087 occurrences.			Extend context		
9 , 2007 <p> More than 300	firefighters	are battling three blazes st	1	More	Full
ne of the island 's tourist	resorts	. </p> <p> The Country Fire	2	More	Full
re Service (CFS) said the	fires	had burnt more than 21,000 h	3	More	Full
ay " still at risk " , many	roads	closed and smoke drifting ac	4	More	Full
ver the mainland . </p> <p>	Discussions	were being held with interst	5	More	Full
g held with interstate fire	authorities	to get an extra 300 firefigh	6	More	Full
orities to get an extra 300	firefighters	to help fight the blazes . <	7	More	Full
efighters to help fight the	blazes	. </p> <p> James Knight , co	8	More	Full
ally blowing the blaze from	Flinders	Chase National Park towards	9	More	Full
aying at the property , but	guests	were evacuated on Friday . <	10	More	Full

Fig. 9.12 Snapshot of the ten most prominent NN2 (plural common noun)

320 occurrences.			Extend context		
refighters , five water bombing	aircraft	and six surveillance aircraft we	1	More	Full
g aircraft and six surveillance	aircraft	were currently working on the fi	2	More	Full
, 2009 <p> THOUSANDS of elderly	people	will be housed in some of the st	3	More	Full
rge concentration of vulnerable	people	in bushland and there 's one roa	4	More	Full
in the Victorian bushfires , if	people	[in this development &rsqb	5	More	Full
ly where it involves vulnerable	people	. " </p> <p> Ms Keneally said th	6	More	Full
and out - there are hundreds of	people	living in nursing homes and reti	7	More	Full
risk from bushfires . </p> <p>	People	living nearby have described the	8	More	Full
ould house thousands of elderly	people	, is before Ms Keneally after it	9	More	Full
t villages or accommodation for	people	with disabilities being built in	10	More	Full

Fig. 9.13 Snapshot of the ten most prominent NN (common noun)

Table 9.4 illustrates the top twenty salient semantic tags in the bushfire corpus and again the mere number therein is insufficient to explore how news values are inscribed in these semantic tags without scrutinizing their concordance lines.

The semantic tags of 'N.5.1+++' (i.e. entire and maximum), and 'A13' (i.e. degree) in Table 9.4, as presented in Figs. 9.14 and 9.15 respectively, are chiefly adopted to maximize the news stories and accordingly construe the news value of **superlativeness**. The extent of bushfire danger in Fig. 9.14 has been described as 'extreme', and the risk in Fig. 9.15 has been intensified through comparison.

In Fig. 9.16, the negative verbs (e.g. damage, destroy) were deployed to vividly depict the impact of bushfires and how destructive they were. This is also the case in Fig. 9.17 where the reporting on bushfires focused on the threatening impact they had on homes, properties and local residents. In Fig. 9.18, reporting bushfire

76 occurrences.			Extend context
gh his consultants admit " during	extreme	bushfire events , evacuation of re	1 More | Full
early this week . But apart from	extreme	weather conditions , the reality i	2 More | Full
ction of new homes in moderate or	extreme	fire-hazard areas and demanded hig	3 More | Full
d windy , is rated a very high to	extreme	fire danger . </p> <p> While rain	4 More | Full
the only blazes in the ACT on an	extreme	fire danger day . </p> <p> Both ,	5 More | Full
ult for firefighters . </p> <p> "	Extreme	heat makes it a bit harder for the	6 More | Full
reau of Meteorology has issued an	extreme	fire danger warning for north-west	7 More | Full
ary 12 , 2010 <p> CATASTROPHIC or	extreme	fire conditions have been forecast	8 More | Full
ria today due to a combination of	extreme	heat , high winds and dry conditio	9 More | Full
nd Daylesford , has been given an	extreme	fire danger rating , as has the Ma	10 More | Full

Fig. 9.14 Snapshot of the ten most prominent 'N.5.1+++' (i.e. entire and maximum)

26 occurrences.			Extend context
get out of the bush and into the	relative	safety of townships instead . </p	1 More | Full
ton and Steels Creek , which are	as	close as four kilometres to the e	2 More | Full
y late afternoon it had not been	as	warm as forecast . </p> <p> ''At	3 More | Full
day and the winds were n't quite	as	strong as expected , so it 's giv	4 More | Full
r in November so its felt like a	relatively	cool start to December , " he sai	5 More | Full
temperatures are not said to be	as	high as originally thought . " </	6 More | Full
" The problem is the terrain is	relatively	inaccessible for trucks . It is n	7 More | Full
lis told AAP . </p> <p> " It was	relatively	small , burning four hectares , b	8 More | Full
m the weather bureau it could be	as	early as 6pm . </p> <p> About 6.2	9 More | Full
Saturday were faced with flames	as	high as 100 metres , a fire sprea	10 More | Full

Fig. 9.15 Snapshot of the ten most prominent 'A13' (i.e. degree)

rabran in the central west ,	destroyed	at least 33 homes and damaged	351 More | Full
troyed at least 33 homes and	damaged	the Siding Spring Observatory	352 More | Full
hectares after beginning its	destructive	rampage on Sunday.On Monday i	353 More | Full
Spring Observatory were not	destroyed	although the Australian Natio	354 More | Full
versity (ANU) facility was	damaged	in the fire.ANU Acting Vice-C	355 More | Full
at the observatory had been	damaged	significantly , including the	356 More | Full
s not seem to be significant	damage	to the buildings that house t	357 More | Full
vatory from being completely	destroyed	is an absolute credit to all	358 More | Full
e , Kandos and Clandulla has	broken	containment lines , putting s	359 More | Full

Fig. 9.16 Snapshot of some prominent 'A1.1.2' (i.e. damaging and destroying)

highlighted the severe danger and risk that bushfires caused to the local area and residents. Hence, the news values of **impact** and **negativity** were realized therein.

The semantic tag of 'T1.3' refers to the time and period of the reported risk events, and it was mainly employed to indicate how recent these events were by explicating the exact date. As such the news value of **timeliness** is constructed (Fig. 9.19).

In Fig. 9.20, the location nouns are modified by the determiner 'the' to their left, by a modifying clause to their right or refer to a specific local area, suggesting that the places are geographically close to the readers, or that readers have been informed of the exact geographic location of these places. The reported news stories were therefore expected to arouse readers' concerns or interests. The news value of **proximity** may be consequently construed.

rea are not under any immediate	threat	despite strong winds gusting thr	12	More	Full
p> And while there is no direct	threat	to homes in the area , it has ad	13	More	Full
uary 11 , 2009 <p> The bushfire	threat	in NSW has eased significantly w	14	More	Full
le of days which has slowed the	threat	of the fire , but at the same ti	15	More	Full
dly . </p> <p> Homes were under	threat	at one point but it has now been	16	More	Full
April 11 , 2007 <p> A bushfire	threatening	private properties in north-west	17	More	Full
ate forest and farmland and had	threatened	a number of private properties .	18	More	Full
. </p> <p> A TFS spokesman said	flare-ups	and peat fires within the bounda	19	More	Full
s and territories , with blazes	threatening	homes and scorching hundreds of	20	More	Full
</p> <p> NSW is under the worst	threat	with more than 90 fires that hav	21	More	Full
A 9800-hectare blaze near Cooma	threatened	15 homes on Saturday as more tha	22	More	Full

Fig. 9.17 Snapshot of some prominent 'E3' (i.e. violent: angry)

223 occurrences.			Extend context		
mmunity of D'Estrees Bay " still	at risk	" , many roads closed and smoke d	1	More	Full
community of D'Estrees is still	at risk	. " </p> <p> It is understood the	2	More	Full
sed in some of the state 's most	dangerous	urban bushfire zones under plans	3	More	Full
and retirement villages who are	at risk	from bushfires . </p> <p> People	4	More	Full
ell protected . </p> <p> " These	risky	developments must be put aside un	5	More	Full
ing a balance between minimising	risks	to the community while maintainin	6	More	Full
an Bushfires Royal Commission by	Risk	Frontier , a natural hazards cent	7	More	Full
ion by Risk Frontier , a natural	hazards	centre , that many people in urba	8	More	Full
inge areas do not see themselves	at risk	. But FESA 's main headache since	9	More	Full
day the changes to national fire	danger	ratings and alert levels had help	10	More	Full

Fig. 9.18 Snapshot of the ten most prominent 'A15-' (i.e. danger)

In Fig. 9.21, the semantic tags mainly pertain to authorities and local councils who were involved in recruiting firefighters to contain bushfires or in updating readers with official and latest news regarding the ongoing bushfires. In this sense, the news value of **eliteness** is constructed in the news reporting of bushfire risks.

Semantic tags in Fig. 9.22, together with those presented in Figs. 9.16, 9.17 and 9.18 directly involve negative evaluation of risk events. Bushfires, being always evaluated as undesirable and sometimes catastrophic, can damage local properties and cause severe danger to local residents, and in this sense, the news value of **negativity** is constructed.

In contrast to news values in news actors and events in the Chinese corpus, the news value of **positivity** was not salient in the Australian hard news reporting on bushfires. The infrequent occurrence of personalization is further evidenced by rare appearance of eyewitness (i.e. attest) in reporting risk events in the Australian corpus. However, this does not necessarily mean that these two news values were totally absent in discursive realizations. Instead, positive human emotions, judgment of human behaviours or appreciation of risk entities do occur in the Australian corpus, albeit less salient than those negative. The key insight provided by the analysis of APPRAISAL patterns into the examination of discursive realization of news values in the Australian corpus lies not in the presence of absence of occasional positive overtones (e.g. rescues) or emotional values of news stories, but situates in how salient or minor these values are in communicating risks mediated by journalists. In short, news values in news actors and events have downplayed **positivity** in communicating risk in hard news reporting by Australian journalists.

	1173 occurrences.		Extend context
	December 9	, 2007 <p> More than 300 fire	1 More | Full
but guests were evacuated on	Friday	. </p> <p> " Every now and ag	2 More | Full
n their property through the	day	but CFS crews were trying to	3 More | Full
aid the family had spent the	day	making sure they were " prepa	4 More | Full
hin containment lines . </p>	February 16	, 2009 <p> THOUSANDS of elder	5 More | Full
ls that this is " a disaster	waiting	to happen " . </p> <p> Powerf	6 More | Full
escarpment . </p> <p> And a	week	after Victoria 's bushfire di	7 More | Full
in the valley . </p> <p> On	Friday	, Ms Keneally told Warringah	8 More | Full
ving the plan for almost two	years	. " It is a large concentrati	9 More | Full
development] have only	minutes	to get out , it would be impo	10 More | Full

Fig. 9.19 Snapshot of the ten most prominent 'T1.3' (e.g. time: period)

	744 occurrences.		Extend context
t Western River Conservation	Park	, D'Estrees Bay and the Flind	1 More | Full
opping up and patrolling the	area	. </p> <p> The D'Estrees fire	2 More | Full
9,400 hectares of bush in an	area	where access was difficult .	3 More | Full
g further backburning in the	area	, while the Western River fir	4 More | Full
the state 's most dangerous	urban	bushfire zones under plans be	5 More | Full
ost dangerous urban bushfire	zones	under plans being backed by t	6 More | Full
nts that prohibit retirement	villages	and nursing homes being built	7 More | Full
eing built in bushfire-prone	areas	such as parts of Ku-ring-gai	8 More | Full
Regan , said his council 's	local	environmental plan had ruled	9 More | Full
ronmental plan had ruled the	area	out of bounds for this kind o	10 More | Full

Fig. 9.20 Snapshot of the ten most prominent 'M7' (i.e. places)

	652 occurrences.		Extend context
urist resorts . </p> <p> The	Country	Fire Service (CFS) said the	1 More | Full
ng held with interstate fire	authorities	to get an extra 300 firefight	2 More | Full
ian , Tasmanian and NSW fire	authorities	to help fill the shortfall .	3 More | Full
ill be housed in some of the	state	's most dangerous urban bushf	4 More | Full
lans being backed by the NSW	Government	, despite repeated warnings f	5 More | Full
nings from fire services and	councils	that this is " a disaster wai	6 More | Full
happen " . </p> <p> Powerful	state	planning laws are giving deve	7 More | Full
elopers the ability to trump	council	rules and Rural Fire Service	8 More | Full
disaster , the NSW Planning	Minister	, Kristina Keneally , has ope	9 More | Full
Oxford Falls . </p> <p> The	council	rejected the proposal because	10 More | Full

Fig. 9.21 Snapshot of the ten most prominent 'G1.1' (i.e. government)

	104 occurrences.		Extend context
s and councils that this is " a	disaster	waiting to happen " . </p> <p> P	1 More | Full
week after Victoria 's bushfire	disaster	, the NSW Planning Minister , Kr	2 More | Full
ible to evacuate them this is a	disaster	waiting to happen , " he said .	3 More | Full
l Commission into the Victorian	disaster	is complete , the NSW local gove	4 More | Full
nal , " Mr Rees said . " In the	worst	cases you will kill people , and	5 More | Full
oid a repeat of last weekend 's	disaster	. Roger Underwood , former gener	6 More | Full
ughes Park , next to one of the	worst	affected areas , the council has	7 More | Full
and . </p> <p> NSW is under the	worst	threat with more than 90 fires t	8 More | Full
n Western Australia on a day of	catastrophic	fire-risk warnings . Firefighter	9 More | Full
t temperatures would create the	worst	fire conditions of the season ye	10 More | Full

Fig. 9.22 Snapshot of the ten most prominent 'A5.1—' (i.e. evaluation: bad)

9.4 Discussion

The analysis of ATTITUDE patterns presented in Chap. 6 has demonstrated that although ordinary citizens are often mediated by Australian journalists in the expression of negative emotions such as 'concerns' and 'worries', the powerful (e.g. authorities, national government) are not particularly judged in a positive way either. There are far more negative discursive stances than the positive across each ATTITUDE feature in the Australian corpus. These discursive patterns are particularly relevant to the foregrounded news values of 'negativity' and also to the downplayed news value of 'positivity'. The relatively high frequency of affect (34%) and emotional reaction (12%) in the Australian corpus are intimately linked to the news value of 'personalization'. To enact emotions of news actors is an efficient way to establish an emotional bond with the readers and thus to attract their attention. The reason why Australian journalists need to enable certain emotions in risk events to attract the readers' attention will be discussed in Chap. 10 in relation to the tightening budget of the Australian press in face of fierce competition from online news and other media (e.g. TV and radio).

The examination of ENGAGEMENT patterns in the Australian corpus in Chap. 8 has shown that Australian journalists are hardly on site in reporting risk events and that they regularly quote the elite sources. Generally speaking, organizational voices were mediated by Australian journalists as more negotiable than official voices. The news value of 'eliteness' is relevant to this discursive pattern. Since quoting the social elites involves human faces in news reporting, the news value of 'personalization' is brought into view as well. The scant journalistic presence and reliance on prefabricated stories from authorities and organizations in the Australian news discourse may be relevant to the news values of 'prefabrication' and 'competition'. Certainly, we need to be in the newsroom or conduct an intertextual analysis to know to what extent journalists have relied on prefabricated texts, but corpus analysis of ENGAGEMENT patterns may have suggested the significance of the news values of 'prefabrication' in Australian newsroom. By constructing newsworthy stories, the Australian press aim to produce interesting stories that can compete with alternatives that attract readers' attention. This finding is linked to the economic pressure of print media, tight newspaper agenda and fierce competition for scoops and for other newsworthy events. In fact, many scholars (e.g. Bell, 1991; Cotter, 2010; Jacobs, 1999; Machin & Niblock, 2006; Sleurs & Jacobs, 2005) have demonstrated that in the developed countries journalists are becoming increasingly multiskilling and increasingly relying on prefabricated news from press releases. This point will be further discussed in Chap. 10.

The market mechanism has been introduced into the Chinese press reform in the late 1970s and escalated in the 1990s. The reform trajectory of Chinese and Australian press will be discussed in the next chapter. The key point here is that the withdrawal of government subsidies has forced Chinese press to compete with each other for advertisements and readers. Driven by such economic independence, newspapers strive for exclusive news stories to overwhelm their competitors. This explains why the news value of ‘competition’ is foregrounded in news editorial meetings in the Chinese news institution under investigation. Competition is in harmony with the news values of ‘continuity’ and ‘novelty’, as journalists are encouraged to develop a new perspective to surprise the public concerning events either reported by other newspapers or previously covered in their own.

The interviews with Chinese journalists show that Party-affiliated papers feed on predictable government events as daily news. Hence, the news value of ‘predictability’ is salient here. However, not all predictable official events are newsworthy by professional standard and sometimes journalists are requested to augment the power elites rather than focus on the news itself. This on one hand brings into focus the news value of ‘eliteness’ and on the other it shows the external influence from the power elites in the Chinese news discourse to constrain journalistic stance taking practices.

Due to the “patron-client” relationship between Party-affiliated papers and authorities (e.g. Lee, He, & Huang, 2007), Party papers have exclusive access to official events and actors, and as such official sources constitute the primary venue for journalists and their affiliated newspapers to occasion scoops to appeal to readers and in the meanwhile to outpace their competitors. Hence, it is hardly unexpected that the news values of ‘eliteness’ and ‘positivity’ are prioritized in Chinese news discourse.

These news values (e.g. positivity, eliteness) may in part explain why the power elites are positively judged by reference to ‘social esteem’ and why their ‘caring’ and ‘considerate’ affect (see Chap. 6 for details) is often expressed by Chinese journalists in reporting risk events. These values are also relevant to the discursive stances in relation to the contracted dialogic space of the elite sources in the Chinese corpus (see Chap. 8).

To gain commercial profits, news institutions and journalists need to demonstrate to their advertisers or investors the great appeal of their newspaper to readers, which explains why the news value of ‘personalization’ is prioritized to the same extent as that of ‘eliteness’ in the Chinese news discourse. The priority of ‘personalization’ reflects constant economic forces upon the news institution, and the political need to disseminate the CPC’s ideology. The latter is perhaps best illustrated by the tendency to please readers in reporting official events.

The frequent negative framing of ordinary citizens in the Chinese corpus is closely connected to the news values of ‘negativity’ and ‘personalization’. These two news values may in part explain why the sources of ordinary citizens are brought into eyewitness risk events, albeit less frequently than journalistic authorial and official voices, and at the same time the dialogic space of the voice of ordinary citizens is always opened up for alternative voices. To involve human faces or voices is relevant to the news value of ‘personalization’, but to downplay the voice of risk makers in news reporting perhaps is indirectly linked to the news value of ‘negativity’ (e.g. verbiage of risk makers may invoke negative judgement of their actions).

This chapter has indicated that Chinese journalism practitioners are trapped in a dilemmatic position facing political security (i.e. to please the political power elites) on one hand and economic safety (i.e. to please the readership) on the other. The news value of impact has reified this dilemma, because it is not only interpreted as influence among readers by journalism practitioners, but also as praise/criticism by authorities. However, Chinese journalism practitioners have developed their tactics to circumvent this dilemma by taking tailored stances in framing news actors of different social status (e.g. ordinary citizens vs. government officials) and in reporting events of different significance.

9.5 Summary

Overall, this chapter has shown an intimate relationship between the articulated and prioritized news values and journalistic stances. To probe more fully into why journalistic stances are undertaken the way they are and why news values are articulated the way they are in Chinese and Australian news discourses, I will examine in the next section the relations between the government and the press, and those between journalists and government sources, the overall purpose of news production, and the payment system for journalism practitioners within the explicit valuation of stories in the press.

References

Allern, S. (2002). Journalistic and commercial news values. *Nordicom Review, 23*(1–2), 137–152.
Bednarek, M. (2006). *Evaluation in media discourse: Analysis of a newspaper corpus*. London/New York: Continuum.
Bednarek, M., & Caple, H. (2012a). *News discourse*. London/New York: Continuum.
Bednarek, M., & Caple, H. (2012b). 'Value added': Language, image and news values. *Discourse, Context & Media, 1*(2–3), 103–113. https://doi.org/10.1016/j.dcm.2012.05.006.
Bednarek, M., & Caple, H. (2014). Why do news values matter? Towards a new methodological framework for analysing news discourse in Critical Discourse Analysis and beyond. *Discourse & Society, 25*(2), 135–158. https://doi.org/10.1177/0957926513516041.
Bell, A. (1991). *The language of news media*. Oxford/Cambridge, MA: Blackwell.
Brighton, P., & Foy, D. (2007). *News values*. London: Sage.
Caple, H., & Bednarek, M. (2013). *Delving into the discourse: Approaches to news values in journalism studies and beyond*. Oxford: Reuters Institute for the Study of Journalism, University of Oxford.
Caple, H., & Bednarek, M. (2015). Rethinking news values: What a discursive approach can tell us about the construction of news discourse and news photography. *Journalism,* 1–22. https://doi.org/10.1177/1464884914568078.
Conley, D., & Lamble, S. (2006). *The daily miracle: An introduction to journalism* (3rd ed.). Melbourne: Oxford University Press.
Cotter, C. (2010). *News talk: Investigating the language of journalism*. Cambridge: Cambridge University Press.
Donsbach, W. (2004). Psychology of news decisions: Factors behind journalists' professional behavior. *Journalism, 5*(2), 131–157.

Fowler, R. (1991). *Language in the news: Discourse and ideology in the press*. London/New York: Routledge.
Fuller, J. (1996). *News values: Ideas for an information age*. Chicago: University of Chicago Press.
Galtung, J., & Ruge, M. H. (1965). The structure of foreign news: The presentation of the Congo, Cuba and Cyprus crises in four Norwegian newspapers. *Journal of Peace Research, 2*(1), 64–90.
Gans, H. J. (2004/1979). *Deciding what's news: A study of CBS evening news, NBC nightly news, newsweek, and time*. Evanston, IL: Northwestern University Press.
Hall, S. (1980). Cultural studies: Two paradigms. *Media, Culture and Society, 2*(1), 57–72.
Hall, S., Critcher, C., Jefferson, T., Clarke, J., & Roberts, B. (2000). The social production of news. In P. Marris & S. Thornham (Eds.), *Media studies: A reader* (pp. 645–652). New York: New York University Press.
Harcup, T., & O'Neill, D. (2001). What is news? Galtung and Ruge revisited. *Journalism Studies, 2*(2), 261–280.
Harrison, J. (2006). *News*. London: Routledge.
Hartley, J. (1982). *Understanding news*. London: Methuen.
Herman, E. S., & Chomsky, N. (1988). *Manufacturing consent: The political economy of the mass media*. New York: Pantheon.
Jacobs, G. (1999). *Preformulating the news: An analysis of the metapragmatics of press releases* (Vol. 60). Amsterdam: John Benjamins Publishing.
Kepplinger, H. M., & Ehmig, S. C. (2006). Predicting news decisions. An empirical test of the two-component theory of news selection. *Communications, 31*(1), 25–43.
Lee, C. C., He, Z., & Huang, Y. (2007). Party-market corporatism, clientelism, and media in Shanghai. *The Harvard International Journal of Press/Politics, 12*(3), 21–42.
Machin, D., & Niblock, S. (2006). *News production: Theory and practice*. London: Routledge.
McQuail, D. (1994). *Mass communication theory*. London: Sage.
Montgomery, M. (2007). *Discourse of broadcast news: A linguistic approach*. London/New York: Routledge.
Palmer, J. (2000). *Spinning into control: News values and source strategies*. London: A&C Black.
Richardson, J. E. (2007). *Analysing newspapers: An approach from critical discourse analysis*. Basingstoke: Palgrave Macmillan.
Schultz, I. (2007). The journalistic gut feeling. *Journalism Practice, 1*(2), 190–207.
Schulz, W. F. (1982). News structure and people's awareness of political events. *International Communication Gazette, 30*(3), 139–153.
Sinclair, J. (2006). The media and communications: Theoretical traditions. In S. Cunningham & G. Turner (Eds.), *The media and communications in Australia* (2nd ed., pp. 13–27). Sydney: Allen & Unwin.
Sleurs, K., & Jacobs, G. (2005). Beyond preformulation: An ethnographic perspective on press releases. *Journal of Pragmatics, 37*(8), 1251–1273.
Strömbäck, J., Karlsson, M., & Hopmann, D. N. (2012). Determinants of news content. *Journalism Studies, 13*(5–6), 718–728.
Tong, J. (2009). Press self-censorship in China: A case study in the transformation of discourse. *Discourse & Society, 20*(5), 593–612.
Van Dijk, T. A. (1988). *News as discourse*. Hillsdale, NJ: L. Erlbaum Associates.
Van Dijk, T. A. (1991). Media contents: The interdisciplinary study of news as discourse. In K. B. Jensen & N. W. Jankowski (Eds.), *A handbook of qualitative methodologies for mass communication* (pp. 108–120). London/New York: Routledge.
Zhao, Y. (2000). From commercialization to conglomeration: The transformation of the Chinese press within the orbit of the party state. *Journal of Communication, 50*(2), 3–26.

Chapter 10
Symbolic Power and Journalistic Stance

10.1 Introduction

In the previous chapter, I have shown the articulation of news values in Chinese and Australian news discourses. However, news values are not the only social-institutional factor relevant to the enactment of journalistic stance taking practices. In fact, journalistic stances and the articulation of news values are both influenced by the exercise of "symbolic power" (Bourdieu, 1984, 1989, 1991) or "hegemony" (Gramsci, 1971) in news discourse.

In this chapter the purpose of examining the ways symbolic power is exercised in Chinese and Australian news discourses is not to simply provide background to news production in each context, but to investigate the mechanism of the exercising of symbolic power as mediational means to enable and/or disable journalistic stances. This is based on the view that the symbolic power needs to be eventually realized in journalistic practices, and at the same time journalistic stances in institutional and professional practices are afforded and/or constrained by how journalism practitioners recognize and respond to (e.g. to sustain or to challenge) the dominant symbolic power in each context.

10.2 Conceptualizing Symbolic Power

Symbolic power is a notion introduced by Bourdieu (1984) to account for the production and reproduction of social relationships and hierarchies of power within daily social practices of individuals. It is a form of power standing in sharp contrast with physical violence. Symbolic power maintains its effect through the misrecognition of power relations situated in the nexus of social practices. To effect symbolic power, the dominators transform their ideology and the associated hierarchical power into social values to legitimate the *status quo*. It also requires the

C. Huan, *Journalistic Stance in Chinese and Australian Hard News*,
https://doi.org/10.1007/978-981-13-0791-1_10

dominated to accept their ideology in the transaction of social values that occurs between them. The subconscious acceptance of these values to represent and evaluate social life by the dominated mass eventually perpetuates the hierarchical social structure favored by the dominators. In this sense, the legitimation of social world is not the product of symbolic imposition (Bourdieu, 1989, p. 21). Rather, the dominators apply to the orders of social life patterns of evaluation (e.g. stance patterns) to make sense of social life. There are always tensions between symbolic powers for the production and reproduction of the legitimate ideology. The volume of symbolic power however rests on the amount of economic and symbolic capital each group possess. That is to say, not all social values bear with them equal weight; holders of large amount of symbolic capital dominate the hierarchy of social values in their interests (Bourdieu, 1989, p. 21). Consequently, the social values preferred by the dominators prevail in daily social life, whereas social values upheld by the dominated are suppressed.

10.3 Chinese Press in Transition

This section sets out to provide historical background for understanding the exercise of symbolic power in news production in the Chinese press. To do so, this section will contour the course of the Chinese press reform in the "New Era" (Yu, 2009, p. 4) since 1980s when the Central Committee of the CPC and the State Council (hence Party-State) launched a national policy to commercialize Chinese press. More detailed historical account of the transitional trajectory of the Chinese press can be founded elsewhere (e.g. Cao, 1999; Esarey, 2005; Hong, 2014; Lee, He, & Huang, 2007; Winfield & Peng, 2005; Zhao, 2000, 2005).

10.3.1 Chinese Press: Commercialization and Conglomeration

The first period of Chinese press reform—**commercialization**—started from early 1980s until 1995 when Chinese print media at all levels were encouraged by the Party-State to gradually achieve financial independence through publishing advertisements, a way of profit-making that was severely prohibited prior to the reform. Since then, Chinese press have been gradually transformed from the traditional State-monopolized model to a State-owned but market-oriented model. However, the rapid growth of newspapers in this period failed to reverse their dependence on State-budget subsidies and 'forced office subscription'. Instead, the press boom nationwide and the financing of all these press had inflicted more economic burdens upon the Party-State than they had dismissed. The fierce competition among Party papers and market papers had considerably undermined the economic base of Party newspapers since Party papers had mandatory propaganda topics to cover in the limited daily pages. In contrast, non-Party papers had a less vested interest in the CPC's ideology and they were delinquent in editorial supervision responsibilities (Zhao, 2000, p. 8; 2005). Non-Party papers often operated at the margin of the Party prescribed areas of specialization by means of illegally contracting out publishing rights (e.g. leasing extra pages to a third party) and selling press cards to unauthorized groups and/or individuals in exchange for financial revenues (Zhao, 2000, p. 14). As such, the ideological power of the Party papers was substantially compromised in the fragmented, bureaucratized and overextended press structure that created a scale management rather than a scale economy (Zhao, 2000, p. 14). The need for the Party-State to streamline the Chinese press structure had never become as urgent as it was in the wake of waxing number of press but waning share of State revenue in GDP in the middle of 1990s.

In the second period (1996–2001) of **press conglomeration**, the Party-State encouraged Party papers to merge non-Party papers and establish press conglomerates, an efficient way to streamline the then fragmented and chaotic Chinese press structure.

However, the establishment of Chinese press conglomerates was mainly the result of the Party-State directed media reform rather than the choice of the market. The Party papers therefore held de facto leadership in the newly established press conglomerate, even in cases where they were less profitable than non-Party papers (e.g. Wenhui-Xinmin Press Group). In so doing, news conglomeration was able to acquire substantial media assets under Party papers and to regulate the chaotic and fragmented competition in Chinese media market (Zhao, 2000). The streamlined local press structure enabled the press conglomerates to monopolize the market and as such increased their price-fixing and revenue-generating abilities. Consequently, the social effect of minor non-Party papers was considerably minimized while the ideological control of Chinese press was achieved at ease by appointing key media personnel in press conglomerates.

Due to the ideological importance of Party papers, press conglomerates were never seriously and effectively transformed into corporations. The economic operation of press conglomerates was not supervised and monitored by the Party-State, media managers were keen to climb their career ladder by keeping a correct ideological orientation at the expense of economic profits of the news institution at issue (Z. Hu, 2003). Political safety still constituted a priority for the Party and the top press managers, as evidenced by an interview with a marginalized executive, "as long as you are obedient and profitable, it does not matter how awful your paper is" (Lee et al., 2007, p. 32). In fact, most Party papers needed to be subsidized by the non-Party papers in the same press conglomerate. It was the non-Party papers that were dominating the distribution market and readership share. This situation had largely marginalized Party papers in the media market and in the long run may compromise their social impact on leading public opinions.

There was a dire need for the Party papers themselves to generate substantial revenues to sustain the production of ideology in news before their social impact was diminished by market-oriented papers. For this reason, after China's accession into the WTO in 2001, non-State capital was gradually accommodated in soft news production and other areas of media operation such as advertising, distribution and printing (Zhao, 2005, p. 204). On the other hand, Chinese Party papers have been experimenting in separating the editorial department from non-editorial departments such as printing, distribution and advertising departments, and transforming non-editorial departments into for-profit corporations. In so doing, the Party can maintain control over the production of ideologically charged hard news and at the same time increase the revenue-generating abilities of the Party papers.

10.3.2 The Status Quo of the Chinese Press

From 2002 to 2014, the primary focus of Chinese press reform was to transform non-editorial departments into corporations that can be listed in stock markets to attract non-State capital, while at the same time keep the editorial department intact from capitalization.

A pilot reform on transforming Chinese press conglomerates into State-controlled sharing holding corporations started in 2003 in several selected socialist press conglomerates such as *Dazhong Daily News Group*, *Xinhua Daily News Group*, *Shenzhen Daily News Group* and *Henan Daily News Group*. These press conglomerates enjoyed privileged policies, enabling them to merge and restructure Party newspapers at all levels in their respective region, and to be registered under the Administration for the Industry and Commerce as for-profit enterprises with modern enterprise systems. In 2004, the Central Publicity Department and the General Administration of Press and Publication (GAPP) approved the deepening reform of Chinese media, which was characterized by a) the separation of non-editorial supporting departments from press conglomerate and their transformation into State-controlled share-holding corporations; and b) the wholesale corporate transformation of non-Party papers.

With the release of the Working Plan for the Deepening Reform of Chinese Media by the GAPP in 2006, the period of 2006–2009 was a break-through period for capitalizing Chinese press. By capitalizing Chinese press, I mean Chinese press were encouraged to attract various sources of capital, for instance, through listing properties in stock markets. The Working Plan explicitly encouraged prosperous news publication and distribution corporations to list their operational assets in stock markets. According to the 12th Five-Year Plan for Chinese News Industry, by 2010 there had been 1939 newspapers published in China, 1251 of them had registered as enterprises, 39 press conglomerates had separated editorial from non-editorial departments and seven of these press conglomerates had listed their non-editorial departments in national or international stock markets.

Despite the media conglomeration since 2000s, propaganda-oriented Party papers performed largely unsatisfactorily in the market and remained "largely loss-making" (Huang, 2007, p. 415). According to an anonymous officer in GAPP, global financial crisis had resulted in loss-making for the whole Chinese media industry in 2008 due to the overdependence on advertising revenues, especially those advertising revenues from real estates and IT companies. Most press conglomerates still remained as public cultural institutions without fundamental reform of organization structure. For instance, the editorial departments still mirror the structure of government departments in a manner that each editorial department is responsible for liaising with designated government departments.

Certainly, the Party-State required a more economically powerful press industry to boost the China's economic development and to legitimate itself when the China's reform has entered "a critical stage and a deep water zone", as claimed by the CPC. The course for further media reform was charted by the Decision on Major Issues Concerning Comprehensively Deepening Reforms adopted at the close of the Third Plenary Session of the 18th CPC Central Committee on 12 November, 2013. One basic tenet of this Decision was to experiment in the wholesale stock-listing of press conglomerates through carrying out a system of 'special management shares' (tèshūgǔ guǎnlǐ zhìdù), a system that could endow the Party-State with the ultimate discursive power to maintain the guiding role of Marxism in the ideology of press conglomerates, while holding relatively few normal shares. Such a system could on one hand diversify sources of investment and eventually release the burden of State capital, while on the other hand firmly retain ideological orientation, arrangement of managerial personnel, control of media assets, supervision of media content in press conglomerates.

In the process of press reform, the Chinese Party-State has selectively deployed neoliberal strategies (Zhao, 2008), through applying neoliberalism in selective news institutions and in selective departments in a news institution. This is consistent with Deng Xiaoping's reform strategy of "groping the stones while crossing the river". However, neoliberalism extends beyond the scope of open markets, privatization and unregulated financial flows to incorporate the governing activities that perpetuate the dominant ideology in disguise of market economy (Zhao, 2008). One such example is the Party's determination in the Twelfth Five-Year Plan (2011–2015) of Chinese press reform to strengthen ideological control over media content through constructing a digital monitor database to gather up-to-date news stories from all Chinese news institutions before their publication. Such a database accords the Party with technological affordances to supervise all Chinese print media prior to news publication (qiánqí jiǎncè), to regulate them when in publication (zhōngqí chǔzhì), and to censor them after publication (hòuqí tōngbào). It also indicates that the Party is moving away from traditional visible administrative control through imposing reporting guidelines to a comprehensive managing mechanism through legislative, technological and economic means.

10.4 Journalistic Stance and Symbolic Power in the Chinese Press

It is widely acknowledged that Chinese press are subject to tight ideological control by the CPC. However, in light of the increasingly commercialized Chinese press in the post-WTO era, opinions concerning this view are starting to diverge. Some scholars argue that the growing market forces will inevitably undermine the Party ideological control (e.g. Chen & Gong, 1997; Hao, Huang, & Zhang, 1998; He & Chen, 1998; Huang, 2007; Winfield & Peng, 2005), whereas others, holding a contrastive viewpoint, envisage that market forces will enhance Party's control (e.g. Barmé, 1998, 1999; Gordon, 1997; Pan & Lu, 2003; Zhao, 1998). Such contradictory scholarly views may be partly due to the fact that the reform of Chinese press is ongoing and that its future is yet unknown. Such opposing opinions, in my view, may also be caused by insufficient understanding of the production processes and the (re)production of power relations in the Chinese press. Studies investigating the Party's changing control mechanism in the transformation of Chinese press since 1980s have been dominated by perspectives from political economy (e.g. Hearns-Branaman, 2013; Lee et al., 2007), interviewing journalists and/or media managers (e.g. X. Lu, 2003; Yin & Liu, 2014), critical discourse analysis of news reports in draft and in print (e.g. Tong, 2009) and grounded theory (e.g. Winfield & Peng, 2005), among others. Despite the illuminating insights these approaches have provided into an understanding of the changing landscape of the Chinese press, they have largely ignored the role of editorial meetings in news institutions as a significant site of engagement where the Party's ideological control has been produced and reproduced.

Access to attending and observing editorial meetings in the Chinese press, especially in the so-called "mainstream" Party papers, has been extremely difficult to obtain. Perhaps for this reason, there have been insufficient studies in the literature on how editors and managers in editorial meetings in Chinese news institutions negotiate and accommodate power struggles over news production. To fill this research gap, I draw on several datasets as outlined in Chaps. 3 and 9, including policy documents issued by the Party-State and by a Party press conglomerate, audio-recorded editorial meetings and editorial meeting minutes, interviews with journalists and senior editors, and specialized corpora of hard news. My discussion below will show that the Chinese press, no matter how deep its reform has gone so far, will continue to be leashed by the Party. The ideological domination has however been masked by the changing ways of mobilizing economic and symbolic capital.

10.4.1 Symbolic Power and Economic Capital in the Chinese Press

While some press conglomerates are experimenting with institutional detachment from the Party's Publicity Department and with registering with the national/local Administration for Industry and Commerce, the Party-State still holds de facto proprietary rights over the media assets and control of their operation since all Chinese press are owned by the Party-State. Despite the monopolized media ownership, the Party-State has at its disposal economic capital to sustain the hierarchy of power.

According to the 'Notice of the General Office of the State Council on Issuing Two Sets of Provisions on Transforming For-Profit Cultural Public Institutions into Enterprises during Cultural System Reform' and 'Further Supporting the Development of Cultural Enterprises (No. 15 [2014])', the newly transformed for-profit news enterprises from previous State-owned public service news institutions will be exempt from enterprise income tax, value-added tax and public property tax. For all newly transformed for-profit news enterprises, the State will provide them with housing funds (e.g. accommodation stipend paid to people working in government departments and/or their affiliated institutions) and social insurance and pension funds. As a further supporting policy, the State provides transformed news institutions with free allocated lands which are owned by the State but their right of use is either leased to non-State-controlled news enterprises or allocated to State-controlled news enterprises as equivalent amount of shares held by the State. In so doing, the Party still retains tight control over Chinese media asset allocation.

Containing competition among local news institutions helps major Party papers to monopolize the market and maximize economic profits and social impact. In addition, the Party disallows the publication of resembling mass appeal newspapers in one local market, which explains why there is only one evening paper in a city. However, as an alternative way to bypass the frozen publication license of evening papers, many cities choose to publish metro papers. In this sense, there is always competition in a local city between metro papers, morning and evening papers. The fierce competition between newspapers in a city is transferred to journalism practitioners through the institutionalized use of carrots and sticks. As prescribed in the policy documents, missing an important news report will usually inflict a fine of 100 CNY ($16) on the journalists who should have covered the missing news, together with a public notice of criticism, as a warning to others, often posted in the bulletin board in the news institution. In contrast, when journalists report the same news event, outperforming peers from competing newspapers will earn a higher performance bonus.

In the same manner as the annual budget of news institutions is determined by the Publicity Department based on regular review of institutional performance, the monthly income of rank-and-file journalists and editors is directly linked to the quality of their professional performance which is quantified through daily reviews and evaluations by a review panel in a news institution. As these rank-and-file journalists and editors are employed under contract which is subject to regular renewal, the pressure for appealing to a large readership and therefore a wide range of advertisers and investors has been shifted from the top managers to journalists and editors working on the frontline of news production.

The economic security of rank-and-file journalists/editors rests not only on the professional quality, number and length of news stories that are published, but also on the level of political risk each news story may result in. According to the institutional policy document, if a news story is considered politically too sensitive to be published, journalists will lose their performance bonuses. If a news story is censored for its negative exposure of the current sponsors of news institution, journalists will only receive 70% of the payment which they would have otherwise received when the news was published. In this way, as the senior journalist (T) whom I interviewed put it, "gradually you have learned where the political and institutional minefields are, and then you will definitely bypass them to avoid making void efforts".

In comparison, the top managers of Chinese media institutions are directly appointed by the Party's Publicity Department in consultation with the Party's Organisation Department, and their positions are relatively secure as long as they keep a right ideology in daily news production. On this premise, the market performance of the news institution is hardly seriously evaluated and reviewed by its parent government authority, as can be indicated by the speech delivered by the director of involved news institution in an afternoon editorial meeting when he was disseminating to managers and editors the essence of a conference held earlier that day by the provincial Publicity Department. He quoted the director of the Publicity Department:

> The Party supervises the work of mass media in three ways. Firstly, to anchor this principle is to keep a correct ideological orientation [...]; secondly, the Party needs to further raise political awareness and to enhance consciousness of responsibility [of news institutions and journalism practitioners] through the system of 'level-by-level management' in which all involved media practitioners, rank-and-file journalists and top managers alike, should hold responsibility and cannot escape blame for whatever goes wrong in a news report. Lastly, it is essential for the Party to build and control media leadership and the media team [...]. According to the requirement of CCCPC, for some leaders who are not eligible for the important post they are assigned, they should be dismissed immediately to ensure the media team remain loyal to the Party, to the people and to the reality.

Certainly there are some changes afoot to redress the imbalance of resources and constraints imposed on rank-and-file journalists and top media managers. For instance, according to the State policy (No. 15 [2014]) mentioned previously, the Party-State will set up an institution responsible for overseeing the use and operation of State-owned assets. The newly established institution will integrate the management of personnel, operation, assets and ideological orientation of news institutions and thus shift the role of government away from running the media to managing the media. Premised on the corporation system established in news enterprises, the institution will better regulate and harness professional practices of journalism practitioners, managing editors and top managers of Chinese news institutions through the implementation of an 'Encouragement Scheme of the Stock Option'. This scheme allows journalism practitioners and top managers to hold corporation stakes and as such they may prioritize economic profits at the expense of their professional pursuit of freedom of speech.

10.4.2 Symbolic Power and Social Capital in the Chinese Press

All Chinese press, being Party papers or non-Party papers, must adhere to the unchangeable principle that the Party supervises the work of print media (dǎng guǎn méitǐ). One recently modified means to consolidate this principle is the conferral of the title of 'socialist press conglomerate' to newly established or transformed Chinese press conglomerates. To maintain this title, press conglomerates must (a) adhere to the goal of advancing socialist culture; (b) follow the socialist path of promoting cultural advances with Chinese characteristics; (c) pursue people-centered cultural creation; and (d) prioritize social impact of news reporting and at the same time ensure economic benefits. Such a socialist title constitutes the key to social capital of privileged official sources.

Socialist press conglomerates, especially their flagship Party papers, are defined as "mainstream" and branded "the most responsible" media outlets in China. Government officials will only feed the mastheads with recent official events. In such a way, readers will eventually favour the popularity and credibility of the socialist press. Such symbolic capital is nevertheless unavailable to non-Party papers. According to my interview with Chinese journalists in socialist press conglomerates, daily news feeds mainly come from five sources: (a) liaising with government departments; (b) localized national or international news; (c) sources from websites and 'Weibo' (Chinese version of Twitter); (d) phone calls from readers; and (e) journalists' private observation of daily life. However, liaising with government departments constitutes their primary and regular source of daily news since access to reporting official events is granted to these liaising newspapers by invitation only. In fact, most Chinese socialist press conglomerates are organized in parallel with the government structure, with each editorial department liaising with designated government departments.

In so doing, government departments and Chinese news institutions establish an intimate bond, and they rely on each other. The government needs to disseminate the political ideology, and the local leaders need to construct a positive image as political leverage to seek promotion, whereas the Chinese news institutions need regular and reliable resources to fill in their daily pages. This juxtaposition explains my corpus findings in Chap. 8 concerning Chinese journalists' endorsement of official sources, and provides insight into understanding why authorities are mediated by Chinese journalists in communicating risks in a positive way.

The other significant social capital that may be mobilized to retain ideological control of news production is to construct a patron-client relationship between the Party and media executives through manipulating access to top executive positions. Based on a case study in Shanghai's media groups, Lee et al. (2007) report three principal career paths leading to top positions in Chinese news institutions, including "(a) rising from the Party background; (b) climbing the career ladder from within; (c) transferring from a sister or even presumably rival media organization" (Lee et al., 2007, pp. 31–32). Whichever the path is followed, the appointed top media managers must remain absolutely loyal to the Party.

One central task of socialist press conglomerates is to report important official events and to report positive propaganda. The primary reporting task, as described by the director of the news institution in an editorial meeting under investigation, is

> To actively engage in publicizing thematic reports on investment in [name of the province], including advantages to invest in [name of the province], advantageous enterprises, platforms and famous entrepreneurs. [...] Negative reports about stock-listed corporations based in [name of the province] should not be published publicly. It is very difficult for our leaders to attract or invite these corporations to start business here. We should avoid giving them a fatal attack by exposing their malpractices.

From participant observation, I learned that in each editorial department there was usually a list of corporations that were typically divided into two groups: those that require protection and those that may be criticized. The corporations that were protected by Chinese press outlets were not necessarily their advertisers. Rather, in some cases they were protected because of their intimate political ties with local authorities. The negative news reports were only targeting those corporations that were neither the regular advertisers of the news institution in question nor the political friends of the local authorities. However, such negative news reports could never be published as long as the involved corporations were willing to "buy" them. This is not to suggest that such a malpractice was legitimated by the CCCPC. Instead, this was often condemned by the CCCPC in principle. Local authorities however had turned a blind eye to such unethical journalistic practices. This was because on one hand local authorities needed the companies under protection for local economy and on the other hand local authorities must allow malpractices of some companies to be exposed to the public as a means to support journalistic professional role of watchdog.

Failing to comply with the authority may lead to the removal of key managing editors from their posts. In the infamous "2013 Southern Weekend Incident", there was a conflict between the Publicity Department of Guangdong Province and *Southern Weekend* newspaper, with the latter under the pressure from the former to make significant changes to the New Year's special editorial. The newsroom staff went on strike to protest against such infringement of editorial freedom. There was no official response to this incident. However, no official response does not necessarily mean that there was no official action taken to deal with this incident. In fact, a managing editor who was working in another news institution and who had learned of the official response to this incident told me in my interview with him:

"there was no official action on the surface level, but actually there have been declining news stories concerning people's livelihood since then". He added

> Of course, no one was arrested because this incident was a complicated issue. But the director, editor-in-chief and some key middle-level cadres were relieved of their official duties by the Guangdong provincial committee of CPC. They have been transferred to other places such as Hong Kong, or to other posts. Some get promoted but to a virtual post without any real authority. In so doing, we can avoid foreign attacks on our press freedom and in the meantime satisfy the needs and requirement of "dǎng guǎn méitǐ" (the Party supervises the work of Chinese press).

10.4.3 Symbolic Power and Cultural Capital in the Chinese Press

Cultural capital may be institutionalized in the form of official credentials or qualification. The control over press publication licenses constitutes one prime source of cultural capital that has been mobilized to streamline the Chinese press structure. Socialist press conglomerates are privileged to stay unbound from obtaining new publication license, whereas non-socialist news institutions need to spend a huge amount of economic capital in exchange for such cultural capital—a press publication license (Cao, 1999).

Control of ideology is also manipulated through the Party's monopoly in (de) legitimating journalism practitioners through issuing an institutionally recognized press card. To obtain such a press card, journalism practitioners must pass an exam testing their knowledge about how to apply official ideology in journalistic practices. There are other mechanisms to ensure that senior editors and journalists have embodied such knowledge. One chief mechanism is to require them to take regular training programs in official ideology. The other principal mechanism is to subject press cards to annual reviews upon approval of news institutions, in the same manner as the publication license is subject to regular renewal upon approval of the GAPP. Good journalistic practices will be rewarded in the form of news awards that are conferred by journalists' associations at local/national levels. These professional organisations officially claim their adherence to the Party leadership and as such the awarding of top news stories may be manipulated by the Party. Such ways of exercising symbolic power is consistent with Gramsci's analysis of hegemony (Gramsci, 1971), a form of power that not only incorporates physical domination, power and control over the use of resources or capital, but also minimizes the journalists' ability to develop a coherent world-view of their own. The professional philosophy that guides Chinese journalists' practice does not belong to journalists but is borrowed from the hegemonic social group (i.e. the Party). In line with Gramsci's concept of hegemony (Gramsci, 1971), this is the key factor that prevents journalism practitioners from effectively resisting physical domination and the exercising of power against them (e.g. Ives, 2004, p. 79).

In addition to various laws and regulations, there are some 'unwritten rules' (qián guīzé) serving to regulate operations of news institutions and practices of journalism practitioners, one such infamous unwritten rule being that of 'paid journalism'. As per my participant observation of several Chinese journalists in their daily practices, for all officially organized news events, journalists received a 'red envelop' with some 200–600 CNY (35–100 USD) after they were invited to 'sign in' in a prepared name list in which they were included. It should be emphasized that only journalists from Party affiliated papers were invited to report these news events and thus were privileged to accessing such economic capital. Organizers of these official events without exception distributed a pre-formulated news report to invited journalists. A journalist from a nationally important official Party paper, who requested anonymity, said in my interview with him, "some journalists nowadays even don't know how to write a news report without a pre-formulated report provided by conference organisers". He continued, "some journalists are so good at taking the advantage of their position in the Party-affiliated papers that they often stop over at the official conferences, sign in (meaning to get the red envelop), get the pre-formulated report and run away".

In the same way as the published newspaper is the most precious objectified cultural capital for news institutions, bylined news stories are the chief source of cultural capital for journalism practitioners. Although the final news report is the product of collaboration between journalists, editors and desk chiefs, Chinese news reports are often bylined with journalists' names only. These bylines on one hand delegate authorship to individual journalists, whereas on the other they create a room for the news institution to step back from potential criticism on some controversial news reporting, as evidenced by the notorious Chen Yongzhou case in 2013. Chen, a dismissed journalist in the Guangzhou-based newspaper—Xinkuai Bao—was arrested by police from Changsha in another province (around 700 km away from Guangzhou) who alleged that Chen received bribes to publish 14 bylined negative news reports against a Changsha-based State-owned company. Although the director and editor-in-chief, and the deputy editor-in-chief of the newspaper were immediately removed from their posts, only Chen himself was sentenced to a 22-month term of imprisonment. Since rank-and-file journalists and editors constitute a professional community of practice with managing editors and top executives in the act of news production, it is hardly convincing that top management can repudiate the accountability of the so-called "politically wrong" news reports. This is because any managers who delegate to their subordinates the authorship to act in the name of the institution cannot deny their role of "principalship" in Goffman's sense (Goffman, 1981).

10.5 Understanding the Australian Press

With four significant newspaper owners overall—News Corp, Fairfax, Seven West Media Limited, and APN News & Media—Australia has one of the most highly concentrated newspaper ownership in the developed world beyond the party-controlled papers of the communist realm. Ownership of the two national and ten metropolitan daily press in Australia is largely dominated by the News Corp owning the only one general interest national newspaper (i.e. The Australian) and six metropolitan daily press with a combined two-thirds share of the metropolitan and national daily circulation. Fairfax, the second largest player, owns the only one specialty national newspaper (i.e. The Australian Financial Review) and three metropolitan daily presses with a combined one-quarter share of the circulation. In comparison, the third ranked player, Seven West Media Limited, occupies only 10% share of the circulation with one metropolitan daily press in Perth (i.e. The West Australian). Direct competition only exists between the two largest players in the two most populous cities in Australia—Sydney and Melbourne, whereas other geographic markets publish only one daily press owned by News Corp in Adelaide, Brisbane, Darwin and Hobart, by Fairfax in Canberra and by Seven West Media in Perth.

Despite such a high concentration of press ownership, the Australian government believes that media are powerful institutions that can influence the ways people perceive and engage in social life. In this sense, media constitute an important role to support an informed citizenry in the act of truth searching and media encourage effective engagement of people in the democratic discourses.

One basic means to ensure media diversity is to make available to all Australians access to a diversity of media voices. To do so, the Federal Government of Australia has established the Australian Communications and Media Authority (ACMA) to oversee media works in Australia through several legislation, regulations, standards and codes of practice. The most direct and perhaps the most effective tacit adopted by ACMA has been its enforcing limits on the control of licensed commercial broadcasting services and associated newspapers. Under current legislation, cross-media ownership is highly regulated by prohibiting any mergers from involving more than two of three regulated media platforms in any commercial radio license area, the cross-media ownership rule that is known as "2 out of 3" rule. In general, ACMA outlaws any mergers that considerably lessen competition in a given market.

Media diversity is measured not by economic ownership per se, but by the capacity of a person to exert control over a given media company through other ways of control.

> Other examples of control are if the person: is the licensee; can control the selection or provision of a significant proportion of the licensee's programming; can control a significant proportion of the operation of the licensee's programming; can control a significant proportion of the operations of the company; can appoint, secure or veto the appointment of at least half of the board of directors; or can exercise direction or restraint over any

substantial issue affecting the management or affairs of the licensee or company. (Department of Media Policy Paper No. 3, 2014)

The emergence and rapid growth of online news medium has revolutionized access to news and has established itself as the chief rivalry to traditional print media in Australia. Accessing news online allows readers to tailor news to their tastes and interests. As such young generation has largely migrated to the online consumption of news, which accounts for the declining readership for traditional print newspapers (Finkelstein, 2012; Papandrea, 2013). The reduction in readership has a direct bearing on the declining circulation of newspaper and has eventually resulted in the shrinking advertising revenue for the press. However, rather than diminishing the influence of traditional media, online news outlets overall provide existing players a vehicle to maintain or increase their influence because traditional newspapers have as yet remained a popular and principal source of original news reporting for online news outlets (Finkelstein, 2012; Papandrea, 2013).

In the Australian context, newsroom is characterized with the separation of "church and state" (Pavlik, 2000), the metaphor for the separation of business from editorial department. Media proprietors and policy-makers choose editors who accept and share their values, and advertising practitioners who are adept in making profits. While managing editors select journalists who could satisfy the professional requirements in relation to the status or nature of the media (e.g. quality newspaper or tabloid, print media or broadcast). Editors and journalists need to collaborate with advertising practitioners to attract a large amount of readers and eventually to obtain economic profits for media proprietors. Subjecting to increasingly severe economic pressures, Australian media proprietors have been attempting to foster multiskilling journalists in newsroom, which undermines the basic news-gathering skills and standards of journalism (Papandrea, 2013). This is because Australian journalists are expected to function as watchdog for democracy rather than mere money-makers for media proprietors. Australian journalists need to operate within a legal framework in which freedom of speech is guarded and guaranteed. However, this enshrined freedom is evanishing and evaporating, partly due to the fact that an overwhelming majority of news media are controlled by an extreme minority of social elites as mentioned above. What has been made manifest here is the seemingly conflicting two functions of journalistic practice, namely catering to market forces and striving to serve the public. On one hand, deviance from the entrenched cultural expectations and widely accepted social values is discredited both legislatively and culturally, whereas on the other hand failing to produce profits for media proprietors cannot sustain the operation of the news institution (Tiffen, 1989, 2006a; G. Turner & Cunningham, 2006).

10.6 Symbolic Power in the Australian and Chinese Press: A Comparison

This section compares and highlights the different ways symbolic power is exercised in the Chinese and Australian press, with a view to examining the link to the articulation of news values and discursive journalistic stances.

In contrast to the Chinese press, Australian newspapers are privately owned rather than State-owned so as to allow people to access a diversity of media voices (Cunningham & Turner, 2006; Finkelstein, 2012; Papandrea, 2013). The Australian press are detached from any State capital or other tax favors given by the government. In this sense, the Australian press are dissociated from any specific political party and government and are thus not obliged to fulfil any propaganda objectives. It is the media proprietors rather than any specific political party that exercise editorial control over news production. Accordingly, the symbolic power of the Australian government is minimally relevant in enacting journalistic stance. Instead, the Australian news institutions possess significant symbolic power to decide what makes news in their newspaper during editorial meetings. In so doing, the preferable ideologies and values that are upheld by media proprietors are enacted and made possible in news production.

In the Chinese context of news production, the Chinese government and the CPC possess significant symbolic power to enable/disable certain journalistic stances. As such, Chinese editors need to toe the Party line in deciding what the Party considers as newsworthy in the enactment of the CPC's political ideology.

Simply put, Chinese and Australian press defer to different ideologies. The Australian press are dominated by a commercial ideology (Tiffen, 2006a, 2006b), whereas the Chinese press conform to the political ideology of the CPC (Zhao, 1998, 2005, 2008). In the Australian press, the ultimate goal of news production is to maximize the economic profits for shareholders and media proprietors while to praise or criticize the government is only a means to achieve this end. The reverse is the case in the Chinese press in the sense that to promote the political propaganda is the end of all Chinese press while to pursue economic profits is only an efficient means to achieve this end, as Sun Zhijun, the deputy director of the Party's Publicity Department, said in an interview with a journalist on 12 March, 2014:

> It is worth noting that the CCCPC always emphasizes the principle of controlling and in the meanwhile prospering public service media sectors and for-profit media enterprises. Even to develop for-profit media enterprises, the CCCPC still emphasizes the importance of the social impact and the social responsibility of all Chinese media institutions and journalism practitioners. The CCCPC will restrain from the so-called 'industrializing' of our media sectors and companies. Thus our newspapers cannot solely focus on circulation of copies.

The different ways of exercising symbolic power in Chinese and Australian news discourses have a considerable influence on the articulation of news values and enactment of journalistic stance taking practices. The news values of 'positivity' and 'eliteness' in news actors and events have been prioritized by Chinese journalists to please the leaders (i.e. the government officials), and at the same time the news values of 'negativity' and 'personalization' have been foregrounded by Chinese journalists to please the readers. In the Australian context of news production, the discursively realized news values (Chap. 9) are mainly concerned with the attraction of readers' attention through construing the values surrounding 'timeliness', 'proximity', 'negativity', 'superlativeness', 'eliteness' and so on, but the news value of 'positivity' is hardly provoked in reporting risk events.

In enacting discursive stances, Chinese journalists tend to construct a positive image of the powerful through mediating how mournful the power elites are to those people impacted by risk events in question, and how capable the elites are in dealing with risks. The dominated (e.g. ordinary citizens) are represented in the Chinese corpus through mediating their 'worrying' or 'fearful' emotions towards risk events and the negative judgement of social sanction of risk makers. In the Australian corpus, the attitudes of officials and ordinary citizens are mediated in different ways as well, but no positive judgement or positive affect of officials are mediated therein, indicating that Australian journalists were not taking a stance to align with the government officials.

The (re)production of symbolic power is also closely linked to the "symbolic relationship" (Ericson, Baranek, & Chan, 1989) between journalists and sources. Gans (2004/1979) vividly depicts the journalist-source relationship as a tango dance, "for sources seek access to journalists, and journalists seek access to sources". Sources need to gain access to public attention and strive to be represented as desirably as possible, while journalists need sources to live up to daily deadline. "Although it takes two to tango, either sources or journalists can lead, more often than not, sources do the leading" (Gans, 2004/1979, p. 116). The interaction between sources and journalists in the Chinese and Australian news discourses differs from each other, as illustrated by the different ways news values are prioritized and different discursive stances that are enacted.

In the Chinese context, the interpersonal relationship between journalists and official sources depends on the nature and status of the journalists' affiliated newspapers. Chinese journalists in Party papers will automatically obtain privileged access to official sources and official events. In the transaction between Chinese journalists and official sources, the news institutions accrue economic profits and the top managers may accumulate social capital, while official sources obtain political leverage for promotion. This explains why Chinese journalists prefer predictable official events (i.e. the news value of 'predictability' in the news selection process), and why the news value of 'eliteness' tends to occur in company with that of 'positivity', as presented in Chap. 9.

Accessing official sources is a form of privileged social capital available to the pro-government press in China. Negotiating relationship between the power elites and the press is key to the enactment of journalistic stances. In this negotiation process, Chinese journalists have taken a stance in alignment with the power elites. To be specific, Chinese journalists tend to contract the dialogic space of the official voice through the adoption of 'attest' and 'endorse' sources (Chap. 8) and on the other hand the official voice is hardly mediated in 'acknowledge'. This suggests that the official voice in risk communication is considered by Chinese journalists as less negotiable than other voices. As such, an alignment is established between Chinese journalists and official sources.

With the tightening budget in the Australian press, Australian journalists tend to rely heavily on prefabricated news from regular sources. The official, expert and organizational voices are the primary voices adopted by Australian journalists in mediating risk communication. However, reliance on the elite sources itself does not necessarily mean a "compromised fourth estate" as suggested by Lewis, Williams, and Franklin, (2008), although it consciously or subconsciously sustains the status quo. What also matters is the way that the elite sources are mediated in news discourses.

The corpus findings in Chap. 8 have shown that in the Australian corpus although the elite sources (e.g. the official sources) are the primary source in mediating risk communication, these sources (e.g. the official sources) are adopted to attest risk events at issue (38%) as much as they are acknowledged (36%). This suggests that the dialogic space of the elite voice is likely to be opened up as much as it is closed down in the Australian news discourse. As such, Australian journalists are not taking a discursive stance to please the power elites as their Chinese peers are.

However, this is not to suggest that media proprietors of Australian press cannot exchange media responsibility with non-media interests. For instance, Vic Carroll, a former EOC of the SMH and a former managing editor of *the Australian* once commented, "all media are potentially compromised when the media owner/controller has substantial non-media interests. They are politically compromised when the non-media interests involve government licenses" (Barr, 2000, p. 7). Without examining the non-media enterprises of the Australian press, this research is unable to state that the Australian press are comprised. But based on my corpus findings about discursive stances in the Australian news discourse, there is no strong evidence supporting a comprised fourth estate in the Australian press in general.

Journalists may manipulate sources via attribution in news texts, but they are unable to manipulate interpersonal relationship with news sources especially the sources of high social status. While sources and journalists obtain their own desirable benefits in each context, the only loser in this "tug of war" is always the readership (Kovačič & Erjavec, 2011), the observers of news texts rather than the participants. This is because the readers do not possess enough economic or symbolic capital to exercise symbolic power to influence journalistic stance taking practices, despite the decision of readers not to purchase the newspaper that they dislike. Additionally, in each context of news production editors and journalists constitute an interpretative community (e.g. Van Hout & Jacobs, 2008) or the "speaker footing" (Goffman, 1981) to interpret news events by social-institutional and professional standard of news values. The real reciprocal communication in the professional community of practice only exists between the rank-and-file journalists, editors and top managers. News is produced *by* journalists, *for* the readers. "The relationship between the producers and receivers of news discourse is that of spectacle and observer" (Scollon, 1998, p. 75). The interaction between journalism practitioners and readers only creates a "podium event" in Goffman's sense (Goffman, 1981). Journalists have "little knowledge about the actual audience and reject feedback from it" and consider readers' feedback as unprofessional (Anderson, 2011; Gans, 2004/1979; Hermans, 2004). "The increased audience interaction will continue to be a euphemism for allowing the public to subsidize the corporation's newsgathering efforts" (Williams, Wardle, & Wahl-Jorgensen, 2011, p. 96).

The "pseudo-relationship" (Cotter, 2010) between journalism practitioners and readers can be illustrated by the prioritized news value of 'competition' in the news selection process (as presented in Chap. 9), and by the adoption of the sources of ordinary citizens (see Chap. 8). In each context of news production, the news value of 'competition' in the news selection process is foregrounded (i.e. in the Chinese context) or provoked (i.e. in the Australian context). This suggests that the goal of attracting readers' attention in news reporting is not to interact with the readership but to compete with other similar news institutions for economic profits. To have a large readership is an efficient means of appealing to advertisers.

In the Australian corpus, the sources of ordinary citizens are less frequently adopted than the official sources or other sources (e.g. sources from experts and organizations) in reporting risk events (see Chap. 8). This is because Australian journalists are seldom on site in reporting risk events and accordingly they are less likely to interview ordinary citizens who are influenced by the risk events in question or who produce risk events.

In the Chinese corpus (Chap. 8), the most frequently mediated sources in eye-witnessing risk events (i.e. attest) are journalistic authorial voice (40%) and the official voice (29%) rather than the voice of ordinary citizens (25%). The endorsed voice of ordinary citizens (e.g. consumers) only occupies 1%, and the endorsed risk makers' voice accounts for 15%. However, in journalists' acknowledging of different sources in the Chinese corpus as illustrated by "shuo", the sources of risk makers (41%) and consumers (24%) together amount to 65% of all acknowledged sources. These findings suggest that the voices of the less powerful sources are mediated by Chinese journalists as negotiable, whereas the voice of the power elites is more likely to be warranted. By "the less powerful sources", I mean those who have little or no economic and/or symbolic capital to exercise symbolic in enacting certain journalistic stance.

10.7 Conclusion

To conclude, the symbolic control of the Australian press is exercised by their proprietors rather than by the government. While the Australian government is unlikely to endanger the superiority of free press through granting and removing news publication licenses, it can regulate journalistic stance taking practices through issuing regulations and codes of practice. In the Australian news discourse, journalism practitioners need to (re)produce the news values and world views of media proprietors who may uphold an ideology of either the government or the opposition to best suit their economic interests. In the Chinese news discourse, the Chinese Party-State has a range of economic and symbolic capital to (re)produce symbolic power in keeping the Chinese press on leash and in sustaining the official ideology in news production.

The examination of mediational means through which journalistic stance taking practices are undertaken has privileged the articulation of news values (Chap. 9) and the exercise of symbolic power (this chapter). These two factors are far from comprehensive to fully appreciate the mechanism of journalistic stance taking practices. However, the (re)production of news values and symbolic power is arguably central to an understanding of the enactment of journalistic stance. This is because (re)produced news values reflect the values and belief that are currently operational in a society or news institution, and they have a direct bearing on journalistic stance taking practices. The (re)produced power relations are sustained by the volume of economic and symbolic capital that the powerful have at their disposal to sanction/censor journalistic stances. However, the length and scope of the book, together with the different datasets collected, would not have permitted a parallel study of news values and symbolic power in the Australian context to be undertaken.

To wrap up the entire research, this book has shown that the control of ideology or social order in news production does not reside in the symbolic imposition (Bourdieu, 1989). Rather, the orders of social life and the power relations are legitimated and sustained by regulation of social practices of journalism practitioners. Instead of directly imposing the symbolic power or the social order onto the personal order of journalism practitioners, the dominators assign values and stance by distributing economic and symbolic capital. The dominators possess considerable economic and symbolic capital to regulate the ways mediational means may be appropriated by journalism practitioners in interpreting news events. For this reason, the (re)production of news values and the distribution of economic and symbolic capital are never static 'context' just out there. Instead, they constitute their respective discourses or practices, and in this sense the enactment of journalistic stance is the "semiotic aggregate" (Scollon & Scollon, 2003) or convergence of different discourses struggling for dominance. In this site of struggle, social-institutional orders, (inter)personal orders, and semiotic resources coevolve with each other (Crichton, 2010). This is one basic tenet of the multiperspectival approach (e.g. Candlin & Crichton, 2013; Crichton, 2010). By the adoption of the MP approach and with the affordances of this ontology, this book hopes to stimulate more insightful discussion and study on stance in news discourse and beyond.

The corpus-based study of stance patterns in this research can hardly be achievable in the same way by manual analysis of a small number of texts. The corpus findings have shown that stance patterns (i.e. the adoption of ATTITUDE and ENGAGEMENT features) and stance categories play a substantial role in discursive stance taking practices. Stance patterns demonstrate consistency in *what* triggers *whose* ATTITUDE in my specialized corpora. The multiple evaluative meanings of a stance marker may be consolidated by integrating insights from the reification of the marker itself in its embedded pattern and the target of evaluation (e.g. animate human beings or inanimate things) (also see Bednarek, 2009a). Overall, this research has illustrated the affordances of corpus linguistics and perhaps pattern grammar in the study of discursive realizations of journalistic stance in news texts (see Hunston (2011) for a more detailed discussion).

Despite the affordances of corpus-informed investigation of stance, the mechanism of journalistic stance taking can only be more fully appreciated by going beyond the mere discursive journalistic stance in news texts. "Saying things in language never goes without also doing things and being things" (Gee, 2014, p. 2). In analogy to this, in taking discursive stances journalists perpetuate or challenge the status quo and at the same time enact certain professional identities. This shows that journalistic stance taking is a nexus of practice, in which the (re)production of prioritized news values and symbolic power is the key mediational means of enacting certain stances but censoring others. The investigation of the (re)production of news values and symbolic power affords an insight into *why* journalistic stances are undertaken the way they are, the knowledge that is hardly achievable with a restricted focus on the discursive aspect of stance. In short, the significance of investigating discursive stance patterns in news texts is that "looking closely at the structure of language use as it is being used can help us uncover different ways of saying things, doing things, and being things in the world" (Gee, 2014, p. 9).

References

Anderson, C. (2011). Between creative and quantified audiences: Web metrics and changing patterns of newswork in local US newsrooms. *Journalism, 12*(5), 550–566.

Barmé, G. R. (1998). Spring clamor and autumnal silence: Cultural control in China. *Current History, 6*(20), 257–262.

Barmé, G. R. (1999). CCP and ADCULT PRC. *The China Journal*, 1–23.

Barr, T. (2000). *Newmedia.com.au: The changing face of Australia's media and communications*. Sydney: Allen & Unwin.

Bednarek, M. (2009). Language patterns and ATTITUDE. *Functions of Language, 16*(2), 165–192.

Bourdieu, P. (1984). *Distinction: A social critique of the judgement of taste*. Cambridge, MA: Harvard University Press.

Bourdieu, P. (1989). Social space and symbolic power. *Sociological Theory, 7*(1), 14–25.

Bourdieu, P. (1991). *Language and symbolic power*. Cambridge, MA: Harvard University Press.

Candlin, C. N., & Crichton, J. (2013). From ontology to methodology: Exploring the discursive landscape of trust. In C. N. Candlin & J. Crichton (Eds.), *Discourses of trust* (pp. 1–20). Basingstoke: Palgrave Macmillan.

Cao, P. (1999). *Zhongguo Baoye Jituan Fazhan Yanjiu [A study of the development of Chinese press conglomerates]*. Beijing: Xinhua Press.

Chen, F., & Gong, T. (1997). Party versus market in post-Mao China: The erosion of the Leninist organization from below. *Journal of Communist Studies and Transition Politics, 13*(3), 148–166.

Cotter, C. (2010). *News talk: Investigating the language of journalism*. Cambridge: Cambridge University Press.

Crichton, J. (2010). *The discourse of commercialization: A multi-perspectived analysis*. Palgrave Macmillan.
Cunningham, S., & Turner, G. (Eds.). (2006). *The media and communications in Australia*. Sydney: Allen & Unwin.
Ericson, R., Baranek, P. M., & Chan, J. B. (1989). *Negotiating control: A study of news sources*. Toronto: University of Toronto Press.
Esarey, A. (2005). Cornering the market: State strategies for controlling China's commercial media. *Asian Perspective*, 37–83.
Finkelstein, R. (2012). *Report of the independent inquiry into aspects of the media and media regulation (The Finkelstein Report)*. Canberra: Department of Broadband, Communications and the Digital Economy.
Gans, H. J. (2004/1979). *Deciding what's news: A study of CBS evening news, NBC nightly news, newsweek, and time*. Illinois: Northwestern University Press.
Gee, J. P. (2014). *An introduction to discourse analysis: Theory and method* (4th ed.). New York: Routledge.
Goffman, E. (1981). *Forms of talk*. Philadelphia: University of Pennsylvania Press.
Gordon, K. (1997). Government allows a new public sphere to evolve in China. *Media Development, 44,* 30–34.
Gramsci, A. (1971). *Selections from the prison notebooks* (Q. Hoare & G. N. Smith, Ed. and Trans.). New York: International Publisher.
Hao, X., Huang, Y., & Zhang, K. (1998). Free market vs. political control in China: Convenience or contradiction? *Media Development, 45,* 35–38.
He, Z., & Chen, H. L. (1998). *Zhongguo Chuanmei Xinlun [The Chinese media: A new perspective*. Hong Kong: Pacific Century Press.
Hearns-Branaman, J. O. (2013). Journalistic professionalism as indirect control and fetishistic disavowal. *Journalism, 15*(1), 21–36.
Hermans, L. (2004). Occupational practices of Dutch journalists 20 in a television newsroom. In K. Renckstorf, D. McQuail, J. E. Rosenbaum, & G. Schaap (Eds.), *Action theory and communication research: Recent developments in Europe* (pp. 355–370). Berlin: Mouton de Gruyter.
Hong, Y. (2014). Between corporate development and public service: The cultural system reform in the Chinese media sector. *Media, Culture and Society, 36*(5), 610–627.
Hu, Z. (2003). The post-WTO restructuring of the Chinese media industries and the consequences of capitalisation. *Javnost-The Public, 10*(4), 19–36.
Huang, C. (2007). Trace the stones in crossing the river: Media structural changes in post-WTO China. *International Communication Gazette, 69*(5), 413–430.
Hunston, S. (2011). *Corpus approaches to evaluation: Phraseology and evaluative language*. New York: Routledge.
Ives, P. (2004). *Language and hegemony in Gramsci*. London: Pluto Press.
Kovačič, M. P., & Erjavec, K. (2011). Construction of semi-investigative reporting. *Journalism Studies, 12*(3), 328–343. https://doi.org/10.1080/1461670x.2010.493321.
Lee, C. C., He, Z., & Huang, Y. (2007). Party-market corporatism, clientelism, and media in Shanghai. *The Harvard International Journal of Press/Politics, 12*(3), 21–42.
Lewis, J., Williams, A., & Franklin, B. (2008). A compromised fourth estate? *Journalism Studies, 9*(1), 1–20.
Lu, X. (2003). Quanli yu xinwen shengchan guocheng [Power and the process of news production]. *Twenty-First Century, 77,* 18–26.
Pan, Z., & Lu, Y. (2003). Localizing professionalism: Discursive practices in China's media reforms. In C. C. Lee (Ed.), *Chinese media, global contexts* (pp. 215–236). London: Routledge.
Papandrea, F. (2013). *State of the newspaper industry in Australia*. Canberra: University of Canberra.
Pavlik, J. (2000). The impact of technology on journalism. *Journalism Studies, 1*(2), 229–237.
Scollon, R. (1998). *Mediated discourse as social interaction: A study of news discourse*. New York: Routledge.

Scollon, R., & Scollon, S. W. (2003). *Discourses in place: Language in the material world.* London: Routledge.

Tiffen, R. (1989). *News and power.* Sydney: Allen & Unwin.

Tiffen, R. (2006a). Political economy and news. In S. Cunningham & G. Turner (Eds.), *The media and communications in Australia* (2nd ed., pp. 28–42).

Tiffen, R. (2006b). The press. In S. Cunningham & G. Turner (Eds.), *The media and communications in Australia* (2nd ed., pp. 97–112). Sydney: Allen & Unwin.

Tong, J. (2009). Press self-censorship in China: A case study in the transformation of discourse. *Discourse & Society, 20*(5), 593–612.

Turner, G., & Cunningham, S. (2006). The media and communications today: Introduction. In S. Cunningham & G. Turner (Eds.), *The media and communications in Australia* (2nd ed., pp. 1–12). Sydney: Allen & Unwin.

Van Hout, T., & Jacobs, G. (2008). News production theory and practice: Fieldwork notes on power, interaction and agency. *Pragmatics, 18*(1).

Williams, A., Wardle, C., & Wahl-Jorgensen, K. (2011). "Have they got news for us?" Audience revolution or business as usual at the BBC? *Journalism Practice, 5*(1), 85–99.

Winfield, B. H., & Peng, Z. (2005). Market or party controls?: Chinese media in transition. *International Communication Gazette, 67*(3), 255–270.

Yin, L., & Liu, X. (2014). A gesture of compliance: Media convergence in China. *Media, Culture and Society, 36*(5), 561–577.

Yu, H. (2009). *Media and cultural transformation in China*. London: Routledge.

Zhao, Y. (1998). *Media, market, and democracy in China: Between the party line and the bottom line*. Urbana: University of Illinois Press.

Zhao, Y. (2000). From commercialization to conglomeration: The transformation of the Chinese press within the orbit of the party state. *Journal of Communication, 50*(2), 3–26.

Zhao, Y. (2005). The state, the market, and media control in China. In P. Thomas & Z. Nain (Eds.), *Who owns the media: Global trends and local resistance* (pp. 179–212). Penang, Malaysia: Southbound.

Zhao, Y. (2008). *Communication in China: Political economy, power, and conflict*. Lanham, Maryland: Rowman & Littlefield Publishers.

Appendix
Interview Questions

Interview questions	For journalists	For journalist educators
How long have you been working as a journalist, and how long in this news agency? Do you think there have been any changes over time in the style of reporting both in terms of yourself and in relation to the news agency?	✓	
What kind of readers do you think your newspaper has? How do you think your perception of your readers influences your writing?	✓	
Do you receive any feedback from readers? And how do you respond to such feedback?	✓	
Where do the major revenues of your newspaper come from? How might these factors influence the stance of your newspaper or your own expressions of stance?	✓	
Could you describe the process of writing a news item from the moment you get the source to the final print version, especially how other parties get involved?	✓	
Do you think media discourse has specific linguistic features compared to other discourses such as textbooks, advertisements, or novels etc.?	✓	✓
To what extent do you think your colleagues from the Marketing section may influence your expressions of stance in your news texts?	✓	
To what extent do you think the media owner may influence your expressions of stance in your news texts?	✓	
To what extent do you think the editors may influence your expressions of stance in your news texts?	✓	

(continued)

C. Huan, *Journalistic Stance in Chinese and Australian Hard News*,
https://doi.org/10.1007/978-981-13-0791-1

(continued)

Interview questions	For journalists	For journalist educators
To what extent do you think the government people may influence your expressions of stance in your news texts?	✓	
To what extent do you think your expressions of stance in news writing may have been influenced by legal requirements or by codes of ethics?	✓	
To what extent do you think the recent change in personnel quota system in China has influenced your expression of stance in news writing?	✓	
Are you subject to any kind of annual verification of your journalist license? Do you think this verification requirement may influence your expression of stance in your writing?	✓	
When reporting Risk events, for example, food safety and/or bush fires (or earthquakes), how is your stance influenced by the views of editors, managers, government people, or the stakeholders in your newspaper? How do you reconcile these factors?	✓	
Do the dangers foreseen in reporting Risk events influence your expression of stance in news reporting?	✓	
When reporting Risk events, whose viewpoint do you usually prioritise?	✓	
When writing international news from the Xinhua News Agency, do you edit it, especially the expressions of stance in it, or do you just paste and copy it?	✓	
How do the daily editorial meetings influence your expressions of stance in the processes of news collection and writing? Do these meetings determine in advance what stance and tone you should adopt?	✓	
What kind of events do you consider as newsworthy?	✓	✓
Do you think Chinese journalists enjoy as much freedom as your foreign counterparts in terms of taking a particular stance in news writing?	✓	✓
What do you think are the factors that might influence the autonomy of Chinese journalists in news writing?	✓	✓
What do you think are the roles and responsibilities of the print media?	✓	✓
Do you think news is objective reporting on the events at issue?	✓	✓
Do you think it is necessary for journalists to take a stance in writing? If so, why?	✓	✓
Where do you usually obtain the news, e.g. from other news agencies or from online sources, or from microblogs?	✓	
What are the criteria for you to select sources: those that are more reliable or those that afford easy access?	✓	
What do you think is the relationship between source opinions and journalistic stance taking?	✓	✓

(continued)

(continued)

Interview questions	For journalists	For journalist educators
How do you check the credibility of news from sources?	✓	
Why do you think sources offer you particular items of news? Do they contact you more frequently or vice versa?	✓	
Do you think some journalists may instruct their subjects to take a certain stance, especially in reporting Risk events? If yes, then why is this necessary? Who may decide to do so?	✓	
Which do you think is more important with respect to stance taking in news writing, citizen sources or elite sources?	✓	✓
When you interview civil servants in China, do you have to obtain any kind of formal permission from them prior to your interview? Is this also the case for press releases? How might what you learned in the interview influence your stance taking in writing up your piece?	✓	

Index

C. Huan, *Journalistic Stance in Chinese and Australian Hard News*,
https://doi.org/10.1007/978-981-13-0791-1

MIX
Papier aus verantwortungsvollen Quellen
Paper from responsible sources
FSC® C105338

If you have any concerns about our products,
you can contact us on
ProductSafety@springernature.com

In case Publisher is established outside the EU,
the EU authorized representative is:
Springer Nature Customer Service Center GmbH
Europaplatz 3, 69115 Heidelberg, Germany

Printed by Libri Plureos GmbH
in Hamburg, Germany